FROM

POVERTY

TO VICTORY

Discovery of Your True Self in the World

- You cannot expect to take anything from life if you haven't contributed anything to it.
- Your path to success lies above you, and you must rise to reach it before it can start working for you.
- Just like a leaking roof needs to be repaired or replaced, if your life has leaks, address and fix whatever is causing them—especially if it's poverty holding you back.
- The way you perceive life is how life will respond to you.
- You are made to be who you are, but not to live without purpose or direction.
- The world is available to everyone, but it opens up only to those who think about becoming successful.
- Life will never grant you power if fear is holding you back and dragging you down.
- Achieving success requires eliminating poverty from your path.

FROM POVERTY TO VICTORY

Discovery of Your True Self in the World

Frederick W. Sonpon

First published in India in 2024 by Exceller Books, An imprint of GE Group

Address: G1, Dream Apartment, Degree College Road, Belgharia, Kolkata, 700056, India

www.excellerbooks.com

Dedication

I wholeheartedly dedicate this book to my grandfather, Nelson Gewleh Nah, and my grandmother, Tanneh Gewleh Nah. My profound appreciation goes to my Spiritual Father, Pastor Victor Dorbor, for your mentorship, which has shaped me into who I am today. I also want to take this time to express my gratitude to my professional colleagues and friends: Senior Brother Alfred W. Tokpa, Comrade Mark W. Torh (though you have passed on), Ms. Edna Freeman, Ms. Joyce Randall, Former Elections Magistrate Arthur C. Y. Duogee, and Logistician Alfred Dunner (you have been missing for some time, but I trust God will bring a change and reveal where you have mysteriously gone).

As professional comrades, we were together on duty, working for our nation in Grand Gedeh County, Zwedru City, when I had the dream of starting this book. You were always curious about what I was working on during the time I envisioned and began writing the book. Your encouragement helped me complete it. This book will surely move mountains and hills, both spiritually and physically, as it helps the children of God achieve their dreams in this world. You will always be remembered for your kindness in supporting this work, even while we were on national duty. History will remember you as some of the best because of your unwavering support. Thank you for your excellent contributions.

Acknowledgement

I will always remember you, carry you in my heart wherever I go, and hold you in my memories, my beloved wife, Anna, and my children, Fidel and Elvis. I also want to express my deep gratitude for the hard work we've done together in striving to make this world a better place. We, who are still alive, owe this to the world.

When I reflect on mankind's successes and how God created human beings, I'm deeply moved. I believe God made everything good from the beginning of creation, but something dangerous happened that turned what was once good into a struggle. Until we wake up and change this, we will remain as if dead, and the world will lose its meaning. This is why I seek to revise this situation.

I also want to personally salute my Uncle Benjamin Gewleh, who kept the dream of pursuing education alive, continuing the legacy of his father, my grandfather, Nelson Gewleh. We live by overcoming the odds, and that means we are already successful—something God intended and preserved our lives for. I salute you all!

Table of Contents

Chapter 1

Your Life Is Shaped by How You Live It

If you want to be good, you will become good in life. If you want to be bad, nature will not deny you the way to become so, because what you tell life is what life will give you. This is simplified in the Book of Galatians 6:7 of the Bible, which says that whatever a man sows, that he will also reap.

This also suggests that life is both a receiver and a giver of either good or bad, depending on how you speak to it, directing the course of such actions in return toward you. Because nature is true to itself, it embraces the way we choose to act and live. If you say to life that this world is a good world and that you were created as good, life will manifest in the same way. If you say that you came to this world just to be down, life will keep you in that same state, cornered. It is your belief that is a factor in defining your purpose and ability to push through. In doing so, if you want to succeed, you will succeed because the steps you take are determined by your beliefs, which guide what you pursue in life and for what reason.

Life can talk, see, and act in defining itself. It is what you make of life, or tell it through your actions, that will be reflected back to you, portraying life as an element that can hear, see, and act.

So, understand that your life can hear, talk, and move. The power of your life to hear, talk, and move is dictated by your actions, meaning you are telling life what it should be like with you in this world. Your actions exemplify your command to the world. If you sit back because you believe that life was not meant to move with people, you will reward yourself with nothing, and nothing will happen for you. The fact that your life can see, talk, and move is the reason we can have dreams, think of something good, and pursue those dreams.

Define your life now. Start questioning your life to understand what you need to do to succeed and break free from personal poverty or deadlock. You must do this because the world is not waiting for you. The world is moving forward, concerned with how you can add value or contribute to the voices of those with spiritual power, economic power, political power, scientific power, educational power, production power, and technological power, all of which positively change our ways of life. By taking positive action, you will help build a good world full of human development. Do the same as others are doing, promoting the world with beautiful ideas and actions.

Try to remove whatever complaints or negativity you have. No matter how long you sit down from morning to night crying, it won't bring about economic prosperity and good health. Get into a questioning mode to understand what you can do to develop from where you are now, especially if you don't see a sense of value in your life. Your negative actions may be causing you to have no respect or recognition. If the problem of lack of success is due to poverty or other causes, it is time for you to begin to fight against it.

Those who learn to question nature about life strive to find solutions. So, what are you doing with your life now? Have you asked yourself why you were created in this world and what you are meant to do with the life within you? Time is ticking away, not waiting for you. Have you also asked yourself why you are still alive and healthy, while others are unhealthy, dead, and gone? You are still living, so you must gain some recognition with the life you have. You must ask yourself whether you were made to be a substitute—without any compliments. Were you meant to be like someone else? If so, what is the purpose of your life? You must ask yourself because you didn't come to earth to live carelessly, be treated poorly, disrespected for no reason, or sit idly without making any contribution. Wake up and ask. In your questioning, you should be able to arrive at an answer to know the purpose for which you are here. When such a questioning attitude is persistently maintained, see it as a way of finding a solution, meaning you are opening the road to discovering your true self.

It could be that maybe you are doing something with your life that is not positive, without yielding fruitful results yet. If you think you were made not to produce anything helpful for this world, ask yourself, what about those who are succeeding? Do you think their efforts to work with their lives are meaningless? Should lazy people expect that manna will fall from heaven for them? Are you one of those who don't value the idea that you were born to succeed? Have you asked yourself whether this world was made inadvertently, and whether it was made for human beings like you, or was it made for different creatures? Shouldn't you be part of those who this world was made for and should enjoy it? Because you may be carrying negative thoughts, I believe this is making you accept that you are meant to be nobody, treated by nature carelessly, and that you have no contribution to make, even to your own life, community, and country. Dishearteningly, you have not asked yourself what your mission here on earth is. If you know you are on a mission, then what are you doing with your life? Why are you not succeeding in anything or creating value to live your life to the fullest with happiness? You must make your mission on earth meaningful. If you know yourself, you will strive to advance yourself rather than sitting idly or letting poverty hold you down, making you appear as nobody on earth. Value that you were created by God with power, and you should show that power in all that you do.

Yet, you haven't asked yourself what you can do to show your true worth to the world by contributing positively. You still haven't asked yourself what impact you can make, by contributing positively to the world that will leave your name remembered. Are you not concerned about this? How do you really see yourself on earth? Do you see yourself as nobody, or what? If you value yourself, you will value your economic growth as well. You were born from the prosperous hands of God the Almighty. This should prove that you are not born to be worthless. You carry a virtue.

Or, I want to know, what are you complacent about in this life? What are you complaining about? Do you think you don't have a space on earth to live? Is this why you believe the world is turning against you? Or, is it because you are embracing a life of being nobody, which is proving you to be nobody and causing you to accept this way of life as a curse? Do you like the idea of suffering in poverty for no reason, and think you should persist in this state? Do you think you were made this way and should stay like this forever? Even time changes, meaning your life must change rather than remain chained for no reason.

Try to develop now. However, if you are yet to realize yourself or seem to accept being troubled by circumstances, have you asked yourself what may be causing this or why things are this way against you? Don't be like others who, from the day they were born, are missing in action on earth. Problems are hiding them. They are like battle soldiers missing in action, held by problems, and never waking up to do something about their problems on earth. This world will not cease to trouble you until you learn to cease from accepting that you were born to be nobody. Nobody can hear about those who don't value themselves. Nobody can feel them. Nobody can say anything good about them. They are just like nobody people in the world. I want you to know this: there is no value in being a nobody. Change your mentality and don't be like those kinds of people. They are such that, even in their own little communities, they can't make any contribution. Some don't even know their way out. Some are complaining from morning to night. They make their complaints like trademarks for people to know them. They act as if they were made for complaining rather than for a purpose, believing they must show their true values to the world. Life was not made to be full of complaints. There is no value in this, no reason for you to accept being this way. So, stop being like those who accept seeing life as ugly with poverty increasing in their world. Some people are just enraged by various conditions of life and blame God or the people around them. They do this because they don't see the power in themselves anymore and accept that they were somehow born cursed. I want to know which way you are then.

Picture this: I came to understand that 'good' and 'bad' are properties of this world and are on a battlefield against each other, each wanting to dominate the other. They have their own people associated with the promotion of each. Each one is fighting to quash the other. If one dominates, that one becomes the power in a person's life, possessing them to act in certain ways. It can dominate a person, and that person will be characterized as either good or bad. In short, if you allow poverty to rule you, it will surely rule. If you allow success to rule you, it will definitely rule you. Find the path of good, which is through God, to discover your true self in this world.

You were born to be who you are, but not to remain who you are. Go for your time of influence by having some impact. While the day of judgment is based on faith's result, your days on earth are based on action and the impact or influence you can make. Your actions to create a positive impact can make people remember you, or if they are the other way around, they won't.

Differentiate yourself from those people who do nothing with their lives. It is a bad thing to continue experiencing evil and suffering as if God didn't create you for His good purpose and to live well. You were made in the image of God (Genesis 1:26). Think of this to know that you carry a reflective power of good upon you because you are made in the image of God. Follow His pattern of good so you can feel the good while still on earth. It is up to you to determine this. Decide to be on either side of life—either on the side of good or bad. Or is the thing that is confronting and dominating you, reshaping your being into something acceptable to mankind? Understand this: it is the point of a battle over life that every human is confronted with either of those opposing elements, each trying to dominate. We are either to be dominated by good or by evil and become exactly what that is. And each element is controlled by a power source, which is from the invisible side of life. God is the source of good, while Satan is the source of evil or bad things happening in our world. It happened that Satan was once called Lucifer, living in heaven, but because of the evil that entered him, he was separated from God and thrown away from heaven to earth. I know you want to know why it should be the earth he was thrown to and not any other place. In my belief, which I searched the Bible to know, he was thrown here because nothing like hell was created from the beginning of the world. If he couldn't be in heaven, there was no other place to throw him but earth. He is, therefore, the source of evil. He is on the way to the place of everlasting banishment. This is why the Bible described him as a thief who came to steal, kill, and destroy (John 10:10). He has weakened nations because of his presence (Revelation 12:10), but God still found a way to redeem mankind.

It is the separation between the forces of power trying to quash each other—good from the hands of God and evil from the hands of Satan. In short, God is the source of good, while Satan is the source of evil or bad. After God created you and me as good people (Ephesians 1:4-5) before the foundation of this world, Satan came down to our earth by way of rebellion and tried to spoil it, turning our good world into a place of trouble, now facing economic and political turmoil as well. But you can separate yourself from the trouble of this world through Christ Jesus if you wish to find the side of good and remain in a place of experiencing such good.

This is the point of conflict in life—these two forces are fighting against each other, with one side wanting to dominate the other. But good must win! Because of these two forces, there is a fight for survival, which you must see as a lesson. Stop sleeping on your life and learn to put up a fight for your success now. Because either force is trying to dominate the other, you should know that life is not just about experiencing good; there will be difficulties along the way, even while seeking success or if you choose to relax. Mankind is not free from trouble. And the door of good is not closed to us. There will still be trouble whether you decide to succeed or not. Put up a fight despite what is happening in our world. Just find a source of good, which is God, to depend on. Stop daydreaming, saying you can't make it. Stop carrying such negativity. Keep in mind that you shouldn't die in the difficult times of this world, which was made for you and for me, as if nothing good can come out of you or come your way. It shouldn't be so when you know that a good God created you, meaning you have some little well inside of you. You should strive to gain some influence if God is acting on your spirit by His Spirit to change your level. As you carry God, see it as carrying the power of good inside. You are not supposed to be carrying or toting complaints and problems upon problems. Identify your identity in God, who is the source of your good.

We, as Christians, are told that if we are willing and obedient to God, we shall eat the fruits or good of the land (Isaiah 1:19). Fight to be covered by your current good that God made you and your siblings so you all can eat the fruits or good of the land where you are. Too many good things should happen in your life—they are in the land before you. You are placed in a good world because God knows that you are good. This is why you must wake up now and fight to succeed economically. The God who made you placed you on an economic, political, scientific, and technological earth, having everything, and nothing is left of that which God didn't create. You must not accept not feeling good or not being a part of the list to enjoy the Earth. Good is here, and you are one of the good. Because there is good with the presence of God here, the plants are still producing food for our good. The soil still contains minerals we can transform. Humans have potential or talents that can translate into ideas for the betterment of humanity on Earth.

To see that minerals are on earth—they are not there to feed angels or God Himself, but they are for the good of human beings, for whom God created them. The soil you see is also growing food to feed mankind. The soil is also full of mineral deposits, showing that God intended good for us as well.

See the values in you now and know that you were made a successful being long before your arrival on earth because your life is traceable to God, who created you. He is a good God. He is not sinful, nor was He living in sin before creating you. No. God even made a land for you and me, rich with resources and able to grow food, meaning the good earth existed before you were born (Ephesians 1:4-5). Our mission here is generally to take care of God's goodness on earth. God made you a landlord all over the world. Discover this and make your life a happy life. Make every day a happy day for yourself instead of making it a day of frowning. You are a wonder that must do wonders because you are made with features of good wonders. This is why you are still alive, which is proof that you have a mission to accomplish for God on earth. You are not a meaningless being on earth. You weren't made by yourself; God created you for a good reason. This should be why you should not be held back by life's circumstances, with no respect being shown for your life anymore. Believe in God, believe in yourself. Imagine you were not with God even when He was about to work or when He finally created you and the world, including the rest of the human race. As a good God, He completed everything as good when He created you and me. You are part of all the good that God created, and He rested on the seventh day after working for six days to create all things.

Your today must be good. Your tomorrow must be as good as well. Your eternity after life on earth must be as good. Because you came from a source, which is God, you will go back to the same source to report to Him how you have lived your life on earth. You are from the hands of a good God, so you shouldn't live below the standard of experiencing good deeds on earth.

Because God's goodness belongs to you, know this: God was not daydreaming when He created you and others. He did it of His own will without anyone asking why He did what He did good concerning you and our world being created. To create you, He didn't need your opinion, but He did it.

Value the story of your creation because it is a great story, meant for good, not for telling lies, letting complaints cover your life, and being hidden in the world. You were taken from the territory of nowhere and brought to the territory of somewhere. This is why you are on earth—a place of honour for you. This is the story about you and me: our creations were meant as a blessing to God and to ourselves. You can't bless God, but God has blessed you and me. By God resting after working on the sixth day, it means that nothing was left to create, including the beautification of your being. You are completed as a good being, in full, which is why you are still living. You are complete, which is why you can have food on your table daily. From your baby state, your parents or guardians took care of you, and you didn't die because you have a purpose that God made for you, which you must strive to realize. Don't let anything that didn't create you ruin your life or make it seem the opposite. We all were made to own the world, which is considered a place of values that we are to possess and exemplify the power of whatever authority God gave to us. We were never made to be dislodged on earth or locked up by circumstances as if you and I were made to be that way.

Picture this: God's plan for keeping you on earth is not intended for evil. You and I weren't made to be silenced by any force contrary to God's order. You and I carry God inside of us, which is why nothing should be carried against you by unknown forces, including poverty. This is why you must see God's success in you and about you and not overlook your existence. Make a difference now! This world will be abnormal until you can get normal. If you haven't yet seen the great power of God concerning your creation, now is the time to see it and begin to walk into your greatness. He says in His word that His goodness and mercy shall follow us (Psalms 23:6). Go for such goodness and mercy now. Forget about your past history and focus on your current history by making a great change come.

You can only receive a compliment if the complaint is confronting you, which may lead you to push out of it, and then compliments from people will be given to you as a victor. This should, therefore, signal an undeniable truth to you, knowing this as a matter of fact: you're God's property, and He gave you a key as landlord to the part of earth you are located in. This is why you still have a means, a place, and a time to think about your life, a moment to shine, and you should be able to wake up, seeking a means of realizing your purpose instead of seeing yourself without one. If you wake up, it simplifies that you may be taking your true position on the earth, leading to you becoming a winner in the time to come. Until you overcome the heart of negativity, you may just be living life somehow. Create a winning spirit in you. Being a winner is something we were born to be because the God who created us is a natural winner. He made you with His winning hands. He made you in His image to do wonders like Him, reflecting goodness and displaying good deeds and values. Nobody can take His trophy of being the best in everything good, as He gives you good. From His hands of good, you were created, so you must be as great as well while spending your days on earth.

If fear is stepping against you, holding you down, life will never step you into power. Being able to attain success requires killing poverty in your way. You must see how great you have been created so you still have life in you, moving as a living being. If there were no value in you, you would have been forgotten by this time. Picture this! Rather, you were made to shine as great. You were not made in your own image, but you were created in the image of God (Genesis 1:26), and for you to show forth your image to this world. Create happiness. Keep your day happy instead of complaining.

You were never made to become a complaining factor. Make every day a happy day for you instead of making it a day of worry and constant complaining. You are a power that should be seen either in the age you are now or from your youth. Because you were born great, you must be a power in your community for people to look up to by doing better than worrying for nothing or letting your life be turned upside down. You were not made to be like rumpled clothes that need pressing before you can be straightened out. If your life is rumpled, you can press it by straightening yourself up now. Nobody will do this for you. Stand up now!

Go to the next level with your life. Never make yourself a spectator in your home, your community, or your country as a whole. God sent you to earth for a mission, and every mission has its own struggle. Your struggle right now could be about setting the pace for your freedom to come.

How are you thinking about your life? Why accept being overwhelmed by frustrations? Nothing lasts forever, so you must ensure your poverty doesn't last forever. End it. What should really be on your mind is that, in God, despite the pains you may be going through, you are on a mission, and you must make sure your mission ends victoriously.

Calculate the power of success and how it should manifest in you, and begin to empower yourself. Time is not waiting for you. In fact, I want to know this: what is your age? Even forget about the age factor because nobody is too late for success. You have power in your adulthood, which you must believe about yourself and start to work on. Even if you grow old, see yourself as a power in your old age by doing something meaningful with your life before you leave Earth. You are made to be a power for your community. You have the power in your workplace to contribute positively with ideas that will change the order of things. You are a power, maybe at your school. You are a contributing factor to greatness in the world. You weren't made to hide in glory in the world. You are genuinely packaged for good, and nobody has the same qualities you have. You are made to occupy the earth, not to be dislodged from it, so don't let circumstances change you.

If your life has a leak, you can patch it up. A leaking roof is either repaired or removed. If your life has a leak, try to repair or remove whatever is causing it, especially if poverty is promoting it.

Put your life together now. This is your place of power. Know that your body has a mission only to function or achieve here on earth. Create this power of being discovered. Don't have the mentality that you don't belong on earth and were made to be controlled for nothing. You aren't an alien to think you should be displaced by evil. Imagine that God made you. This is why you must create something as well. You aren't an enemy to be dislodged from earth. The only enemy of God that was dislodged from heaven was Satan. You are not the one dislodged from heaven. Here on earth, you are placed to create power while you are alive. This is your place, so know that you were long ago made successful here. You don't have to travel to other places or different parts of the world, believing that those are the only places where you can have a good life. Right where you were born or are located is where your success was born or located to show up for you. See it as a fact and begin walking into your greatness, live with its power, and seek success now without sitting and complaining all the time. By complaining constantly, you will be proving to the world that God made you to be a complainant—a sign of a lack of purpose. You were never created for that purpose. He made you and me in his image, meaning to reflect good in everything. You must reflect good deeds and expect good things to happen in your way, not see yourself being led away from good. See your life as a representation of God on earth. This is why he considers those who believe in him to be his sons or daughters (John 1:12). Go for that status with your life. You must show forth such value because you were created in his image, not in the image of any other being. Therefore, you carry values that can change your world positively, not keep you in bondage. Be a light that shines for people to feel you. Just be positive about your life. Be like an eagle on the wing. You must be like that because you were made with power, not made to be powerless. Those who carry power learn to display it.

So, start to count the days you expect to make a change from retrogression to achieving greatness by showing forth whatever you have to the world. When you are successful, as a child of God should be, you are telling the world that the Almighty God who made you is a good God.

Count the days you want your compliments to come. Start to set up the foundation for those days to come. As a great God, He indisputably gave you and me power to preside over the earth and its riches so our lives can be lived to the fullness of His glory. This is what God is concerned about: you must display good and not evil. You must not let poverty take over your world without knowing what to do with your life.

Prove to the world that God made you for the purpose of good and not for evil. Do you see what He has done for you? He is still keeping you alive because He wants you to have an impact on life. And it was only human beings He gave such power to who were supposed to rule the earth and enjoy it, not spirit beings. He didn't give this power to any non-living things, minerals, or resources. These can't talk or do the things that human beings can, which is why He gave power to humans as the caretakers of the earth and its possessions. He did this by making you a part of those who rule the earth. You and I weren't born when God gave us this power, even before we were born or behind our backs. He decided your elevation before you were born on earth. He made you and me rich before we even came into the world, which is why the earth is full of riches that we found here. Before we were conceived by our mothers, He made way for our elevation. He intended for us to come to earth and show forth His power of goodness upon us. This is the reason for your elevation and why you are still living, part of the world's people, and not in the ground yet. You aren't put in the ground as a mineral but placed on the earth's surface to show forth the wonders of your creation. You didn't die before your mother was to give birth to you because you have a mission to accomplish on earth. He made you, therefore, a landlord of the world to rule as a king or queen. He did this by letting you be a part of those presiding over the world as well. You are not here without value. You carry the values of a great God because you were made in His image. You must influence others through good deeds and attributes that others will appreciate about your being, along with your Creator, who did this for you. You aren't here as a spectator on earth. You were given the power to take care of it. You aren't here to be subjected to difficulties by unknown forces which are not part of God's plan for you. Realize this power. He made you a great person, which is why you are still breathing and have a chance to make a change. This is why nobody can be exactly like you; your DNA is attributable only to God. Wake up now! Use the power in you to possess the world instead of letting the systems of the world control you. Can't you see that you are made with power? Well, if anything contrary is happening to you, it means something is wrong, fighting against you, and you must acknowledge that it exists and begin to fight it out of your way now.

You have a great world that you are placed in, not to be displaced from. Wake up! Keep in mind that you are born to win and believe in yourself. Look around you and see the world within you, which should be a good world as you live life to the fullest. This world may be waiting for you to develop, and until you do, the world will not reflect development either. See the world within you and develop your life now. Ensure your success, no matter what, to make it to the top and shine in the world—as a light-bearer rather than bearing shame because of poverty. You were never made in darkness, cornered for nothing, because the God who made you is a God of light. You must shine like your God while you are still in this world.

Value yourself, believing that you were made a landlord over the world. As a landlord, you were made a great caretaker. This is why you shouldn't be suffering with poverty holding you down. You are made powerful, and for this reason, you must have respect wherever you are and exhibit this similarly by giving respect to others and accruing respect. Understand that the world is your place to possess and display in glory, not to be depressed. Carry this mentality within you and begin to reshape your life for the good. You must not live here by letting poverty take hold of you, cornering you forever. Refuse to be down. Refuse to let the elements of the world make you turn your back on your God by blaming Him for poverty. He created you and made you live in a world full of all good things that can make your life prosperous. You may be suffering because of poverty, but bear in mind that you still have time to make a change by bringing your values out to the world, meant for your time of sufficiency. Let sufficiency be your next level rather than perpetual lack.

If God didn't mean well for you, He would have long ago cut you off from the earth or not allowed you to stay on it, or you would have remained in your mother's womb without coming to earth. But He didn't do that by killing you. This is why if you decide to plant anything concerning your life, it will grow because you were made with the properties of growth and prosperity.

This world is made for you, just as it is for others. See it as a world so rich that you must be a part of it, enjoying its riches by being on top. See it as a very beautiful garden full of roses, which God created for you and me. This is why you must be positive, and circumstances must not corner you. Be positive in the sense that if people who don't want to see you rise tell you that they didn't make you, but God did, they don't have the power over you to keep you down forever. Tell them that everything on earth has a tenure and that your tenure of poverty is coming to an end now.

Wake up now! See the richness of the soil around you. Even the soil is fertile, so you will not lack if you start planting some crops. Perhaps let's forget about the real soil for now. Your mind is also fertile soil for good ideas that can be turned into products for you to sell to the world. You were made to displace, not to distress. You must, therefore, get to work by using your mind to start the process. Make your mind valuable by developing positivity. Think of this: the day you put your mind into power, you will have then put your life into power. It is the source of your greatness. Success is sourced from your mind.

Don't worry about how others think of God. See how wonderful God is to you and me, especially in the good of earth's creation, including what He did for humans. He did all these good things concerning the earth, having riches and good soil, because He never wanted you and me to be hungry and suffocate. He made good soil and made sure there was rainfall and sunshine, so that when we planted our crops, they developed, producing our food. He knows you need to live a good life from your work. He knows you were made to shine, which is why this world is not empty. You see! Despite all that, He has given you potential or talents as riches you possess. He also placed some riches on and within the earth for you to retrieve and enjoy. If you don't want to make use of your talents, He shows us a way out: you can live, especially if you see a reason to join forces with others who are succeeding or already successful.

Stop creating distress in your life. It's as if you're thinking that God didn't create you for a good purpose and to live a good life in this world. Start to recreate yourself by developing a new mindset. If your soul is troubled by what may be going wrong with you, perhaps due to poverty, which is preventing you from being successful, know that you can do something about it. If there are no minerals in the place or country where you are, making life difficult, remember that He gave you talents or potentials beyond physical minerals, which can still bring you success. When you tap into them, they will make hunger go away. No doors of opportunity are closed to mankind despite our ways. God loves us, but He doesn't like our ways. Carry the mindset of a victor. If there are no diamonds in the ground for you to dig up, there are potentials or talents within you that can create a market with a product you invent, securing a patent right. Your talents could manifest in various ways. If you've learned to play a ball game, golf, make music, create a movie, or sell something already produced by someone else, even online, you will still be discovered. You are successfully meaningful and must live successfully on earth rather than in disgrace because of poverty. Begin to say yes to life, to affirm that you will make it. Your yes to your own life will bring what you desire closer to you if you're willing to change your situation and take action. So, let your yes empower you to stand up and take on the challenge of overcoming poverty. Take a step forward, and hardship will step away from you. This is how success operates.

This should be a lesson for you now to overcome your economic struggles. Do this by acknowledging the fact that you were made a landlord over the world. You must take part in enjoying the world instead of suffering in it. You aren't a tenant of this world, but God entrusted the world to you and others to take care of it. This is why you don't see spirits living on earth, but it's you and others like us, with flesh and blood, who are meant to live here. You are not a tenant who must be given notice by any being other than God, who sent you to care for the earth and has the right to end your days here.

You are not a tenant on earth but are part of those who own the world. God says yes to you, and you must say no to circumstances. You are not supposed to be dislodged by circumstances created by evil people or by the systems of the world made by mankind. Understand this: the only counterfeiter I know who doesn't belong to Earth is Satan, the spirit being. He is the only one who was given notice in heaven. But on earth, you belong to this place and must shine.

You are here to create your power on earth. Realize that you were made long ago as a landlord over the world, and you must begin to push yourself now. Get into motion, and success will be pushed into your care. Understand that any force of darkness causing you harm on earth is a negative force. You are placed as a landlord, and as a landlord, you must see yourself as a caretaker. Contrary forces meant to fight against your well-being want to deny your purpose. You need to know that you are a good being.

Fight against negativity. Poverty, like any negative element, comes from the devil, and you must fight it. Don't let it become a landlord over you, making you feel trapped as if you were landlocked, and causing persistent lack in your life. Understand that anything contrary to your success means you will carry shame, dullness, lack of attraction, lack of wisdom, lack of respect from others, stagnation, and more. These elements were not part of your creation. Imagine you were made in the image of God, which suggests that you must reflect goodness. This should make you realize that you belong to a place of light and should live as a light to the world. You belong to a God of joy, so you must be full of joy as well. You were made with a shining power because you are a property of God Himself, who is light. With this understanding, know that you are made with full attraction, meaning you should learn to influence change, influence people positively, and influence better conditions in your own life. You were made solidly, as a concrete being, originally meant for good things to happen in your life rather than being devoid of good. Recognize what is wrong with you now that may be preventing you from realizing your true self. If it is poverty, change the condition before it brings disgrace. Say no to negativity, where poverty is manifesting in your life. Say no to the shame that poverty can bring upon people. Say no to the disgrace that poverty might cause, making you overlooked and undiscovered.

You must see the world within you and work it out for your good. Determine a great world within yourself by improving yourself. Do it by defining your world—a world that is full of satisfaction. Make the change happen now.

God was never a mean God, as evidenced by what He did for everyone by creating this world for us. He had no obligation to do it, but He did. If you want to refuse God, then refuse yourself. If you refuse yourself, it means you are pushing God out of your way. If you don't want to develop, it means you may be suggesting or telling the world that it shouldn't develop either. It's as if you are the one causing this world to delay in development.

So you see! If you want to prevent good things from happening in your life, then refuse creation itself and know that God did it for a purpose by putting you on earth for a good reason. He made sure the world was full of riches for you, for me, and for others to enjoy. If you look at the surface of the earth, you will definitely see some of the riches—especially humans being endowed with ideas that can bring riches or help to change their own conditions and for you to join the list of those powerful people. If you go deep inside the earth, you will also see tangible riches for your benefit. So, this world is not empty or broken, which means you shouldn't allow yourself to be broken, either. It is not a different world where others are living rich and happy. Don't think that this world is different and no longer has resources for us to enjoy. This world is the same as yesterday, today, and will be the same tomorrow as God made it. As long as we are still alive, it is God's will that we enjoy its values. You and I are still here, proving that God is keeping us for the purpose of His good.

Know this further: your location is a place that should be better off. You are in a part of the world where your position is for you to try to grow from there. Your position is to be ahead, not left behind. Your position in that part of the earth is to make sure you know what to do with your life. Your position in this part of the earth is to bring out your creative ability to the world that would market you. If you start to think right now, you may own a patent for an invention you will discover. So, you aren't a displaced person on earth. This must not make you feel that you aren't one of the owners or caretakers of the earth. Appreciate yourself; you are worthwhile and must live as worthwhile while yet on earth. Take your place in living a life of relevance rather than being taken out of place by any means contrary to God's will for you. Stop regretting why you were created and start succeeding. Your time is on the way if you can make your way now.

From the day you are able to do something with your hands, know that you are on the way to your success.

Join me then. I am propagating the power of God's goodness. I am bringing my talent out to the world through the books I write. They are bringing some returns. You must try to establish and propagate your talents too. Have no trace of keeping negative thoughts in your mind. Believe in yourself. This is the power I want you to have.

Take your position on earth and know that you are part of those who God made to own the earth. Seek your recognition now. Do so because this part of the earth where you are located is not ground zero. Rather, it is a place for you to showcase yourself. Walk with power; create your financial discovery. Create the economic power of ownership or being a caretaker of the earth, and preside as a landlord.

Be positive about your life rather than thinking negatively. If you think negatively, it means you don't value your creation. I want to know why you are thinking negatively in such a manner. Why think that the world is different and that you don't have a place here to progress? What makes you think that you don't have a voice for people to hear about you as a great person that others can speak about? What really makes you think you can't end poverty in your life? Is it poverty that is causing you to think negatively in this way? No. Stop thinking and acting like a nobody, causing your physical self to appear poor—or seeing nothing good happening in your life. Why allow poverty to be a master in your life like this? Your today may be bad, but it doesn't mean your tomorrow can't change. Make a change now! Have you ever heard that poverty was there with God to help Him create you? Did God ever ask poverty, or the creator of poverty—Satan—to help create you or the world? Why allow poverty to rule your world as if it were a member of the things God put together in creating you? Poverty didn't create you, and it was never part of the elements God used when He worked on you. Know that you were created rich, which is why you are on an earth full of riches. This is why you don't go hungry every day. God wants you to show your talents to the world by giving yourself a push. Your nation's government didn't put you on earth, so don't think that the government should be the one to help you before you succeed in your problems. In fact, take note of this: the earth you are on was here before you and me. It is a place for your position, not for your disposition. Don't think that this is a different earth from the one made by God long ago, which is still full of riches. You will never see God, who is in spirit, come to enjoy the earth; only you and I will. A spirit can't eat. It doesn't have tangible physical power to do anything. Only humans, made of tangible flesh and blood, can do things of physical power. If your mind is a problem in your life or is emptied out or without ideas, it suggests that the world will be completely emptied and without anything. You and others having ideas is the reason this world got to develop by people from every part. Maybe you could be an inventor of something that the world can benefit from. You must see yourself as someone who determines what the world should be like. You are the one the world may be waiting on for that part you occupy before development can take place. Stop carrying a negative mind that you are nobody. Start to develop your life so that your development can have a positive impact on others and on the landscape you occupy to develop physically. If you put life in yourself, it means you put success in you.

I believe that you are the light of the world, which is why you are found in the light of day in the world and not belonging to the dark. You are the one your family's history may be depending on to have value for others to respect you and the family. Make a push in life now rather than letting the push of poverty get you off track! And you must see it as bad to think that you were made to be nobody on earth because of poverty eating you up. Refuse poverty! Take it out of your way. Until your mind is depleted of talents or potential, know that your actions are depleting the world of values or giving it a lack of development or resources. Put yourself to work so that the world works.

Stop thinking of a new earth you should be reborn into before you start making a difference in your society. If you think you need a new earth, your life should be that new earth that you establish. You are not a second-hand being but a double-handed being, having the power to create and not to be destroyed.

You are here, and your power as a great person must show. You belong to a class of good people on earth, which is why God will never let you sleep hungry. You belong to the class of good, which is why you are still breathing and able to think and create something with your hands.

Both good and bad people are living on earth. Good wants to dominate evil, while evil is fighting to dominate well. Both groups are fighting to dominate the other, and I know the good shall take over. You are one of the best people on Earth, which is why you are part of the seven continents of the world. You are on an earth that is not different. It is the same earth divided amongst the seven continents containing conglomerates of races. It isn't new either. This earth will definitely remain only changed if your life changes to help improve it. This change, I believe, will come; it is the earth concerning your being that should be changing, concerning your personal life that is expected to change for the better. See the earth, therefore, in you. Value it in you to wake up. Appreciate it.

It is essential for your mind to differentiate you from others as you live successfully on Earth. Your body or race should not make you think that you were never made to succeed because of your race. Even in Africa, white people are succeeding. Even in the West, black people are succeeding. It is not about your race differentiating you from others. We all are destined to face physical death in the body, except for those who will be alive when Christ returns and will be spiritually empowered to rule forever. They will be differentiated. Be part of the list of the good people of the earth, and prosperity should be your portion.

Start to feature yourself on earth. There is no way you will be part of a team and want to win a championship without putting yourself into action. What you should know is this: a person, whether black or white, has either black hair, black pupils or lashes, red blood, water inside the body, the same five senses, and so on. You aren't different from other people who think that their colour makes them successful instead of you achieving success. We all are made as humans containing those properties. The difference you have is the difference you can make to change situations around you and impact the world. You are a character who must exhibit the power of God to show that you are made to influence.

Some people in different parts of the world think they are too privileged or born with riches to be successful without the hand of God approving it for them. This attitude is common among many black people I know. They make the issue of their colour a problem in their lives by blaming God for making them black. Some black people think they are black but were meant to be white. And some white people think they were made to be superior to all races. If we think by our colours and locations that we are the best, why do we face hunger, lack permanent systems, experience economic failures or face death? Anyone who thinks they are better in life than others should be able to conquer death as a superpower.

Nobody is better in this world than the other. We are the same. So, nobody is better than you. What truly makes us different is not our colours or races but our beliefs, characters, faith levels, and so on. These differences are shown through our actions. But we were all born naturally from the wombs of women before science attempted to change this. What we have in common is that we will all likely grow old, not live on earth perpetually, and face death, suggesting that nobody lives forever; we all have the ability to dream, confront economic problems, face hardships, experience pain, and so on. Nobody is perfect and will never face any of these challenges. Even Jesus himself felt the pains of hunger because he was human, moved about on his feet preaching, received threats or insults for the good he did from evil people hating him, and faced death and resurrection at last. His resurrection is the power behind Christianity. So, what makes you different from others, or others different from you? You are human, just as those people are human, too. Our common denominators in the body are the same.

If we were different from each other, we wouldn't have been on the same earth. We wouldn't be concerned about holding together as a world's people, seeking world peace, forming the United Nations and other organizations, and seeking human cooperation and collaboration. Or, you need to tell me whether you are truly different and to what extent you are different. Is it because you are poor or rich, which makes you different? If you are different from others, why do we all live on the same earth? Why can our countries face economic stagnation despite the schools we built that should have lasting solutions to life but don't? Everyone is concerned about having a permanent solution regarding our health crises, political wars, global warming, and so on. Why are we facing these terrible medical problems? With all these, why are humans killing each other if we are civilized people of the world?

So, don't mind your colour. It isn't the thing that should make you feel superior or overlooked. You shall die someday, even if you were the richest person in the world. You can't buy your way out when meeting with God, hoping to stay on earth forever. Age has made us all timed. Therefore, see a brother or sister around you as yourself.

I am concerned about your economic growth, so I strive to improve for you to help people. You must rise because you were created as a solutionist, which is why you are part of those who own Earth through the help of God. It may surprise you that the only white person I purely know of who is good in character does not depend on his or her colour, a physical feature, for such. If he or she is white, he or she might have some features of a black person, such as some parts of his or her hair being black, having black pupils or lashes, and many others. Universally, we are humans, with nobody having power over the other. I remember the only man who came to earth and wasn't defined by his color but proved by his character that he had helped the world—Jesus Christ. He showed mankind the power of a universal race that complements all races based on the character of the person he lived. His purpose in coming to earth was to lift mankind. To unite us, this is why he said the spirit of his Father is in those who put their trust in him because they are one. Greater is he that is in us than he that is in the world (I John 4:4). You are in this world, but the world must not be in you. The systems of the world must not keep you poor and without a purpose. You carry power. You have a universal DNA that makes you one with other races. To complement this further, he made you and me the lights of the world and a city set on a hill that can't be hidden (Matthew 5:14). He didn't limit the power of light in you that should shine over the world. This light shining over the world means you are a supernatural power to all people or races, despite the locations of those people or races.

Understand the concept of being black or white in this world. The only black person or white person is someone who tries to segregate. This person has a black heart, is evil in ways, greedy or corrupt, bitter, conspiratorial, blasphemous, a counterfeiter of truth and God's word, etc.

Jesus' heart was not black or white in any way. His heart was a merry heart, not even white by perception. Rather, His ways were purely holy—a character the world must have, which He demonstrated to all races, irrespective of their origins. We all can embody the qualities of being "white," not by colour difference but by embracing the ways of God to promote ourselves and our world. We must show love toward our fellow men as well. In some way, we can all be as white or black, especially if we practice dark ways, live in darkness by promoting evil practices, or cheat people, which may be based on the kinds of hearts we carry toward each other. Your completeness by creation as a unique person and your location on earth doesn't determine how black or white you are. It doesn't matter who bore you; that does not determine how poor you may be or not. What matters is how you see yourself and how you behave in the world. God has blessed every human being, which is why every country has resources—meaning every part of the world is rich or has minerals. It has people with ideas that can change conditions, even for those from that part of the world. God blessed the entire world, which is why people are able to think and invent things for the improvement of our lives. You deserve comfort in life. You carry the power of radiance to reflect goodness upon yourself and others.

Your success requires a powerful weapon: faith. Develop the belief that you were fashioned for good. By doing so, view this earth as your property, which you must enjoy and value. Nobody, regardless of the colour of their skin, is different from you. We all are on earth with the same characteristics. Be aware that it is the same earth, with all humans possessing five senses being the same.

Recognize the power you have concerning the head on your shoulders. We are naturally born without any resources that were to be in our hands before coming to earth. In short, nobody came to earth with a diamond in hand. It is the same earth your forefathers and foremothers were born into and left you as part of their lineage to continue the family's history. This place is for you to believe in yourself, work to obtain your glory, and ensure that you showcase that glory. Be wise. Stop looking for another earth because you are facing hard times, expecting it to be a paradise or different from what we have now. Create a power here. Stand up against odds and stop allowing poverty to define you. Take your place on earth rather than being displaced, displeased, and kept abnormal by circumstances. If you continue to allow poverty—a disease that can diminish people—to define you, it will project you as someone with no contribution to make on earth. You are not a stranger on earth. Picture it and take your position to enjoy the earth. Stop living in relegation on earth when you are a landlord.

This is about taking on your power and displaying it by overcoming poverty. For me, it may surprise you that I am doing the same by finding my place on earth to be recognized. I am doing this because I see the earth as my own and must showcase the talents God has given me. An example of showing my relevance is this book you are reading, which is a product of my potential. God gave me the mind to think of it, and by developing this subject, I was able to create this book, which I know will give someone like you hope when you read it.

You don't expect to take anything from life if you haven't given anything to it. Life is about give and take. Do something so you can achieve success. This is why your frequency for success is located right up, and you need to go up before you can make it work for you.

I am giving you hindsight so you can start to understand that the best struggle to go through and succeed is when you are in Africa, a place where opportunities are rare, and you must fight your way up. We turn our struggles into lessons but do not die in them. Learn from my African success so that you can succeed by reading about it. I believe in myself, so I see the earth as my place of honour rather than as a place of dishonour. Develop a happy spirit and fight to succeed.

Work during the time you walk on the earth's surface as a place of habitation, not in fear. I walk like a bold man every day. Even if I haven't yet acquired all the riches in the world, I don't let myself worry about life. I make time for change and work to bring about whatever change is necessary. I believe in myself. I know for sure that the greatest riche to have in this world is having God first. He was the one King Solomon sought for wisdom to rule his world. The second thing to seek in life is health. These are the valuables of life. Because I have God and health, even if I don't have anything or food to consume during the day, as long as I am taking steps to obtain it and believing in God, confidence builds up in me without giving up hope. See life as a process that must go through stages before a final product or fruit can emerge. This is like a product in a factory that goes through processing before becoming a final product to consume. We are all in the factory of life that must be processed for the good that lies ahead of us. You must have a foundation set up before you can harvest for the future you desire. But many people don't want to be processed for the good lives ahead of them. They just want to walk into success without working for it.

I see myself as a winner without carrying a negative mindset, despite my conditions. I adopt the mindset of a winner, believing that I must rule my world rather than having the mindset of a loser. Create a weapon of faith within you. If people don't have faith in God and in themselves, they walk through life with hopelessness. Carry faith. Think as I think. Walk as I walk. I know that the earth was made for me, and I believe this strongly and work hard to keep my place recognized. I want my voice to be heard for the things I have learned to do. I know the earth is my home, and I will not be displaced or suffer any displacement as long as God is with me. And God is with you, which is why you still have the life of God in you. He gave your life, and you must depend on Him. You didn't make yourself; God made you. Because you didn't make yourself, neither you nor anyone else can determine how long you will live. I trust God with this fact: He placed me here on earth with power. I don't believe He placed me here to be powerless or without value. I don't see myself as a tenant on earth. I boast that I am a property of God and must realize this glory by having the world hear about me. You can create faith in God and in yourself to understand that you are on earth for a mission and that this is the place of your power where you must achieve success. Don't let the world overcome you. It is because you weren't made for the world, but the world was made for you. I don't see myself as an occupier who came to earth by chance. Because the earth was made for you and me, and it was from the same earth's dust that He created us and gave life to each of us. Such a life means having life in everything. This shows that you must demonstrate the power of your relevance because you are a property of the earth. You must not be displaced by any element or spirit being other than God, whose holy hands created you and placed you here for a good purpose. You have to work to realize your values. Do this because God will be pleased to see you in power and displaying that power while depending on Him.

I boast that the earth belongs to me. Say the same to yourself. Justifiably, I hold God to this. I remind Him every day. If my faith starts to weaken, I pray to Him to help me with my problems. I can say that I was never made to be put down by circumstances on earth. I believe in myself and say that God put me in power long ago, so I must walk on earth with power. I believe that God made me to be a landlord here, so I make sure to stand my ground as a caretaker. You must stand your ground, too. Develop such a faith—carrying a positive spirit—by being optimistic.

You are blessed, so work with your life by showcasing the blessings God has given to you. Aim to be great rather than letting poverty trouble you. Can't you believe that you were made to be successful? Perhaps we are troubled in this world to understand that something spiritually went wrong, which we must try to correct. Begin by saying no to shame or disgrace following you perpetually. Say no to poverty and its shame. Say no to evil forces trying to bring you down. They didn't create you, but God did. God can't be a wicked God who created you just to make you suffer. No. Look at what God has done. Imagine, even before our births; He made the earth a place of celebration for everyone to enjoy its values. It's as if, before our births, we were all given invitations to attend the party of coming to earth and enjoying it. This is why you don't know how plants grow our food or how gold, diamonds, crude oil, and other minerals were created. They were freely given for us to enjoy. And God did it. You weren't there to ask why He created those things. You weren't around to ask why He created heaven and earth. But He did it, and you get everything here. You must enjoy everything here. Start to think differently now. What are you thinking about? We are here for a success party. Join God's success party to understand that every resource on earth is for your good and mine. Get in the position to start reclaiming your place to enjoy the resources of the earth. This is why you are blessed even by reading this book. Believe in God. The God who made you and me was never mean. This is why you are on Earth, which is full of riches. Serve yourself by bringing your talents to work for you or by enjoying the earth's resources through learning something. It is like a buffet to learn to serve yourself with whatever riches the earth has.

I greatly remember this verse from the Bible in Galatians 6:7, which says that we must not be deceived because God is not mocked. Whatever a man sows, that is what he reaps. If you sow for yourself that you are nobody, you will definitely reap the result of being nobody. If you sow for yourself that you were made to have power, you will definitely work to bring that power into the world. Stop carrying negativity in your mind that you are nobody coming from a cursed family.

The boundary of your success depends on you to create. In short, the amount of riches you want on earth depends on you. This is why you must understand that the world is looking for thinkers like you, not just takers. You must picture that the world is not a different place without a spot for you until you wake up and do something meaningful with your life. You need to be different in your thinking and in your actions as well. The difference you make in your thinking will determine the difference between your today and your tomorrow. You need to be different in how you see things around you by appreciating God for being alive and with you. You need to be different from being lazy. You need to be different from having financial limitations. You need to be different from living in fear, which rules your life and causes you to stop valuing yourself.

See the earth as being full of riches, for you to have your share of those riches like others are doing now, showing their marketable selves to the world. There are several things you can do with your life to achieve success. If you start a business, you will grow. If you obtain knowledge, you will have a service or work that pays off. If you bring your talents to light, you will own a patent, and others will pay you for your talents. You have the power of knowledge in you, and until you work toward discovering that knowledge, you may just be a spectator daydreaming on Earth. Start attending the party of the Earth to enjoy its values or resources. They are for our good. You must because the riches on earth were made for you and me. So, why are you thinking negatively about your life? You need to think positively, meaning you must see yourself as valuable and stand up to life rather than letting life stand against you. Stand up to whatever problem of poverty is bringing you down. This thinking of bringing about a change means you will empower yourself. This thinking means you will value making efforts to change your current condition and be a help to others once you overcome life's challenges. Be a fighter now. Put yourself in a positive mode first. Build a vision of a great self by thinking positively that you will make it in life. One day, I want you to smile as an overcomer. When you start to smile, let the world know that you are no longer the ordinary person who once had no value but has succeeded.

Stop looking for another earth, thinking it should be different, where you can live without living in this present one we all have. Change your thinking, change your life. Stop looking for a different place of redemption without depending on yourself to create whatever redemption needs to be while on this earth. This world has everything you need. Stop looking up to people and thinking they should help you before you can succeed and escape poverty. Stop trusting in man because man will only help you but won't learn for you; you must strive to learn something for your life. Man won't work for you. Make your own world a good world now!

Stop thinking negatively about the earth we have now being different from the one that was made before. Stop carrying the belief that the time will come when riches will fall from the air for you rather than taking your place on this earth and working to be showcased. The opportunity to be alive is for you to do well. To be alive on earth is an opportunity for you to start creating relevance. Stop daydreaming of another new earth that will come before you gain your purpose. Stop being too religious and not doing what you need to do now in your body by showcasing the values God has made you with. You are poor if you accept this, meaning you are saying the world should remain poor forever. You are the world. If you fight to become successful, you are saying that the world should become successful, too.

Are you hoping for a new heaven to come where you will have a place before realizing your true self? Make today a good one. Stop waiting for a tomorrow you have not seen yet. Every tomorrow requires working in your today to prove its existence.

What I believe is that everything related to heaven has a start in the physical. If you want to be in heaven, which is glory, create the means here now. This earth is for you and me. You and I make up this earth, you see, which is full of riches and currently engulfed with troubles, which shouldn't be the case. God didn't make it for trouble to be against us, either. Neither did God make it for animals alone to live here. God didn't make it for the things of earth themselves, including the animals, to take care of it except for human beings like us, who were given the power to take care of creation, including ourselves as humans.

You can only change the earth if your mind is changed. You can't deform the earth because you didn't make it. The only way to change the earth is by having an impact. When you develop your life, the earth will also develop. If you fail to develop, you may not want the physical earth to change. It's like saying you want us to keep living in backwardness because you don't want to join others who are inventing ideas that are changing our statuses. So, your life and your society all depend on you. Stand up to life instead of stamping yourself in poverty as if you have no power in you to live better. The earth is a place of blessing, not a place of suffering. Tell the world that you will show forth the values of God upon you by realizing your true self. Being an image of God is a fact you must embrace, meaning you must reflect good in the world. And you can never make good reflections in the world if your life lacks purpose or meaning. Create that spectrum of a good society from your thinking and actions, and see if the society won't remember you for what you will do in the end.

Do you really want to see a good and developed world? See the earth in you. Make the earth in you shine good and better, rather than sitting without a mind for changing your level. You can never change the content of the earth if the content of your thinking, character, blood, and actions are patterned on the same level of not wanting to succeed. Whatever beauty you want in your life on earth is housed right within you. Start thinking about taking from life what you want to live your life on earth. Whatever you want to see in this world, know this: by working on yourself first. Until you can create a power of success upon yourself, the world will continue to infuse troubles upon you. This is the world you see, as things are, pushing things towards each of us. Every trouble of life is being pushed against you by the world, so you must wake up and push back. It's like those things you don't like are being pushed toward you as if you must accept them. Poverty is one of those things pushed into life from the unknown. Refuse to let it continue to affect your world. You should give to the world rather than letting the world push things towards you. Give it light. Give it the power to develop. Give the world a sense by becoming a contributor of ideas.

Know this: it is an indisputable truth that the world you want to see, probably that should be good, starts in and with you to change it. If you wake up to change your personal world, whatever is far from your shores to enjoy will fall right within your care. This is why you should know that your personal world, which you can change, is your life and the environment you live in. This is where the changed world needs to begin. There is where the changed world must show up, reflecting you are carrying values, meaning the power you will know by fighting to realize your true self will determine this. You can become excellent if you make yourself an embodiment of values and not disgrace. People without values cannot be respected. Until you create that value, it is as if you are just considered a stranger on earth, continuing to wander into different poverty troubles.

You need to change your mind by removing negativity and also need to change your environment to feel happy and great in the end. This is what you need to stop carrying a poor mindset about, which leads to creating a poor self and, eventually, a poor society. You must understand that you are part of the society, which is the earth we live on now. You are to contribute to its growth depending on how you view it by making your individual growth possible. No one in this world is an island, so you must see the importance of helping develop the world, especially as you gain power over yourself and add to the many inventors or service providers in the world. Generally, we are on earth to provide service to God, to humanity, and to ourselves. On the basis of service to God, we must put Him first in all that we do. Second, you must value that society depends on everyone for its survival and growth. The determinant of who you are in this world is the reason you don't live here anyhow. Third, you must do something with your life and character. Each of us is rewarded by nature based on how we choose to live our lives. This is why we live together on earth—to contribute. While in this stage of life, start creating meaning in your life. Don't be like those who don't value the good in themselves. Those who can't even contribute to their own lives are the people hiding at the back doors of life. And you were never made to be like this. Those kinds of people are unknown to others and don't wish to be respected as well.

Chapter 2

Reinventing Yourself

Dortu was a strong boy everybody in his town adored. He was highly recognized, having no equal because he was tough and swift at winning a fight against anyone or beating his colleagues in their little town. He went around picking on his friends, even forgetting that, despite his strength, steel can cut another steel, and he needed not to think he had no equal. Sometimes, some of his friends would lie to each other, accusing him that Dortu was going to fight for them. Each time Dortu heard his name in any of the friends' mouths, he became very irritated and wanted to fight the friend who mentioned his name, either because of the matter or for no reason at all. Because of his strength, his own friends would run away from him. His parents in their little town saw him (Dortu) and believed that, because of his strength, he would be successful. Dortu was never encouraged to like going to school. He depended on his physical strength for everything. At a certain time, his parents saw a moral in this and believed that his strength was enough for his success in life, and he never even cared to have gone to school to learn something for life.

He grew up and started having children. One day, his son asked him a question that he couldn't believe for being so brave to ask. The boy asked because things had changed economically in the town. Here was the question the boy asked him: why was he so strong in body and had fame for his strength, but that strength couldn't be used to help change his family's or their economic status? The boy's question touched him. As life turned out, Dortu saw that his strength sagged. Many of his friends whom he used to beat became successful and owned properties. But Dortu, without a skill, ended up becoming a security guard for some of the same friends he used to beat. It was from that point that he learned his lesson and understood that life was not about the size of a person's body to believe it would bring success. Neither could it be about the location from which the person comes, the family's background, or the power in the body that could bring success. He realized that it was good to learn to be wise. Since that time, Dortu has learned his lesson and has become a changed man.

Many people in the world behave like Dortu, trusting in their physical strength or their own skills without depending on God to learn to be skilful in life. King Solomon, during Bible days, didn't ask God for riches but asked God to give him wisdom. This is why the best thing we need in life is wisdom. So, suppose you are someone going about without knowing your position on earth, perhaps depending on your body size, family background, or feeling comfortable working for others throughout your life. In that case, life may naturally retire you due to age. There is a time for everything, and you have to work while it is your time. Don't wait until you are old to decide to succeed. Change your mentality, change your life, and the environment where you are. What you need to be able to develop is a new self by learning to put your mind to work for you.

Success is not far from you until you are willing to take your life forward. You were made for success by God a long time ago. This is what you need to understand about success: take it as something anybody can obtain. You just need to be willing to create a new self. To do that, be willing to change your thinking, change your confession by learning to say good things to yourself, and change your associations. You must help to change so together we can change the world. You and I are the world or earth that should change, which you must concentrate on changing concerning yourself. Your development should prove the value of taking a step and adding to others who are developing the earth. Think of this! What you should beware of is that if everyone chooses to live at a low level, the earth itself will be low or underdeveloped. So, see yourself as the true earth that needs change based on valuing your growth. You have to do something about your life because, without you and me, the physical earth won't exist. You were made to rule the earth, which you must wake up to now. Value your life. Understand that you were made to own the earth but were never made to be owned by it. In short, you should determine what becomes of the earth by adding your voice or potential development.

This earth is for our habitation. If you believe that the earth is made for you and try to change your status, you will definitely make it. Fight to create your power here on earth. Don't let anybody rule you in an evil way. Don't let anyone try to suppress or push you down to nothing, especially when you have no voice of your own.

Because of greed, poverty is often promoted by powers just to keep low people down to serve them. Don't let poverty rule you because of laziness. Create your financial power by discovering your future now. Stop waiting in vain, letting poverty eat you up. Stop waiting and complaining by giving credence to the power of poverty. Stop waiting for men to help you before you can succeed. Stop waiting on your community's leadership. Stop waiting on your country's government. Fight poverty now. Understand that poverty was not part of God's creation when He made you. So, don't let it turn you otherwise.

I remember biblically that everything good was made in heaven and earth complete by God within six days. Nothing like poverty was part of the elements of creation for mankind. God created the heaven and the earth, including human beings, and poverty was not part of this.

You are not a counterfeit person by letting poverty turn you into a subject of it. If you don't want to change your level and continue to keep poverty confronting you, it is like making yourself a counterfeiter. Stop living in a state of regret and disdain. So, stop seeing yourself as if you can never make it in life. See your life as original and not a fake being. You are a decent creation of God, and you must be respected by succeeding as well. Stop letting poverty keep upgrading itself against you.

Picture this in your mind: you were successful long before coming to earth. This is the reason you are here. You can bring whatever success or virtue you carry out to light. Create a purpose for a new beginning. Start creating a new self now by thinking. Imagine how you have been created in the image of God. This should be a reason to make you reflect well on Earth instead of the opposite. You came from the good hands of God and were made in His image. Stop thinking lowly anymore. Create a new self that will be respected.

Those who know their Lord and God shall do exploits. This is why you must change your life by adopting a new mindset. To create a new self is not about keeping an old mind, old ways, and overlooking yourself or deceiving people. Put up with a new self as a way of living in a new world better than the old one where you had no purpose to show. A new self should be about concentrating on sharing good things rather than shedding frustrations and complaints. A new self must empower you for good in this world and later help others.

I guess the reason for your suffering might be that you have been unable or unwilling to create a new self. Maybe you are just overlooking yourself because of the conditions you are currently facing. Perhaps it is because you have been limiting yourself, thinking that you are never made to progress. Put away the old self that creates so many limitations and makes you think you will never make it. Maybe your conscience over your life to learn to improve yourself is yet sealed up and keeping you down. Your new self should see the world as a place of power and blessings to enjoy, not as a place of suffering.

I remember that when I first started travelling out of my country, I hoped to create a new mindset in myself. I was tired of living in an old environment with the same friends who had no interest in learning or growing. Things have changed in my life. Ten years ago, the person I am now is quite different from who I was then. This is why you must create a new self that will be respected in the years to come. Stop carrying the same person you were perpetually, even into old age. A new self should not be about folding your hands to be pampered. A new self is one that sees the world and wants to rise above rather than letting the world sit on top of you. It is not a self that is depressed for nothing and conquered by circumstances without knowing what to do to change your level. A new self is one with a marketable vision, bigger than the ordinary eyes that harbour regrets and complaints. A new self should be about having new perspectives, new ways, new expectations, and a future full of prosperity. A new self is about having new associations and new influences and creating some impact on your society, believing that after succeeding from your old self, which carried shame, you can now contribute positively. A new self is to be occupied by the spirit of God that dominates your ordinary spirit. A new self is a conquering spirit you must have. You must have this because you didn't come to earth just to be depressed or live without purpose. You didn't come to earth to be held in bondage. You don't come to earth as a spectator while others succeed, and you are left without hope. Change that. Achieve a status of a conqueror. As a conqueror, you don't create a spirit of limitation about yourself. You must be empowered to succeed. Start to create a spirit of being a victor rather than a victim on earth. A new self is one that sees a spirit of fertility, where happiness becomes a part of life, creating smiles and kicking poverty out.

The world is made for everyone, but it is only open to those who think about becoming successful and to successful people. Be on the list of those. You must open your world now! It takes a belief in God to drive a belief in yourself before you can create success.

If you can picture this about your life—that you are made to determine who you are to become—you won't have to keep sitting and complaining about life. Just put up a better version of yourself, meaning you should adopt a better self by thinking positively and working towards the future you want to have. Stop imagining a better life as if it will come out of the blue.

Be determined to change your level now. In every struggle, there should be a redeemer, and you are the redeemer of your own life until you take steps to realize this about yourself. You are the redeemer of your own life; this is why, if you are hungry but nobody can know the intensity of your pain except you, you must speak up. If you are a young man or woman without school fees to pay for your education, see it as a difficult economic situation that may be confronting you, which nobody will understand unless you move out to tell others about your situation. This is how life works: not everything can be solved by others until you see a reason to wake up and fight for yourself. Beware that there are some things in life that people can't always do for you, and you have to be willing to initiate the steps for your own lifting before you see others come to help you. Start planning for your tomorrow now. Make your life a city for the future. Create a city within yourself that should be very good. Stop giving up on yourself and surrendering to hardship. It is never too late to try and succeed. If you are facing difficulties because of the actions of others or because you are creating such a situation yourself, you don't have to remain stuck in it. If you are trying to enslave yourself due to your own mindset, why can't you wake up and fight to change the condition? Start working now so that your tomorrow can change. We are the world, so make your own world a better place. Determine a means for your life to matter in the future. Determine your level and strive to live your life as a great person, starting from where you are now. Take control of your life by making a determined effort to fight poverty. You can change the world by changing your mindset. A reflection of any change should be evident in your actions. This is why you should know that no amount of sitting idly and letting countless hours go by can bring about a change in your economic status. Make up your mind now! You can also change the world by not letting poverty follow you throughout your life. It is wrong to see poverty continually affecting you. Stop building a temple of poverty in your life. The reason is that you were born into a world that is rich. God created this world as a paradise, meaning you must live as a king or queen here. Overcome negativity, which keeps you from becoming a successful person in the world. Begin to live like a winner by giving yourself the power of life.

Make a change now because, as you grow up, life will continue to develop with its own problems, especially as you age. I guess you were once a baby and have now reached adulthood, so you must learn to grow up now. Make your economic growth possible by following the stages of your life; as you age, you must also develop in prosperity. Perhaps you have become an adult. Next, you will become an older person. So, what are you doing with your life now? Age doesn't matter; if you want to succeed, you can succeed. Do you want to keep living as if you were born to be nobody? If you believe that you are made to be a nobody, you need to ask whether the God who made you is a nobody. No. God knows that you deserve a good life, which is why you are born into a rich world. Just as you may be counting your old age coming, start working on your success stages as well. Everyone has an inevitable final stage of old age. This is why you must work during your lifetime before it is too late. You are not here forever, so you must make an impact on Earth.

If these factors are acceptable and meant to be believed concerning you and life, why are you wasting your life away, wasting your thoughts away, washing your future away? Your negative behaviour is like washing away your progress on the shores of the Earth. You need to know that life depends on how you make of it. Don't ever think that your power to develop should be seen only if people help you first. Wake up now! Tell the world that you were never made to be a victim, as if you are a cursed human being who fell from heaven like Satan. Be positive and realize that you are a victor, which is why God sent you on a mission on earth. For this reason, you must strive to live happily.

Stop sitting among those who accept being nobodies while you are in a world full of riches and must do something to develop. It is the truth to realize that you belong to the territory of serious-minded and successful people, which is why we are on earth.

If your situation is such that you don't have anything today, create the means to provide for the things you need tomorrow. Stop sleeping for nothing. Stop crying for nothing. Whatever good you believe you need tomorrow is possible if you start the process today. Have a winner's spirit to reach the level of satisfaction that success can bring. When you reach the level of having your needs met, try to go to the next level of having your surplus met. This is why, if you are persistently experiencing a lack, it is not a life you should continue living.

What you give to you today will bring whatever surplus stage you desire. Your life depends on you creating your surplus stage. You live in a world of abundance that God has provided. Be a financial hero or heroine in this modern world.

Don't be concerned only with your current state without planning for your future. You can change your poverty condition and discover your potential. You are made with power, not without it. You carry the image of God, not anyone else's image, which you must believe in yourself. Nobody should determine your destiny by waiting for help before you make changes to your level. It is the value you carry that causes the elements of the world to turn against you. Stop hiding yourself. You are not the only person in this life, nor are you the only one facing challenges. Others have suffered before you but have overcome. Be like those who fight to succeed and enjoy the beauty of the earth. They are successful because they laboured. They might have seen a bright future and worked towards it. See your future as bright and make a basis for your success now.

Difficulties are like barriers. They can place you in bondage, like having your hands and legs tied. What breaks barriers and helps you reach greatness is not creating complaints but finding the power of victory to overcome obstacles. See your challenges as opportunities to grow and keep fighting instead of giving up. Believe in yourself! If you focus on frustration, you will create your own detention. If poverty is a problem in your family, create a strong will to fight and overcome it. Nothing should allow poverty to last forever in your life. Stop letting poverty control you. This is an act of giving up on life. Take action against poverty by first believing in yourself. Be a victor in the world. Be a confident person who learns to speak positively. Develop a habit of always speaking against poverty. Tell the creator of poverty that you are more than an overcomer and will fight to overcome it. Confess that you are made in the image of God with the power to create change. Say to life that you will live a good life by destroying poverty. Let your life reflect good, not evil. Focus on God, who says that you are created in His image. Bring out the image of God in you with power.

See yourself as valuable. It is because of the good inside of you that the forces of Satan work against your life. Satan inflicts evil upon humans and the world, aiming to turn the values of God into something different. Satan uses people and creates systems through them, including promoting greed. He creates hosts of people and systems to spoil their world. Until you embrace God within you, your life will lack meaning on this earth. Seeing the good in you means seeing God in you. If you see God in you, you see the power to never give up. If you succeed, you will prove to the world that the God who created you is a good God. You are made to transform your world into a good place. You are powerful because you are here to take care of God's creation, and nothing should push you off track from your purpose. You are made to progress, not to regress. The nature of progress in you is the reason you didn't remain a fetus in your mother's womb and why you didn't stay a child forever. Life progresses through stages, and you must grow. Try to make a difference now. You are made to make a difference, not to be distracted by poverty. You aren't meant to be weighed down for nothing. See the power in you and take your stand in the world.

You may be going through a time of scratches on your life, obstacles mending, or trouble confronting you, but you must understand that the time of glory out of these unnecessary troubles is still ahead of you. Keep fighting. You will make it through God. He was never late when He created you. He was never evil when He worked on your good life. Because He completed you as good, life is still in you. This same God is still on the throne and knows the purpose for which you are still living, making sure that you discover yourself by looking up to Him. You must give Him a signal about your life before He will work through you. If you think He made you just because He wanted you to suffer, you are proving Him wrong. It is like throwing God away from being a good God to you. You are taking Him as evil. He never proved Himself evil or wrong in any way either. He is just a perfect God who knows why you are here and must accomplish His goal concerning your life. He is very mighty and knows the time you have to develop if you are ready to hold onto the truth that you were created to progress or be made to live in good.

Chapter 3

The World Is Not Getting Better Until You Get Better

I want you to see a good world in yourself. If you develop, you will see a good world with your life, meaning the physical world you see will also be developing. The concept of a world has to do with humans. If you sit down without thinking about doing something about your life, you are telling us that you don't want development for all of us. The world is waiting for you to develop now.

Many ordinary people are still thinking about how the world could improve economically while they are sitting and waiting for that kind of world to come. Stop daydreaming about wanting success out of the blue sky. This is why you must create your own government of success. Believe that there is no good government in this world except the one you establish, which should be a good government. Anything good you want in this world should start with you creating it. Create financial power by securing your future.

Stop being like those who are daydreaming, waiting for a better economy, and reminiscing about past economies they felt were good but who no longer think of developing further, instead choosing to complain while they sit. Apply the mathematics of success, which involves workable steps initiated before arriving at the solution stage. Stop being like those who are blindly and hopelessly waiting for a good government to bring a different glory of prosperity to them. Stop hoping for a better economy through such a government and whatever systems they might come up with. They are waiting for that good government without working to make their own lives reflect the benefits of a good government.

You won't find a good government for mankind until you create that government for your life. Here are some evils affecting mankind's economies around the world. Inflation is one of them. It will continue to affect us to the extent that it will keep confronting our nations' governments and systems. This is why you must stop thinking that prices will reduce in the world without fighting to reduce your own economic tension. Beware that prices will continue to increase. And it is possible that they may even reach hyperinflation at times. Frankly speaking, deflation will never be favourable for ordinary people who may think they will get a little rest when it occurs. For manufacturers, deflation is not favourable either because it may lead to reduced profits. The cost of raw materials for production is not the same across the world, so when goods are produced, they are priced based on the cost associated with these raw materials. Labor and other expenses or overhead involved in processing the goods must be added before determining the profit from them.

Be aware that there is seriously an economic stretch on the world. This is due to economic pressure coming from consumers' demands for satisfaction. Everybody wants the best out of life, which comes with pressure and pain.

Let me give you an example to help you understand how the world is changing and facing economic strain. Take the case of Apple Inc. in the USA. If Apple creates an iPhone for sale due to consumer demand, but the raw materials for the production of the phone are expensive, the company will check its profit line based on the production cost. It will not produce the phones without considering whether it will make a profit by the end of the day. This means that the cost of profit gained after producing the goods will be added to the selling price. Apple will not want to lose money, as it is a business aiming to make a profit from its goods. Therefore, Apple will not seek data from poor people around the world who demand the phone but complain about the price. Apple won't consider how these people feel about the price, especially those who are making demands, before producing the phones. If the cost of materials is high, the company will pass that cost onto the consumer. So you see, if the company were to produce without considering the costs, it would be making a business mistake and would likely incur losses. The company must produce based on demand and ensure it doesn't fall short of profit despite the production costs.

This is a problem for many poor nations and people because of how they view the developed world. The developed world doesn't care about how poor nations feel about the cost of production before producing goods that will satisfy them.

Therefore, understand this economic concept and stop daydreaming about a better economy while you are seated. In my country, Liberia, for example, since the end of its civil war in 2003, ordinary people have not observed global economic trends. They still discuss the economy before the war, which they felt was good, and regret why a war was fought for change if the change has led to a worse state. Many wonder why there was a war if the economy was not going to improve in the future— meaning the current state is worse than it was before. Many thought that fighting a civil war was meant to bring economic change or prosperity without them having to work for it. It can be seen these days that the war has damaged the economy beyond its already bad state, leading to even more economic struggles. There is population growth. The majority of Liberians had better diets compared to these days. Due to increased poverty, exacerbated by the civil war, people eat poorly and are jobless, causing economic strain. So, ordinary people are still hoping for a good economy while daydreaming.

Today, many ordinary people and so-called leaders or politicians are in the same boat, daydreaming about better days expected to come. Due to global inflation, Liberians don't have to keep dreaming of better days without working for them. To achieve a good economy overall requires effort. The economic condition of my country is so bad. Resources are scarce, and the population is increasing. Foreign investment is limited, which could have supported the economy and improved the exchange rate by promoting livelihoods.

But I see this as having dead hopes for better days among Liberians. Some are still daydreaming persistently about how their successive governments will bring about better days, seemingly without the people learning to work for the better days they want. Today, more foreign individuals control the economy. And as daydreamers, these Liberians are still regretting why the country went to war if things weren't meant to improve. The wrong has already been caused. If I were they, the Liberians, I would never hope for a better day without improving myself. They must see the world as a changing world, requiring people to work more than before instead of wasting time complaining about their governments. A better economy will not just come if the people aren't sensitive to themselves by learning to take control of their own lives through hard work. Many personal economies are down, and they must strive by first learning to improve them. To work on their economies, they should begin by valuing themselves, and then their leaders will adopt similar attitudes that will drive a national course toward better change and improved lives.

But see the reason why I say that the world is not getting better until you try to see sense in making your life better. See the world within you. Determine how that world should be. Stop letting the world determine you by doing nothing.

Suppose you took the time to read the world's economic statistics these days, starting with those from the seventies. In that case, you will understand that inflations and stagflations continue to trouble many economic places around the world, impacting every sector. Manufacturing materials are increasing in cost, causing ordinary consumers to fall prey to struggling times. These economic antecedents make consumers feel the pinch of the high costs of goods being produced, and the burden is ultimately shifted onto them.

See how the chain of economic suffering can be with prices increasing. It works this way: as wholesale prices increase due to rising costs from raw materials, the burden of cost increases is shifted onto ordinary consumers, who are at the end of the goods being sold. As production costs increase, wholesale and retail prices also rise, causing consumers to feel the impact of increased prices because businesses want to make profits. Wholesalers and retailers must add the costs to the goods and determine their profits after including these costs.

Some businesses are required to pay taxes despite the cost of production. As the burden of taxes increases, they pass the burden of tax increases onto consumers by incorporating the costs into the prices of goods.

You must make a wise economic change. Stop expecting a good government to appear out of the blue. Every government depends on taxes paid by individuals and businesses to operate. The government can hurt more than help to improve lives in society due to its reliance on taxes. Without taxes, capital projects that benefit the entire citizenry will not be implemented. To increase tax collections, the economy should create more businesses, which will employ more people and pay taxes. Investment coupled with manufacturing can better improve the economy compared to an increase in services where the government prioritizes employment. If a country depends on natural resources, and their prices decline on the world market, it creates more economic hardship as well.

This issue is not unique to your country alone; inflation and economic hardship are confronting many countries. The world has changed. Taxes are increasing everywhere because manufacturing costs are rising. As businesses pay more taxes, the problem is that the burden of these increases, as mentioned earlier, is placed on consumers through wholesalers and retailers. These businesses shift the increased costs of taxes and production materials onto consumers, who pay for them to satisfy their needs. However, if there were a strong government in place that understands the economic complexities and implements better regulations or policies, such as controlling prices, consumers wouldn't suffer as much. Without such regulations, consumers will continue to suffer due to high costs for raw materials, which could hurt both them and the entire economy. Ordinary people need to understand that nothing is getting better economically in the world for them. This is why the best economy to focus on or improve for yourself should be your personal economy. If you improve your personal economy through hard work, nobody would think of retiring from it. This is why you should see the world within you that should improve, starting with improving yourself. Until you succeed in this world, you may not achieve the economic satisfaction you need. Create whatever is necessary for your personal economy now. Start learning something that will benefit you and later have an impact on society.

If so, to say that you are still thinking negatively because you hope that a good government would come and rescue you from poverty, see it as a daydreaming exercise to be avoided. Don't entertain such notions. What hurts your personal economy must be fixed by you, and nobody else will fix it for you until you decide to do so yourself. Create your economic power because you own your life. Apart from God, nobody owns your life, and you shouldn't depend on someone else to help your economic condition. Stop daydreaming about better days while you are still seated or behaving passively in your current bad days. Your bad days today should be the basis for you to prepare for your better days to come. You have to work it out. This is why you must stop relying on mankind to improve your situation and instead start helping yourself now.

Just get to work now. If you were to put an economic scale on inflation and other elements of the world's economy, especially if you were to collect the various commodity prices in the marketplace where you live and compare them with current prices—starting with the prominent ones, particularly focusing on data from the eighties up to the nineties—you would realize that nothing is improving economically due to inflation. For example, a Nike sneaker that was sold cheaply in the nineties is no longer sold for the same price in the 2000s. Similarly, a Toshiba laptop sold ten years ago at a low cost is not priced the same this year. This proves that the stronger the world becomes with advancement and population growth, the harder the living conditions become for ordinary people, who are forced to deal with the burdens of advancement and inflation. If an American Airbus were to produce a new plane for travel between West Africa and America, the cost of travel for this route would not be the same as for other areas. The owners of Airbus would not ensure that passengers pay less due to inflation. Travel routes within America, even from one state to another, will have different costs. The cost for traveling from West Africa to America will not be the same as for other routes. Even if the cost were compared, the poverty condition of those traveling from America to West Africa would not affect the company's pricing. All passengers will pay the required fare. The owner of Airbus will want to make a profit. If the plane offered only a single class ticket and poor people had to travel, they would be forced to buy that ticket if the plane was the only means of travel available. Poor, average, and rich classes would only be distinguished by the ticket class, with no exceptions made based on financial status. This is why poor people, even in developing societies, are getting poorer because development imposes burdens on everyone. The demands of advancement force everyone to adapt without consideration for the poor. For example, if cellphones become a standard means of communication in a town, everyone in the town will have to buy one because it has become essential for communication

Ordinary people are pulled into chains of development somehow without having the excuse not to. This is a reason why you must develop because advancement comes with its own pattern that can force people to adapt to it. You don't have to keep living primitively by refusing to use a phone. In another sense, if you live in the city and are supposed to pay a water bill or an electricity bill, you can't bypass this by refusing electricity.

Here are some reasons why many people are suffering in Africa: Governments in Africa aren't doing much about the trend of advancement in the world, which their nations must follow to learn to transition everyone with this trend.

This is causing economic hardship because nations in Africa aren't keeping up with development. For example, while classrooms in America use screens to teach their children, many classrooms in Africa still use blackboards and chalk. This delay in advancement causes people to lack the basic concepts that modern life brings about. Poverty is one reason many people live below standard.

Entering into advancement, even by poor nations, is part of the trouble related to global economic warming. To me, global warming doesn't necessarily mean that the ozone layer is getting hotter and hotter. Rather, the world should focus on the global economic concept, where communities that were once producing or depending on crop production are becoming increasingly distressed. These industrialized nations continue to pour the wood of development onto poor people and their nations, creating more global poverty that affects lives. Consider that poverty and dangerous power are more about warming lives just as the ozone layer creates heat. Address your personal economic global warming instead of waiting for the world to help you.

This is why your personal government is the best government to have, as it should make a difference and allow you to have an impact on the world. This shouldn't be your problem, thinking that the world should improve as a reason for not working to improve yourself. Be the best you can be by striving upward. By going up, which I believe you will achieve because reading this book will give you a push, is a point where recognition comes through for the world to know you. You can't be recognized or talked about by merely sitting in one place and daydreaming. Those who are recognized in the world today are those who worked hard to achieve it.

If you came to my country, Liberia, the governance systems are disoriented. Workers at both private and public levels don't have fixed pay structures. As inflation increases, wages or salaries seem to decline or remain stagnant. Social security structures and pension schemes in Africa are similarly inadequate, year in and year out. There is no better social security system. Based on my experiences working with the National Elections Commission of my country, many employees who die on the job have no proper benefits. If a person dies, only three months' salary is often paid to the family of the deceased. After the three months' benefits are paid, the deceased's name is immediately removed from the employment list. The family of the deceased is then left disappointed due to the lack of further benefits. This must be fixed. Because of the pay structure in Liberia, workers don't easily save. Leaders or lawmakers mostly don't plan for the future of government workers in Africa. I see this as a factor that causes brain drain in Africa. This is why getting old in Africa is so difficult. Educated people often seek better livelihoods outside their countries in Africa.

My state or government and its institutions are completely inadequate as they promote these kinds of evils. It hurts to see that nations in Africa are not learning from the past and improving their systems.

Think of this now! You can help change your level and fix the issues in our various societies. Start a new economic world order for yourself that is full of power. You should never live only on meager resources, struggling with survival. Create power within yourself and create economic power in your world.

What are you doing with your life now? Know this: the world you may be looking at, hoping to improve through your imagination of a better economy, will not get better without you taking steps for your life. You can influence the world by learning to improve yourself. You should think of a great world and act to make sure that vision becomes reality. Understand that improving your economy won't just happen overnight until you wake up. Make sure you wake up to fight for a change in your level. If you fight for a change, you will face no financial limits. No matter where you are located in the world, you will be able to buy whatever you want anytime you wish without worrying if you learn to seek out money. Create your economic power to live in peace instead of worrying. This means that, at all times, you will be financially relevant and valued by the world. Have money to always spend. Once you succeed economically, you will live your life the way you want without worrying about the economy. It is important to note that every economy depends on money to function. This is why you must work to earn money. When you succeed, you will have financial power comparable to those in developed countries, and your location will no longer limit you. No one is better than you until you learn to improve yourself. Nobody will be freed from economic difficulties unless they work to free their own life. Economic difficulties can make people overlook others in society. If you are successful, you will be placed in the same bracket as those from the developed world. Your success will remove you from the bracket of the poor or average people because you will have created a power that brings you recognition. Your background or location will not measure your life; you will have money to spend and travel anywhere in the world. Your financial power will place you on the shoulders of the world without your background or location limiting you. This is the power I want you to have. Achieving it will give you financial power that will take you to places on earth and add value to your longevity. Surely, if we were to list wealthy people, you would be counted among the rich globally. If you have money, understand that you will have no boundaries to live unhappily economically. Life will no longer be a harsh situation where poverty has control, and economic prominence will become a new aspect of your life. Fashion yourself to live a good life.

To be successful is good for you, so fight for your advancement now. You must have money to spend in the world's economy. Once this is achieved, you will be able to spend money anytime you want without worrying about having enough. This is what poor and average people do; they worry about money and look for it. But this will not be the case for you. You will be able to travel anywhere in the world, potentially helping those in need. Right there, you will have no economic limitations and will be recognized as an economic power in the world. You will move from a life of complaining to one of sufficiency with appreciation. The issue of poverty requires you to handle it. Fight to succeed, and you will be found positively in the bracket of the happiest people in the world. Many people are unhappy due to poverty. Remove it from your path. Succeed, and you will not stress over how to buy this or that. You will have a voice economically as a person to be remembered by others. You will be celebrated as a beacon of success.

When you achieve sufficiency, you become a power rather than a powerless being subject to shame. You will be celebrated rather than overlooked by the world. It is as if having your position unknown to the part of the world where you are located is better than being found in shame and disgrace due to poverty. You carry the power of your greatness, meaning you must wake up and do something to reach such a level. If you do not succeed, you are creating a silence around your greatness, making the world stagnate.

Blame yourself rather than others if you do not develop. While it is visible that your body parts are functioning, it is a shame that you are unable to use them effectively. Create a new self with the power to help the world become a better place.

You don't need to think about survival by checking ordinary prices if you are successful. If you don't strive to improve, nobody will improve you just like that. Stand up to life now.

One thing I know is that if you take your power in the world economically, you will carry financial power that others can benefit from. You will make a difference in the world, potentially helping others. You need to make an impact. Be concerned about your economic growth. A changed world is needed, and you need to wake up and create it. Stop waiting for the world to improve before you improve personally. Even though you live in the world, don't let economic depression follow you. The world you see should be viewed as corrupt, and you should help improve it. You should determine what the world should become, needing correction every day, by being part of those who make those corrections. Play a role in the world rather than letting the world dictate your life negatively. We were not created to be opposite to one another but as images of God and His likeness to become impactful.

God didn't make you for the world, but the world was made for you. You should determine its pace with you. You should improve it rather than letting it deprive you, which is impossible to accept. Be a caretaker of the world and act now. A person like you should work during the day rather than wait for nightfall. Nobody can work in the night—meaning at old age—without having a pension. In short, when you are old, it is not the time to expect to start working.

One thing I know is that if you can't empower yourself now, the world will overpower you by creating unexpected suffering. Because the world can't help people, there are many poor people. Imagine some parts of the world are extremely rich and could help others who don't have or are slow to reach their potential, but those rich places are not helping. Today, the global heat is a result of what industrialized nations are doing. Their factories are producing more heat, affecting the ozone layer. If you see people acting evilly and suffocating others, see this as turning God's world into nothing. God didn't create the world for this. He created the world as a paradise for you and me. It is the concept of a personal paradise you should fight to create. Picture this in your mind and start creating your happiness. If you deny the importance of creation, which is intended for the good of God, and think you don't need to believe in God or fight to discover the new you, then stop blaming the world.

Follow the pattern of education. You should not spend your whole life studying to become somebody and then, at the end of your studies, die or have nothing good to contribute to your life and society. We learn with the hope of making our lives and the world a better place.

Take your stand now and showcase your power in this world. Stop sitting and complaining. Stop delaying your life by worrying about tomorrow without taking action. You need to take steps now for the future you want to be great. Stop waiting for better days without moving forward with your life. Time is running out; act right now.

Chapter|4

"You can be late for a program but you can never be late to have success, if you go for it."

– Frederick W. Sonpon

Stop Carrying a Poor Mind

Be a contributor to the world by putting your mind to work instead of sitting idly with a mind that is not active. Work with your mind, work with your body, and work on your entire life now. Initiate the process. It is through work that a return will come.

This is the power the world needs: our minds must work for us. It is the best superpower to create for your life. Currently, you may not have money, but you were born with riches because of the talents or potential you possess. They are the hidden riches inside you.

Understand this: the world doesn't need the power of complaining, creating unwanted stress through you. Rather, the world needs the power of invention. It also doesn't need the power of laziness, which increases poverty. So, see the world as your place of power, not as a place where you are powerless and invisible, without the means to show your talents. You were placed on earth to make a display of your character. You are not hidden underground; you are placed on the surface. This shows that you are to do good work and showcase whatever good is about your creation to the world.

The way you see yourself might be the reason your world is not improving yet. There lies your problem. How you think of yourself may be causing this, perhaps with poverty holding you down. You might be seeing yourself as a nobody because of life's trials. You may be going through some trials, but it doesn't mean you should stay in them forever. Poverty trials were made for you. Don't let them defeat you. See them as a way to polish you for the success that should come by fighting your way up.

However, your biggest problem might be that you are carrying fears. Maybe you see yourself as a nobody. Or is it the other way around? You may not be succeeding yet because you might be carrying a fear that only those with commendable backgrounds are destined to succeed. If this were the case, God wouldn't have placed us on the same earth. So, no one is better than you. Make yourself a valuable being without overlooking your life.

Stop building a reservoir of negativity inside you. It is an act of negativity akin to building a reservoir of poverty. You are not a negative entity because you are placed in a rich world. If you are carrying the negativity that you were born to be nobody, change it. If you are creating a negative reservoir in your life, know that you will only become its sole driver, especially if you can't change your thinking and your life.

I have noticed that many people are personally chained down because their minds are occupied with negativity. You were not created as a negative being. You carry value because you have talents. Change your thinking, change your life.

Some people are builders of negative reservoirs. They are filled with negativity. They create fields of negative grounds, not thinking about their lives or others. They seem as if they were never meant to succeed. Because of how they see themselves and the world, they lack good spirits of happiness. From their youth to their adult years, they remain the same almost forever. Strive to develop a power in yourself to become a great person in this world. Fight for this. Wake up. This world needs you more than you may need it, and you must determine what should become of your own world. This will add value to the world at large. Keep in mind that the world needs you to create something substantial or innovative that will be recognized and valued, improving all human lives. You could hold a patent for something you create. Why are you wasting time learning to put your mind to work? Stop keeping yourself down. Nobody will help you develop until you empower yourself for a change. If you keep yourself in the dark hole of poverty, you are limiting yourself and suggesting to the world that you are half-dead. To exist is one thing; to change your status is another. It depends on you to elevate your level. You have the power to succeed and shine. You were never made to be defaced by economic hardship.

Carry a mind of victory. Nobody in this world was ever made unsuccessful. Because we are all made successful, that is why we are in a rich world together. Just wake up and look ahead to your future; you will work towards achieving greatness by working it out. There is no mistake about your creation. Picture this: because every human being has success or values endowed within them, we are made in the image of God. Also, we all have talents or potentials inside us that are good elements which can bring each of us to light, depending on how we treat them by developing from them. Start tapping into yours now. If you can sing, start practicing to succeed in that now. If you are a cobbler, keep pressing on in that now. If you want to sell pure water as a source of your future greatness, start doing that now. The small things you do are what faith is built upon, leading to bigger things. Plant the seed of your success now while you are at your early stage.

It is not a mistake for you to face poverty now. It is a matter of being polished by waking up to succeed from poverty. Nothing good can happen for a person until you learn to work out the good to come. There is no mistake about you. You are here on earth for a good purpose because you come from the good hands of a great God who made all things, including us. There is no mistake concerning you and the world. You are just missing the steps of success based on the kinds of thinking you keep having. Perhaps you are fooling yourself by not believing that you are carrying some values of greatness that you must strive to bring to life for the world to benefit from, including your own life. Those who have nothing to offer to earth are the ones who are dead and gone. But you are still here, meaning you have something to achieve probably before you get old and leave earth. Think of this right now!

Understand that success will only be possible if you learn to follow its rules or patterns, which are not ordinary rules but patterned on the culture of the majority where you may have never thought positively before. Success has a different culture in that only a few thinkers who see themselves as winners, not as mourners, embrace such a culture. Until you learn to see yourself as a winner, you will only widen the scope of being a complainant over life. Create a thinking room by not thinking ordinarily about your life. Sometimes have quiet time and think about how you can make it. Look around you and see those succeeding to understand that there is no magic about them.

Buy some books to read. Meditate on your life so that in the next few years, you must not be the same person that everybody knows as being nobody and living in poverty. Start working both day and night with the hope of succeeding. Make sure to improve yourself. Stop sitting. You can never be paid for doing nothing. And understand that nobody is better than you until you start to value and improve yourself now. Start making a difference now. Start adding value to society by succeeding. This is why society needs you to develop now. This is why society depends on people like you to help. You are one of those who will do something to make society better. Step out of the little closet of negativity now! Dump away the negative mindset of keeping poverty as a property with you.

Be one of those who will discard a lack of fulfilment and bring in a life of achievements. Be one of those who will employ people by the time you succeed. You need to see the world as a place of honor for your life, not as a place of dishonor. And honor for your life can't just happen until you work it out. I guess you may be denying the purpose of God in creating this world, especially if you do nothing about your life and see the world as a place of dishonor, living dishonorably. Stop proving it wrong by your actions, suggesting that God is a liar and created you only to see you do nothing positive with your life on earth. You are not a substance to be treated anyhow. He gave you authority just as He did for the first two humans (Adam and Eve) to rule the earth and even subdue it. You are part of the generation of those first humans. Stop hiding the power you have in you and begin working, showcasing the power of your greatness to the world by helping society with your success.

What you should know is that complainers are not thinkers. Complainers are not promoters. Complainers are not valuable workers. Complainers are not inventors. Complainers are not creators of ideas. But those who can create or invent are those who think positively. And thinkers don't sit with the majority who are complaining and never think of helping their own lives and society. Thinkers learn to isolate themselves for making discoveries during quiet time and to think of good ideas. They work out whatever good ideas they conceive by proving them right to the world. If you want to start moving forward, develop your thinking room. It could be in your house. Do it by picturing the world as a valuable place, and that you should be of value to contribute something positive to it with your ideas. So, learn to buy books and start reading about other successful people, their backgrounds, and how they might have made it or continue making it. Every successful person has a story to tell the world about how they succeeded, which should be a lesson you can use to turn your situation around. What I know about successful people is that some might have gone through very terrible pasts, perhaps compared to yours, which they overcame. Their stories could help you rethink your life instead of giving up or doing nothing in the world.

If you make up your mind, you will be paving the way to a future that should be bright for you. Your mind is the first thing that was given power before your body. It was given to you as your power, a base for the start of your life so that you can use it. See it as a rich box that must produce valuable ideas. Until you start warming it up with thinking, it will remain as it is. Books can help warm up your brain and start formulating ideas for changing your level. It is a reservoir of resources because it holds the inventions you see from people who put their minds to work, leading them to live good lives. You can do the same. Your mind is a rich box, full of ideas that must be shared with the world. Maybe you could be an inventor of a sweet or nice cake that bears your name. Or, you could be an inventor of something movable. A trade needs to start with ideas that will develop into the production of goods. This can happen because you have talents or potentials inside you. They are a store of values. I see them as invisible goods inside your head. You must think them out so they can become physical products. You don't need many ideas. A single idea can make a difference for you. And you don't really need many people helping you before you make it. You don't need to beg to start improving either. The same five senses that successful people have, you have as well. And they are not in a different world but in the same world we all are in.

I guess you want to know how your mind is considered a rich element. It is full of riches and should be emptied out based on what you do with it. Know that your talents or potential are invisible goods. Know that the service you provide is good and can market you well. Know that opportunities coming your way are goods that can change your status until you learn to improve your thinking. They can market people as one's marketable goods. You were marked long ago by God as possessing some marketable goods in the form of talents inside of you.

Develop a sense to do something about your life now. And how does one do this? Make use of every opportunity given to you by people. See those opportunities as goods in service based on the trust people have in you. Embrace this concept. To better manage what has been entrusted to your care, ensure that it also helps to change you for the better. Know that your character can sell you as a good, and through it, better opportunities from people could come to you. Even if you are an inventor selling your brand, if your character is bad, nobody will want to buy your product. Character is a product of life that can sell people, and you must value yours. This is why you don't have to waste things that people give you, which are part of opportunities to manage. Your progress could be based on some of the opportunities you were given. Every blessing doesn't come directly; sometimes, it can come through people indirectly. This is why you must also value gifts from people. Some are opportunities. Make proper use of them. Potentials are riches inside you as gifts from God. Create a marketplace for such goods now. I am doing the same with my ideas of writing books. I write books that come from my inner thoughts and bring them into the physical state through publishing to sell. They are my marketable goods available to offer to the world to create some money. Yours could be different from mine, but know that you have goods inside you—referring to your talents or potential. Tap into them and stop waiting in vain.

Move from ground zero with your life. From your point of economic difficulties, you must go on to a place of prosperity if you can work it out.

Be like a winner. Understand that God created every human being with potential or talents. These potentials are ideas that must be turned into products. They must be turned into physical goods when you take steps to bring them to light and market yourself, especially in this book you are reading. It is an idea from the potential that God gave me, which I brought from my mind into a physical product. You created a purchase by obtaining it. It came from my spiritual side or inner thoughts. You have the power to invent something as well. Just be willing to exercise your brain by learning to think and harnessing that power.

It is part of the gift of God to me, specifically based on this book. Everything you have been told is about having the power to let your potential or talents be shown to the world. This is the message you must get from this book you are reading.

I have shared part of my potential, and others need to hear about yours too. You have yours that the world must benefit from. Just make a move and start thinking about your future now. Look at this example: if I were to sell even one million copies of this book you are reading at a cost of one United States Dollar each, I would make one million dollars, minus the cost of production. That would be a substantial sum. It shows that an idea turned into a product can generate money. Give something to life before life gives you something in return. This is what potential is within us. We must create a plan to bring that potential to the world. By doing so, you could become the owner of a patent, and the world could pay you.

Start to think positively about your life now. You could be carrying a negative mindset, which could be causing delays in your life.

Let me elaborate on how you may be carrying a negative mindset. Some of these signs might be:

- You don't see the world as a big place with your own place in it. You view it as small because you have a limited mindset about your own life. You don't picture yourself as part of it, contributing to it.
- You isolate yourself due to poverty, making you feel like you don't fit in society or with other people.
- You don't see your life as valuable and in need of improvement.
- You see money as evil instead of viewing it as a tool that can serve you if you learn to make or manage it.
- You are lazy and haven't thought about empowering yourself or making improvements.
- You wait for a push before you can learn to push yourself.

- You overlook things entrusted to you that could help change your life.
- You are not trusted to manage anything because you don't see success as something you must achieve.
- You overlook others' successes, thinking they were born with advantages or that their success is due to evil rather than attributing it to their efforts or God. This mindset makes you not focus on earning money or becoming rich.
- You aren't able to manage yourself.
- Maybe you think success falls to earth and is intended for others but not you.
- You surround yourself with negative people who are your friends.
- You waste your life with men who have no future to offer because they also live loosely.
- You value your body so much that when you get a small amount of money, you rush to buy clothes or use it, often regretting the expenditure later because you didn't spend it wisely or invest in something with better returns.
- You don't plan to invest money at all, possibly because you lack dreams. This lack of vision is causing delays.
- You see your background as a hindrance rather than thinking of improving yourself beyond it, which may be limiting you.
- You are always too weak to do positive things that could change your situation, possibly due to spiritual problems or reasons that make you feel destined for poverty.

The way you think of yourself, your environment, and how you respond to life will determine the kind of person you become in the future. Start preparing for tomorrow by taking the actions you take today. Stop letting your life drift aimlessly. Don't you know that we are getting older with each passing day? Develop the power within you to push yourself. Only by pushing yourself will you make a difference and attract opportunities.

You are part of the world and should help determine the power within it, rather than letting the world create a negative force against you. Know that life doesn't lie to anyone. Just as two plus two equals four, nothing less or more. Until you add value to your life, regardless of your location or country, life will give you only what you don't desire. Some people aren't poor by choice, but because of their past actions or others' greed, they are poor. You must give value to your life by planting seeds that will grow into a future harvest. Look at farmers: those who plant during the season have the opportunity to harvest later in the year. Create your own farming season. So, what are you planting in your life? What are you doing that will lead to prosperity? According to the common law of receiving, you must give before you receive. In short, if you want to reap a harvest by learning something, you must go and learn now in that field to develop a profession.

Chapter 5

Lessons from Successful People

There are several lessons in life you must learn as a way of positioning yourself. For you to succeed, you must first learn from your past and determine what you want to become in the future. Look at your background, including the problems of poverty you encountered, and try to determine what is good for you to work towards in the future. Reflect on those things that caused your life to be degraded, and try to change your story. One of the biggest mistakes to avoid is having life within you but not doing anything meaningful to progress. Why can't you also learn from the most successful people in the world and start to shape your life accordingly? Many of those successful individuals started from nowhere before reaching their current levels of success.

Success doesn't fall from the blue sky. This is why you must stop expecting manna from the sky, as it is not meant to fall solely for you. If you think success can fall from above and that God will grant it to you, that is impossible. The only falling success for everyone is the rain that helps our food grow. But it isn't possible to see a diamond fall from heaven that is intended just for you. The only possibility in life, which God has made available for all, is the creation of a single world full of riches for each one of us. Your talents will never be depleted, and you will not face global warming affecting such resources. It is a world that came about from God's thinking. Because God thought of what He wanted to do, we must also think to create all that we want. This is the same world that man was made to take authority over and subdue. It has all the values of life within it. Start digging into your mind to uncover the values inside you, as you will need to establish a new market for yourself. However, some people are not willing to start digging by thinking and doing positive things that will bring out the good inside them. God didn't place you in a territory of frustration and poverty; it's not a reason for you to accept being that way. See that God, who made you, is a successful God. He did not create mankind without resources, which is why the world is still full of riches. They are made for you and me. Until you put yourself to work, you won't feel like you are part of the world and enjoying its resources.

Live so that you are successful and happy rather than living in poverty or mediocrity and complaining constantly. Consider why you were made. You were made good by God, which means you should live well rather than suffer. Be a controller of your world and live like a queen or king on earth. Start meditating on this and work towards it. You must, because time is not waiting for you. Stop having a poor or average mindset and claiming that you have no reason to exist. Turn away from the road of poverty. Make a turn now. Get on the path of successful people. Watch your thinking. You must rise before you can help those who are down. You must develop so you can own a company and employ more people in your country.

Start thinking like successful people. You carry God within you, not men, so your development shouldn't depend on others. Find your redemption in God and in your efforts to apply that which will make a difference for you. Embrace a big mindset. Erase the negative thinking that money is trouble for your life and the world. People who say this are wrong. They are wrong because money drives the economy. If you don't have it, you won't be able to buy anything or contribute to your nation's economy.

You see! According to statistics, many of the crimes committed in the world are mostly by poor or average people. Being poor or average is not inherently bad, but don't accept being poor or average. Understand that the reason you are in this rich world created by God is for you to also live richly. God loves this about you. He doesn't want you to suffer because you are hungry or unable to feed yourself. Fight to succeed through your labour.

Some characteristics of successful people that you should aspire to achieve one day are:

1. Successful people don't see themselves as limited.
2. Successful people depend on the power of their minds and will by learning to push themselves.
3. Successful people eat healthy food that adds value to their lives and helps them live longer than poor or average people, who eat just anything without nutrients or values merely to survive.
4. Successful people look at the bigger picture rather than the small details, compared to poor and average people who have limited perspectives about themselves and the world. Everything people do is sometimes seen as insignificant by those who do not think positively or act accordingly.
5. Successful people view money as a tool to serve them, whereas poor and average people see money as evil and are reluctant to have it. They work hard without figuring out the flaw in this view, instead learning to create money by planning for the future.
6. Successful people learn to give more and are blessed with having more, unlike poor and average people who don't always have and can't give due to their poverty, becoming poorer over time.
7. Successful people avoid borrowing for unnecessary reasons, whereas poor and average people borrow and borrow without intending to repay.
8. Successful people make themselves powerful in the world rather than depending on the world to give them power.

9. Successful people work for themselves, unlike poor and average people who spend their lives working for others.

10. Successful people are less troubled by economic problems and support the economies of their lands. In contrast, poor and average people are burdened by economic issues and may resort to evil practices to support their lives or focus on receiving from their lands.

11. Successful people can build refined lives for themselves, whereas poor and average people often build scattered lives or live in precarious economic situations. In short, successful people are more organized compared to poor and average people who live haphazardly due to their poverty.

12. Successful people take risks to invest, focusing on becoming richer, whereas poor and average people risk their lives working for employers or struggling without having anything to show or invest in because of their minimal incomes.

13. Successful people work fewer hours and are often close to their families, creating happiness. Poor and average people work longer hours and stay away from their families, which may create bitterness and a lack of love within their families. This can lead to children becoming wayward due to insufficient care from parents or guardians. Many major crimes are committed by people from poor or average backgrounds.

14. Successful people learn to invest further, unlike poor and average people who don't invest but spend almost everything they make, always finding money insufficient.

15. Successful people complain less and less randomly compared to poor and average people who complain daily for no better reason than their limited resources to meet their wants and needs.

16. Successful people are more likely to tell the truth compared to poor and average people who lie daily to survive or to manipulate situations.
17. Successful people create their own pension schemes by working for themselves and saving to set up businesses, whereas poor and average people rely on government pensions and continue working for their employers.
18. Successful people quickly address their pressing needs with available money, whereas poor and average people may struggle to find means or money, often giving up and relying on external help to solve their problems due to poverty.
19. Successful people pay more in bills and taxes, supporting government tax programs or developments, compared to poor and average people who pay fewer bills or taxes, often complain, and sometimes avoid paying their share.
20. Successful people give to or receive less from the state compared to poor and average people who have limited resources and rarely consider seeking more from the state.
21. Successful people live richly compared to poor and average people who live cheaply and complain about spending money.
22. Successful people experience fewer criminal activities at their residences, unlike poor and average people who often face higher levels of criminality in their areas or become involved in criminal activities for survival.
23. Successful people give more compared to poor and average people who don't have the means to give.
24. Successful people live happily and longer compared to poor and average people who are often stressed while searching for survival and die young.

This should give you the power or sense of life to work skilfully toward becoming successful. Understand that it is better for you to succeed and be rich than to be poor or an average person who will always work hard for others or support the dreams of the people or institutions they work with, instead of learning to work for themselves. They support the dreams of others in that way. Think about this now. Know that the best economy to have is one where you learn to create money by working for yourself.

Don't be a slave to yourself, to others, or to your society, especially by not doing anything to change your status. Know that you belong to a people made by God, who should always strive to be great and contribute more to society. Don't have the mindset that society should do more for you than you do for society. It is a dependent mentality you may be carrying if you think that way.

Understand that the biggest enslavement in life, which you must learn to avoid, is having your personal economy controlled by others. Some people, before they can survive in this world, make themselves dependent on the fact that others have to give to them before they can survive. It is a limiting situation to rely on others for sustenance without creating your means of feeding yourself. Don't believe in the popular saying that not everybody on earth can be successful. Stop enslaving yourself with thoughts of low self-worth. The control of your life starts from your mind, which I want to be filled with thoughts of good. It is a power that comes from your spirit if you see value in yourself and start to have confidence in your ability. It is your soul that controls your happiness, and you have to keep that inner person happy by doing things that will bring you joy. And you must work to be successful.

You have inner power, with your spirit being the source. It is not a power that leads you to create a life of dependency syndrome or to make complaints that only increase your burdens.

So, it would be a great thing to celebrate, especially if you become successfully rich. This will make you a good giver compared to being a good receiver from others because you are poor or average. Societies need givers, not takers, who are like tanks, hoarding things for themselves or expecting that their national governments will dump resources on them before they survive. Such receivers know how to take in but never learn to give out because they are average or poor. Until you develop the ability to give, stop taking from what is not available in the world.

Chapter 6

"Your frequency for success resides within you, determined by the mindset you possess. However, it will only begin working for you once you elevate yourself. Activate this inner power by striving to change and raise your level."

– Frederick W. Sonpon

Why the World Is Declining

One of the biggest mistakes I see in the world is that the world's population doesn't support each other much. People are more self-centred than selfless. I see this happening within most families in Africa as well. At the community level, it's the same. Everybody is becoming selfish due to the growing influence of individualism. Worse still, the corporate life situation, where people are working hard just to make a living and leaving their children behind, is contributing to this. Children are left to take care of themselves or are placed in state-run schools or care units, leading them to grow up more selfish while family values are declining. These days, our children are so engaged with technology that they are exposed to things detrimental to their well-being, often beyond the awareness of their parents. This highlights the fact that we are no longer fostering love or maintaining the collective or communal culture of promoting love. Our children are growing up selfish, and we, as parents, are too focused on survival or advancement, which is detrimental because we lack the time to stay at home and associate with our children, leaving them to fend for themselves.

How can a teenager march into a church or school and shoot people, which is commonplace in America? Society is developing stressful conditions and hardships for many reasons, with drug abuse and racism being major factors.

The bad effect, which seems to be destroying society, is that nobody wants to be trusted. Many young people in my country, Liberia, are no longer trusted. Corruption is increasing in the public sphere. Individuals with money who try to help ordinary people often fall victim to the lack of trust in our society. This is causing poverty to increase. I read the history of some people who received help to improve their lives and start businesses, but those trusted to run the businesses ended up squandering the money due to a lack of basic financial discipline.

Sometimes I wonder why. It's not that there aren't people who can help, but there is a lack of trust in society.

The blessings of God can sometimes come indirectly to people. Some blessings may come in the form of someone helping you to start your journey toward success.

This is when you realize that character matters in life. Until you learn to build a good character, you may struggle. Destiny helpers may pass by, and you might think that God isn't blessing you, but until you succeed in building good character, it may be difficult for you to succeed financially. To manage money effectively, character is essential.

However, many people in the world don't respect the importance of building character for success before seeking success. Today, the world is facing a problem of character deficiency. It is creating fear for everything—fear for survival, fear of life, fear of losing jobs, fear of global warming, fear of war, etc. These fears come with emotions that are affecting our lives and are the basis for our struggles. You must be able to control these fears instead of letting them control you. Start by overcoming your economic fears of not having money by working skilfully to lift yourself out of poverty. Stop letting desires work against you, especially if you do nothing and allow poverty to consume you.

I must say this loudly: character is the foundation of seeking success, and this is dying in the world. You must develop a character for success that should be joined with other qualities in order to become a winner in life. In short, what you offer to anyone in society is the character you have. If you are a business person, the character of trustworthiness in doing business will create loyal customers for you. Therefore, work on your character because it reflects your fears and emotions. The way you think also influences the way you act.

Don't let your character die despite the challenges you may be facing now. If you look around, you will see that there is a reason why the character is dying in the lives of many. Modern life is causing the character to lose its value.

What is now a popular element that some people are promoting more is corruption, which is becoming rampant. It is bringing public dissatisfaction and creating trouble in our various societies. Don't let its trap grab you. The damage to character is leading the world in this direction of a lack of trust and infighting. Because every human being needs to improve their character, begin to work on yours now. Develop a new character for success, not just an ordinary character that may not be taking you anywhere. Don't let this general lack of character that holds society down continue to follow you. Help yourself so you can help others in reshaping the world. Let the world see that greatness starts with you and me. Enter the arena of success. Know this: the world needs good and strong people, not bad, weak, or lazy people who contribute nothing. So, begin to use your mind and work on your life now.

You are the world. What shapes your world is the character you display in it. You should determine the power that exists in the world. The world will not have power if you are not empowered to show the good inside of you. If you succeed, I believe that many people in your area or country will notice, and some will want to follow your example to succeed. If you remain idle, you could be holding back the blessings or successes of many people who, through your ingenuity, creativity, and hard work, might have succeeded. This is how I see life: sometimes, our blessings are interconnected. We just need to push each other to reveal them. This is why you must develop a business or success-oriented character that will make you stand out. It is the character of success that some people have learned, which allows them to move through life differently from the majority. They are just different people. Until you learn to be different in your life, you may not be going anywhere.

Falling into a Trap of Early Rejection

I went through it all, being affected by the wind of neglect. As soon as I was two years old, my mom left my father and even left home to be with my stepfather, and they started living far away in a different region of my country. I was then left in the care of my grandparents on my mother's side. This all started in 1978. I was about two years old when my mom left me with my grandparents to take care of me. I was partly abandoned because my parents were very poor and couldn't even afford to take care of me.

Despite my grandfather and grandmother having their own children to take care of, I joined the list of their family as a grandchild, becoming somewhat of a burden for them. I became my grandma and grandfather's boy. They didn't have much, considering the poverty they faced, but they did their best by helping me start schooling. They set me on the road by looking at the future with hope, expecting that I would become a successful man by making millions through the empowerment of education. The desire to learn something is essential because nobody is born with knowledge; we all start learning the various lessons of life through people, experiences, and other sources. This is why our ability to learn from others, buy books to read, listen to audio, attend seminars, etc., is the sum of our education that can either shift us positively or negatively. Education is the most powerful tool you must seek. If you gain power by using your mind, riches will follow.

Despite the harsh words from my grandma as she struggled to raise me, I didn't abandon the education I received from such an upbringing. I became a strong child. She still loved me, but what often led to her insults was the fact that life was very tough for her family. Having me as another responsibility created an additional burden on her family. My father couldn't come around, and worse, Grandma never received good news from my mom, who was far away. She couldn't even hear from my mother. Grandma did what she did with the hope of training my mental state. She troubled me with insults, and sometimes, I felt degraded by them. She had a habit of insulting me by abusing my father whenever she was angry. But that didn't mean much to me as a boy. I knew that with such insults, she wanted me to become a strong man. I can remember some of her harsh words, which I have decided to write down. Some of her insults included calling me a devil's child and neglecting my parents. But I couldn't take the insults to heart or hold anything against my grandma. These words were part of the culture of bringing up children in society, meant to make us strong enough to withstand insults from older people. This sort of training was meant to teach a lesson. But most people, when insulted, let their emotions control them. However, the insults were intended to teach me to exercise restraint in life.

As young people in Niffu Town, we were taught to respect older people, no matter what. Even if they treated young people badly, we were told to respect them. No child was allowed to abuse an older person in public. It was considered a big crime to do so. This was the culture I grew up in, where older people always had the upper hand over younger people. Even if the younger one was right, the older person was favoured. If there was a problem between two people, one younger and one older, the older person would always win because older people were protected, and they were expected to protect the younger ones. There would be no investigation if a younger person and an older person had a conflict. So, I was raised in this kind of environment and accepted it, as my grandma always insulted me, calling it an act of training. I saw this as a sweet way of polishing my life by learning to have restraint. She always told me that I needed to first attend a "mental school" of training before I could learn anything else. Therefore, you must learn to attend a mental school of learning to restrain yourself before you can become successful in this world. Discipline yourself to manage money, study about money, and learn about values that can increase your financial worth instead of diminishing it by creating more expenses and liabilities in your life.

Some people eat more than what they make instead of learning to invest what they earn by first learning to save and invest. Also, learn to develop a character for business because you could come across destiny helpers who might have attitude problems. You should know how to live and deal with them. Don't let your emotions control you by becoming angry with your destiny helper just because they say something unfavorable to you. At workplaces, some people get vexed for no reason, especially if their bosses don't favour them. They want favours for job promotions and salary increases. You will always have people who will hate you for nothing. They may do this because of the star you have. The best thing you can do to make your star shine is to learn to work for yourself. Nobody will better shine your star than you will.

Some bosses or destiny helpers may seem rude but may not necessarily be bad people. They just have emotions they don't control. You have to control your emotions when dealing with them. Study those kinds of people. You may find such attitudes in the workplace, at school, within an organization, etc. Life requires us to start somewhere before we achieve the success we expect from it.

Take a cue from what my grandma did. One of the lessons I learned from this was how to swallow insults by controlling my emotions. It helped build a spirit of meekness in me relative to the culture I grew up in. Not that it was good behaviour from her, but it helped make me the person I am. I learned to live with people by studying their attitudes. Study people, and you will better know your way through life. But if you don't know your way yet in life, your first lesson should be to learn to study people and understand how to live with them.

There was no concept of child's rights considered during those days before 1989 when Liberia's civil war erupted. Because of the war situation, the world has taken a different trend concerning society. It is no longer the case because of this child's rights movement increasing in power, where nobody can just beat a child from my town any longer. If a child misbehaved or did something wrong, you had to tell the parents first or take the complaint to the police. But you are not allowed to beat a little child, even if that child misbehaves or does something wrong. This was the culture I grew up with. Such a culture has been discarded because rudeness has become the order of the day, promoted by the public. The state is more focused on protecting the rights of children and mothers, leaving men to be treated as slaves in society because of democracy.

Modernity has had some adverse effects on life. Today, young people can openly smoke in public, take drugs, abuse anyone without respect for age, etc.

My father didn't even care about me during those days because he, too, didn't have much. His parents brought him up in poverty, which forced him to abandon them and move to Niffu Town after leaving Sass Town within the same county of Grand Kru. He should have shown concern and love for a child like me, but he didn't care. He needed to be a responsible father then. I was left in the care of my grandparents. I must tell you my story so you can't let go of those ugly pasts and focus on your life to help yourself, especially if you had an ugly past like mine or even worse. Despite my difficult upbringing, my grandma and grandpa were the ones who struggled to ensure that I got started with schooling.

I often wore tattered clothes because my parents couldn't afford to buy me clothes or essentials. They, too, were struggling in poverty and had their own children to support.

Many times, I had to walk barefoot around the whole place until my grandfather managed to find some money to buy me a pair of slippers. Poverty can lock people up in disgrace and promote suffering.

For a while after a good number of years in this situation, something happened. My mother wanted me to stay with her. At the time, she had left home to be with my stepfather on a mission. That's how, in 1988, I left Niffu Town. It happened like this: at age 11, one day, I heard my grandfather tell me that he got a message from my stepfather that I was about to travel to my mother for schooling and leave Niffu Town. This news felt like heaven coming down upon me. It was like news from heaven because I was about to leave the rural, economically difficult terrain. It was close to December in 1988 when my grandfather, my little uncle, and I left home. It was a funny and terrifying journey. Travelling from Niffu, my little Uncle Benjamin, who was then travelling to Buchanan to stay with Uncle Stephen, and I boarded a canoe belonging to my grandfather early in the morning, making our way first to Greenville, Sinoe County. From there, we would get into a car to travel to Buchanan, Grand Bassa County, where my uncle had his house. Later, I would continue to Lofa County, where my mom was with her family, as my final destination. For days after hearing the news of my travel, I felt like I was already in heaven because I believed my dream of building a new future was about to begin. I couldn't even think of eating. For the first time, hearing such happy news, tears drenched my brows heavily.

What I still remember and will never forget is that my travelling bag at the time, due to the poverty level, was a black plastic bag in which I put my clothes. I wore shower slippers from Niffu Town to Greenville City, then to Buchanan City, and finally to Monrovia City. Travelling from Greenville City to Buchanan City, my Uncle Ben and I had to sit on a makeshift seat in a mini-bus. We had our palms held against our knees, squatting slightly on our makeshift seats (not normal seats).

Awkwardly, we were seated with our backs facing the direction we were moving towards. It was not the normal way of sitting, where one faces the direction the vehicle is moving. Instead, our backs were turned toward our destination. The area where we were seated was designed for people to relax their legs, like for those sitting in the nearby seats. Frankly speaking, we were moving like cows being pulled in a direction by force. We could only see the backs of those seated in front of us while they were looking at our faces and seeing behind us. For almost a whole day, we travelled like that from Greenville City to Buchanan City. It was on a gravel road. The dust from the road covered our entire faces and bodies inside the bus. And we all saw it as a normal way of travel because the road wasn't paved.

At the time, my mother and her family were on vacation in Monrovia City after they left Lofa County on a mission. I was to join them before we were to take off for Lofa County, where my stepfather was serving as an instructor at a teacher training institution, which also had an elementary and junior high school for me to join my little brother and sisters. A year after we arrived on campus, the civil war broke out. My family and I survived by engaging in subsistence farming. We did this twice in two years. We also started making gardens where we could grow various colours of potatoes.

Despite all the struggles, my life has changed. To have a better future like I do today, I didn't take my education lightly. I used to love studying and reading.

Don't let your present condition make you think the world is against you because you are poor. You just need to change your mentality, and a new world will begin with you. I remember that Christ Jesus knew the current world of mankind was spiritually damaged due to the way mankind lived. Because of this, one must accept Him as Lord and Savior, which will set up a path to a new world. Therefore, 2 Corinthians 5:17 says that if any man is in Christ, he is a new creature. He came to recreate the great persons of God differently. He didn't come to destroy the physical world; He came to destroy the old inner man that caused your life to be meaningless and restore you to honour. In short, you are going to start a different world, so you don't live the same way, full of pride, bitterness, and corruption, which suggests that the spirit of God left you. He wants to bring back the spirit of God inside you by helping your new self. It is a gradual change, but you have to be willing to accept it. This is why you must also be financially new by overcoming poverty. You have to develop because nobody was born to be poor. This is why we are in a rich world.

It is the same with success—you have to be willing to make sacrifices before a level of change can come relative to such success. You must be prepared to start a new world and not live as ordinary. To become rich, you must develop financial discipline, an exercise that may be tough for you as you begin to achieve this. It is the difference you make between your current state and your past that will bring about a different version of you, allowing you to live in a more glorious future. This is how the future version of yourself will be discovered. Learn the physical act of going to school as a way of discovering different aspects of our lives that should have knowledge where previously there was none. When you obtain an education, you should use it positively. Your education must not cause you suffering or create conflict with society. You must help to add value to your society with the education you obtain.

So, why focus so much on your past? Can't you learn something for your life? Success is never achieved on a silver platter. Stop sitting around. There is no well you will dig and never find water. Stop sitting and waiting for a better day out of the blue sky. To sit without doing anything for your future promotes inactivity, which could even affect your mind and body, causing them to decline. Imagine you were to buy an engine to supply electricity, but you didn't turn it on. Would that engine produce anything? No. This is how life works—we are made like machines that must be turned on before we can produce. A fear of God and education help us do this. Learn something with your hands. Imagine a man like me who never knew anything and never had any means to think there would be a better tomorrow, but God changed my situation. I didn't sit around complaining from morning to night without taking a step. What about your case? What is too hard for God to do? You can make your life work just as my life is working. What I couldn't do or afford before, I can now do or afford. See poverty as a disease that can limit people, and you must fight against it by learning something. Education can't deny people. You will get results. And that's how life goes—you must give to life before it returns value to you. Learning something for the future is an act of giving to your life, giving you power for the future. Your education will bring a return through the work you do. The work will bring in money, and money will bring satisfaction by meeting your wants and needs. And satisfaction is about fulfilment in economics. You must be fulfilled by having the means to always spend because you will have money without struggling for it.

I must boast in God for you to know that He can bless people regardless of their backgrounds. He can bless anybody. This is why He gave the whole world to everyone, whether wicked or good. And God's intended purpose for your life can't be for you to suffer, even in poverty. He lifted you and me since the foundation of the world.

Do something about your life now. I gave you a glimpse of my background story to help you begin rethinking your life, to put life in you, and to stop complaining. Nobody is better than you if you wake up and try, and you will succeed. Look at what God did concerning creation. None of us was with Him when He was about to start creating the world, but He did it because He wanted mankind to have a place like Earth as their own. Even in heaven, there is no special heaven for angels other than the heaven He Himself resides in. But for mankind, He created a home for us, which didn't happen for the angels.

After God had thought about what He wanted to do concerning creation, the next step was to apply some effort by working out what He had thought, letting His plan come to fruition. This is the Almighty God who made all humans in His image and likeness (Genesis 1:26). It depicts power and attraction, which you must take note of so that your life reflects good if you can believe in Him and work your life out of deadness. Our God is not dead, so you are not supposed to be dead because of circumstances turning you upside down and inside out.

Life can sometimes be hard, frustrating, painful, and degrading to the extent that one can regret why it has to be this way, but that doesn't mean you should give up. Life will come with trouble, and you have to look for the good inside the troubled state. Value how God is good to you. You can never go to God to ask Him why He decided to create you at the time He did. Despite your complaints, there is no way you will physically see God to ask Him why life is so troubling and full of struggles. He told mankind from the beginning the trouble sin would cause if man sinned. These are the consequences mankind is confronted with because our forefathers and foremothers—Adam and Eve— sinned against God. They were warned not to do the things that could cause trouble in their lives and the world, but they failed to follow God's instructions. God knows the purpose of all things. We are told in the Bible, especially in the Book of I Thessalonians 5:18, that in all things, we must give thanks to God because it is the will of God for our lives. The will of God is that you should be polished by circumstances and become a victor in time after you have gone through it all. Remember also that any person who is about to rise in life must start from the bottom before going up. Picture this from our birth situation—nobody came into this world with anything or as a full-grown person before passing through the mother's belly. We were first little children before we started growing up big.

Why then can't you picture this also concerning your success? Bear in mind that anything that must go up starts from the bottom. Start your success with the little steps you take today before reaching the point of your glory. It is only from the top that you can see around you or be able to help somebody who is down and probably take that person up, but you must go up first. The power God gives each of us is based on the power of our minds, which changes our levels. It can create that which wasn't created by first thinking it out. It can even be destroyed if you decide to be evil with your mind. It is the source of creating marketable goods by bringing your potential out to the world. It can think of ideas that will lead to success for each of us. When ideas are working, your body will be working along to shine. These ideas can bring about a good economy for anyone. Imagine, this is why we go to school to learn—because we want to change our levels by exercising the knowledge we get from schooling.

Through the manifestation of your mind working for you, whatever you harbour in your mind or within a dream form will come to light if you can take steps concerning it. Having a dream is like your spirit man grabbing a gift to bring to your physical self. You have to put the spirit-man into motion with the gift by bringing it into a physical element for the body to enjoy its values. This is why you must discover your true self by discovering your new world. If you don't do so now, nobody will discover you. Put yourself in a life mirror to reflect the good values you have and show them to the world. Life is about making a reflection of what we have inside of us by bringing it to light and proving it. Stop hiding at the backdoor of your life and realize that you were made to be displayed. You were made to be displayed, which is why you were not placed inside the earth but on the surface of the earth, to show what you have to display in good. When the time of having no use comes, which every human being may be confronted with—meaning you will have been dead and gone—the ground becomes the next place of final habitation, except for the soul that would stand before God because you are here on a mission and will have to report back to God. But for now, you are not old yet and not dead to be buried in the ground. You are positioned on the surface to learn to be displayed for good. You are still living, which is the basis for you to do living things instead of sitting and doing nothing, which may be causing your life to be without purpose yet. Only living people, having the power to know this, are able to move.

You must struggle for a reason now and later struggle out. So, don't mind how things are for you today, but work to leave the struggle level in order to attain your glory in time. Whatever pains you may be going through, you will overcome them. It is out of struggle that peace and joy come. Put your head to work before your life can work, allowing the society you are in to feel the impact of your lifting.

Tailor your life in a way that creates an asset instead of living in liabilities. Making yourself an asset means adding value to your life. The biggest asset you have ever had was the possibility, made by God, of having access to the world. You were made to have access to Earth because you are an asset. Because you are an asset, God sees you as valuable. This is your purpose. Anything that has no value lacks a purpose. Nothing is really wrong with you being down for now, but make a way from down to up. Your name was never written in the Bible as the person born to be poor, either. Check it! Only the mind you carry is causing you not to progress. Until you put your mind in power, your life will not be empowered to succeed either.

We must be able to push ourselves from the point or stage of no value until the glory stage is reached based on discovering our lives. Make the world discover you. God will not deny anyone a reason to succeed if that person works to activate the good inside them. You must wake up now. God knows your needs. Until you move, they will be without solutions. Our being down shouldn't be considered a regrettable moment by placing blame on God. But see your life or situation as a period of preparation. Don't mind hard times and say you were born to be in hard times. See it as your preparation period for the lifting ahead of you.

If you want to be successful, learn to read and check to know the history of successful people. You must take a cue from the Bible, which says there is a time for everything. No great person discovered in the Bible didn't start from a lowly state before becoming successful. Picture this as well: you will never be promoted if you are already promoted. Promotion will only come if you are at a stage of need that would lead to it. This is why you don't mind what is happening to you right now but begin to put life in you, having a mind developed without wavering, knowing you will succeed and that nothing will stop you from succeeding. Carry such a mind in you and begin to walk your way up. Your promotion is on the way if you can rise up from your poverty bed and begin to put life in you. Begin to mine for your glory to come now. Be able to take some steps now and see what your tomorrow will be like.

Really, having hope for a better future is not built on nothingness but rather on something, which makes it a hope to have for the future, and you have to work it out. Develop hope that your future will be better off and begin planning for it now. Nothing is impossible for a person who wakes up and decides to try to succeed. It is in your application of power to succeed that will bring about your employment into the future. Apply some effort before you get the result of success. Think of a change for you to be a great person instead of living in perpetual poverty as if you don't know your way out of it. If God didn't mean for you to succeed, He wouldn't have put you on this great earth. You are not here by mistake. There is an underlying reason that you must succeed. You must do the will of God here while living in glory. This is the time for a change for you that should someday come, especially if you keep pressing on. You must be bitter about your condition today so that the sweetness of your tomorrow can be possible. Don't have bitter poverty today, and let the same continue tomorrow without having time to enjoy either. Your tomorrow should be glorious, and it should be your time of compliments rather than your time of detriment.

Until you turn your life on, nobody will turn you on or make you go high or succeed. What you must learn and cultivate about your life is that God has given you power, which is why you are still alive. Stop sitting! Stop complaining. Stop depending on people to make it for you. Depends on God and on the effort you apply. Look up to God and see the kind of future you want by creating it now. If you don't make up for the future, it will never be the way you may expect it to be. Be focused on what you can do now rather than sitting and doing nothing about changing your level.

God can never deny you a place of honour until you start to create it. He was never mean to you; He has put talents or potentials in you that are your personal riches. Besides your personal riches, He put some riches in the soil so you can join hands with others, especially if you haven't discovered your talents yet. Everything about you and the earth is full of glory. Stop living like you are spiritually blind. Stop blaming God for not blessing you. Just try to develop faith in yourself and make a push. While making a push, remain focused on the process. Start training your mind and body by giving yourself power rather than sitting without empowering your life. Turn on your life now.

Start building a new version of yourself now. This new self must have a financial essence and a future that will create an impact on others as well. Know that you are to build a new version of yourself that will prove to the world that you are not ordinary anymore. By not living an ordinary life, you will not be found in an ordinary place, associating with ordinary people, or consuming ordinary food without nutrients. Look for money with the hope of being considered successful, of having a changed life and family, and of impacting those around you. You must fulfill your potential rather than being defaced on earth, having nothing positive to prove about yourself.

Think of this: by looking at the tower of any communication system, you can understand that obtaining frequency or transmitting it is achieved by building the tower up, which allows the power of frequency to emerge. The frequency for communication isn't built from the ground but rather up. You are made as a person with a frequency, and you must go up before your frequency of success will signal who you are. The power of frequency comes from above, which is why towers are built upward, not spread on the ground. For your success, the tower must start from the bottom, meaning from your zero-stage, before you see it rise. Your frequency for success will work well only if you elevate yourself; until you go up, it won't activate. In short, nobody will hear about you if you sit without doing anything. People want to know who you are in the world and what you can do. Your ideas are probably the elements that can bring about change in the world, where you are meant to change society by adding your voice and actions.

I want you to make money and go further by creating money through engaging in business ventures. Let money work for you. Don't see money as a burden if you have it to spend. Money should serve you by having it. Create a time when money will be looking for you instead of you chasing money throughout your life. This is the habit of poor and average workers. They chase money throughout their lives, learning greatly but never learning to work for themselves. Bear in mind that when old age comes, and you are still working for others, you are looking for money instead of letting money serve you by having your own businesses. No matter how smart you are by obtaining a great education and working for institutions or the government, if you don't learn to work for yourself, one day you could retire from whatever company or government you may be working for.

The act of making money should be turned into creating money. If you have a job, you make money by being paid for your service. You must have a fabulous job. Let your expertise pay off. When you start to earn money in this way, you should also go higher by creating money through adding trade to your life experience. This is why not every dollar you make while working should be spent. Save some so you can invest in the future. When you learn to work for yourself, you can live life in the best way without financial limitations. Invest in productive ventures that will create cash for you. This is where money makes money grow. Your growth should come from your experience of having businesses running. It is better to work for yourself than for others if you want money to grow in your hands. By learning to invest, you develop a growth mentality. This is what you need so that every dollar that comes into your hands isn't just consumed, but you will learn to save a portion of it first. You can better determine what you want your life to be like when you learn to work for yourself.

Every greatness has a start, which is not based on just sitting or expecting others to do it for you. You don't have to daydream about this. It starts with small things you do now, which will eventually turn into big things. One thing I know is that the bigger you become by successfully holding your ground, the better you will be as a help to others. So, learn to invest. Stop looking at money as a troublesome element to have. But the only thing I know about money is that if you don't have it and are working for others, it is as if money is using you because what you make will not always be sufficient to satisfy your needs and wants. You can better use money if you learn to create your own by investing. Some people carry a small-minded attitude about holding money, thinking it is troublesome to have too much. If having money is bad, why did Solomon in the Bible become a rich man? Why did Father Abraham also become a rich man? Why do you see people go to learn something that will market them for tomorrow? The world will not work if we all don't enter our productive arena of learning to work with our heads and hands.

You are just who you are, and until you know what you want to become, the change will not come for you. Be empowered by having money to use rather than letting money use you. Don't mind those who attribute having money to the devil, especially if they have too much to spend. But those kinds of people never attribute the sad thing of having too much poverty in the world to the devil creating it, because they accept being the way they are—struggling or not having money at all to spend and enjoy their lives. It is the poor mentality they carry about money.

Your idea can only fix you if you can get it out to the world from within you. You are just yourself until you try to change, especially if you want to succeed.

If you think that money is of the devil and by not having it work for you, why struggle all through your life looking for money then? Why go to the market every day to buy things using money? Everything about the business world we live in, for which you are able to buy food, is money in exchange that makes this business world work. Or, what is it that since you don't have money now, your life is facing economic difficulties? If you had money, you probably wouldn't live where you are suffering economically, perhaps. Or, you wouldn't sleep hungry or complain for nothing if you had money now. This should prove to you that you need money to solve your problems. And go beyond the level of solving money problems by dealing with money. Many people solve money problems and never deal with money. You can only deal with money if you learn to invest it. Solving money problems is what the working class does more by catering to their expenses.

See how money works. For example, leaving your house to go on the street and riding in a car involves spending money. The clothes you probably have now were bought with money. So, why be bitter about not having money? Stop carrying a negative mentality about holding money. See it as an instrument that should serve you. It should serve you, but you don't have to kill yourself by working extremely hard, looking for it tirelessly, or using any evil means. Money is made to serve people, but you are not made to serve money. Many people in this world serve money. They seek money to the point of not having time to worship God. They pursue money even to the extent of harming others. They are slaves to money. This is not the purpose of having money. It should serve you. God will not condemn you if you work to succeed. The height of life you want to reach depends on how you take your steps toward it.

It is bad to be in the world and to be down for no other reason than being poor or always broke. Stop being unable to contribute meaningfully to the world economy. Create a means to earn money and be able to buy. Stop letting others determine what you should have in the world without you deciding for yourself. If you let dependency take over your life persistently, you are telling the world to determine what you should have. If you allow the world to give you what you want, only poverty will continue to come your way. You have to wake up, work skilfully, and create your own world of prosperity. Poverty can make people eat anything without having a choice of diet. Remove yourself from such an arena. Reach a level where you begin to make choices about what you want to consume.

You were never made to be just a consumer on earth without learning to produce and make an impact on others. Lack of production is a problem in the world, where people face extreme shortages due to increasing dependencies from laziness.

You can succeed. I have taken my stand and joined the arena of producing people with my ideas by learning to write books from imagination. Writers are also producers, just as singers are. Through writers, movies are produced that keep us entertained and happy based on the beautiful stories they create.

This is an everyday activity of exercising to write a story because I am determined to be on top. I hate poverty and dislike sitting idle while doing nothing to change my life. Because of this, I am writing books for marketing. Books are ideas or thoughts that should create markets by educating the world. And good education is what the world needs.

If I think of a story while observing and write it down, turning it into a book, it will definitely generate sales. Since I had the dream of becoming a writer in 2010, I haven't sat on my dream because I know that God has a reason for giving me that dream. Nothing good can be achieved without God, who is the source of good. I am bitter about poverty because I have felt its effects. Imagine coming from a rich country where the people are poor. It is due to greed that successive governments in my country have failed to improve the lives of their citizens. You may come from a country like that, too, but you don't have to kill yourself or sit idly without doing anything to change your situation. I remember that my great-grandparents, from both my mother's and father's sides, felt the pinch of poverty and worked hard to ensure I could go to school. What they wished for in the future is a result of what I do by producing books. You only need an idea to change your level. It doesn't require many things.

I keep working toward my dream, nurturing the power to reach my best state. I keep nurturing the dream because I want to be the person I know I deserve to be. I keep nurturing it, learning from others through the books they have written, and I continue to buy and read. I have to keep nurturing my dream because the best is yet to come until I reach the level that God knows is my apex, for which He gave me the dream.

One thing I want you to know is this: I feel fine when I am spending money to help somebody or buy the things I need without begging. I feel fine using money to travel to places I want to go. I feel fine that I don't have to beg people but make it my duty to help others. I feel fine that I don't wear those kinds of clothes I used to wear as a boy, which were torn up between my legs when no mom and dad were around. My power has come through having success. It was a fight to achieve it. I can determine the kind of brand I want to spend my money on without worrying before spending. The same God who did it for me can do it for you. He just wants you to make the effort.

But there is no way a person who is poor can feel fine in life and help other people while being poor themselves. When you are poor, you lack one of the powers of life, which is economic or financial power. Poverty is hurtful. It doesn't pick and choose. Sometimes, it makes a person frown all day long due to not having money and thinking about how to get money to spend. It is a limitation you must avoid. This is why you must not live your life persistently in poverty or being average. An average person also frowns just because they are tirelessly looking for money. No matter your status, you will have to pay some bills, and those bills won't show mercy.

If you don't have money, it creates worry in your mind about survival. When there is a pressing need, worry can arise because of the pressure involved with not having money. The more you worry about survival, the more stress it can bring. But if you had money, you would see happiness and smiles because you wouldn't be worrying about your finances. Create a spirit of giving by having money. It creates smiles when you give to somebody, and that person says thank you. But when you are poor, you won't be a giver. Rather, you will be termed a taker because you can only take from people. Financial power will not fall into your hands if you don't have that power. If you have money, your heart becomes stress-free. It brings about good concentration. Anybody who understands the value of having money tries to invest every dollar. You can do the same and learn to invest your money. Stop viewing money as if you aren't supposed to have it and keep some for investment. I want to know which is better for you: not having money and worrying about it, or being stressed out looking for money? Most of the stressful people in the world are those who don't have money and are looking for it to deal with their pressing needs. Go to a hospital and see this. Conduct a survey. The happiest people are not found in places where people are stressed out looking for survival. Where the economy and political power are favourable, you will see more happy people than those who lack these things to promote their economies and governance.

Get to know that my life of financial stress and not having money, which felt like living in a hole, is no longer the life I live today. I may not have riches, but God has taken me to another level. You must reach your level, too. From a hole of poverty, I am now up by the grace of God. When poverty confronts you, it creates problems. It can slap people because of the pain it brings. It can reduce the values of people and turn society upside down. Join me in fighting your own poverty. I have left my life of financial limitation by the grace of God and have reached a level of financial power and relevance. When money is in a person's care, it somehow becomes a showcase to the world. You will be called a city on a hill that cannot be hidden because many people will look up to you. Jesus saw this when He described us as the light of the world and a city set on a hill that cannot be hidden (Matthew 5:14).

Society will then depend on you and value you. Society doesn't depend on those who don't want to contribute anything to it. It is the concept of having an impact that makes you a light of the world. Society also doesn't look up to those who are poor and expects society to give them what they want. For example, I want you to tell me this: between a giver and a poor person who doesn't give, who would be celebrated by society?

Carry a mind-set of being able to help the world. This is why you must create your own power now by making your own world so beautiful that you must succeed. If you make yourself fine by creating your new world, it means your world will be as fine as you show it from the inside and on the surface for others to appreciate. If financial stress is what keeps eating you up, you won't be able to create happiness by smiling on your face for others to appreciate.

Chapter 7

"A leaking roof is either repaired or removed entirely. If your life resembles a leaking roof, address the issue by fixing or eliminating whatever is causing the leak."

– Frederick W. Sonpon

Learning from Your Personal History for Greater Progress

You can make history if you learn to develop and learn about your own history. Life is about making history. Your history could be a political, economic, or spiritual history that the world will learn from and depend on you for, remembering you for contributing greatly in that way.

Each person on earth has a history of poverty to tell. The reason is that we all came to earth without any riches, except the riches of having potential that we had and must motivate ourselves to bring to light. Only on the earth upon which we have come do we discover that the world is a rich world. None of us, from where we were coming from, knew what was on earth before we arrived. But we met everything here. The only riches you have and came with are the potential or talents. This is why they can't face any global depletion or global warming. They are infinite riches we are endowed with. These weren't visible for anyone to see in your hands while coming to earth until we had to come and start thinking about how we could produce from them. You and I are uniquely made. The thoughts you have inside of you, nobody else has. The skills you have to creatively do things nobody else has.

I tried to understand this: nobody in this world will want to further learn anything if he or she doesn't first learn something about him or herself. Learning starts with each of us.

The question of learning is to know what you have done with your life, who you have helped, and how you can be remembered in this world. Learning about yourself means knowing who you are, discovering your purpose in this world, and bringing out the purpose in your creative ability instead of sitting with your life as if you are denying yourself a purpose. You learn about yourself to take control of your world instead of letting the world take control of you. Learning about yourself also means being able to have a voice in the world. You learn about yourself to become part of the list of successful people making meaning of their lives, instead of forming part of the list of complainers or people suffering economically, as letting society overlook them or not feel the positive values they may have to show to the world. Some people, because of their level of laziness, have insults as their constant companions. Learning about yourself also means discovering what you will do while you are still alive that will make a difference in your life by bringing out your potential. You learn about yourself by thinking about what is possible to know about your potential and learning something that will bring those out to the world to market you.

At this present moment, have you been able to discover the person you were made to be? It is the first history you need to know. You need to understand why you didn't create yourself, but God created you, so you may figure this out. If you have seen a lesson about your greatness, you must start working on it now. Nothing you can do physically will be accomplished without your spirit realm providing it. You can enter your spirit realm by putting your mind to work and thinking positively. Have a quiet time to think about what you will do to change your poverty condition. Put the ideas you think of on paper.

Since you have gotten to know yourself, have you been able to learn something that will help you contribute meaningfully to your life since you were born? If you have not, are you not improving because you are sitting with your education, or you don't have any yet? If you haven't learned anything in your life, now is the time to start learning. A good reason to learn is that you should be one of the most successful people in the world. You must move from poverty to the next level or a place of restoration of your power and greatness, bringing out yourself for recognition. Learning about yourself also suggests that you need to know what your weaknesses are and work against them instead of letting your weaknesses hold you back.

For example, one of my weaknesses was laziness. I used to love sleep. Also, I had the habit of starting good ideas but never continuing with them. Learning about yourself includes seeking opportunities before you. Any weakness of habitual things you do that causes you to waste money should be seen as a delay. The things that work against you are reasons you are yet to be recognized. Take some spiritual and physical actions to fight against such issues. You were never made to be down for no reason, and you shouldn't let old age find you in a state of stagnation. If you identify lessons about yourself that will help you better see the good in your future and strive to correct your life, you will move forward into that future. You were placed in this world to have a voice and financial power at last. You have the key to your greatness; you shouldn't miss out on this. Try to open the doors to that lifting now. All you need to do is make an effort, which will determine your way out of poverty. Nobody will do it for you until you see a reason to succeed out of your poverty deadlock.

Nobody will know you better in this world and make you succeed more than you can know yourself and fight to succeed. You must be able to tell the lesson of who you are, what you can do, what you are made of, how you can assist others in finding their places in the world, and so forth. You need this to succeed so you can have an impact. If you never tell your own lesson from experiences of difficulties and learn to improve by looking into such a bad history, nobody will tell the lesson of how you ought to become. You will tell your own good story. Tell the world the lesson of your importance and harness your potential instead of letting the world tell a lesson of suppression created by poverty. People are waiting to read the good history of your success. People want to emulate you. This is why you must be ready to tell the story of how valuable you are and bring those values to the world.

Let's look at my own lessons, which I learned before thinking of what I could do to learn the lessons of others and change my world. The first lesson I learned about myself was to discover who I am. Once I discovered this lesson, the next step was to press forward to succeed by showcasing my worth to the world. My other lessons, some of which were very challenging, include:

- I knew my parents were born in poverty, so I needed to try to become somebody and help myself first, and them too, through education. My forefathers or parents could not have had opportunities because their parents didn't have the means to help them succeed. Because of this, they passed the trouble of poverty onto their children, both born and unborn.

- I learned that nobody could redeem me out of poverty if I didn't try to help myself and build an impact for others coming after me.

- I learned that I couldn't correct my poverty condition in the future, but my children would walk into a vicious cycle of poverty as well.

- I learned that I was insulted during my youth by individuals who saw me as nobody because I was very poor. Even in high school, some friends called me degrading names due to my poverty.

- I learned that I needed to fight for myself in life instead of depending on people to do it for me. Some days, when I lived with my grandparents or later with my mother, there was nothing on the table, especially during the civil crisis in my country. I had to go into terrible conditions and make farms for my family to survive because the war hit us while on a mission.

- I knew that success was not reserved for special people; anyone who tried without giving up on life could be successful.
- I learned that some people who were successful didn't succeed through magic; they worked hard for a change in their lives.
- I learned that there is a different life for the poor or average person compared to the rich, and I desired to be in the rich class by working skilfully.
- I learned that there is too much poverty in the world, affecting my extended family, and I needed not to add my family to that list of poverty, but rather be a help to everyone by succeeding with my life.
- I knew I needed financial power for the future, which wasn't possible through empty imagination.
- I learned that the only way to have an impact on the world was to strive to develop.
- I learned that my steps to greatness required learning something for my life instead of sitting and complaining.
- I learned that my parents didn't build a good house for themselves, so I needed to try to change that history.
- I learned that I came from a large family with no money, and I needed to succeed in leaving a legacy.
- I learned that my mother and father did not marry, so I had to grow up not to follow the same path.
- I learned that I needed to be my own boss one day because I received insults from some of my bosses who overlooked me at the time. I needed to change that story for my life, believe in it, and work hard so that one day, people would serve me, too.

What life teaches should be lessons we can learn from and use to change our current and future conditions. This is a lesson I learned, and I told myself that I would become somebody great in life. Learn from the many insults you receive because of your poor condition, as people around you call you names. Picture my condition then, and use it as a good lesson for your life. I didn't overlook myself anymore. I kept trusting in God. This was positive thinking—I didn't focus on the past but on the future in order to change my current and future condition. Don't let anyone's insults hold you down.

The size of the underclothes you wear in your youth won't be the same in adulthood. As your size changes, let your status change as well by learning to free yourself from poverty. This should suggest to you that as you grow older, whether you like it or not, economic problems will come, and you must deal with them. You won't be able to avoid them.

This is why life can create its own lessons for people, either positively or negatively. Depending on how you treat life, the lessons will come as expected or sometimes unexpectedly. There are many people out there who want to hear your success story and follow in your footsteps. But at this point, nobody wants to hear about how you are poor or lazy and never succeeded. Good histories are told of those who make good history, and bad histories are told of those who make bad history. You need to ask yourself what kind of history you want to make of your life.

If you consider these life lessons, they could help you learn from your past or current state and change your future. This will help you find meaning in your life and not give up. The best way forward in knowing yourself is to think of the pains of poverty you are going through or might have gone through. Perhaps you have been insulted by people who overlooked you or said you were poor and worthless. People might have insulted you or your family daily, saying you have no value to offer society. You might have been a drunkard, but you can change that history. The overlooking of you in your community, perhaps because you don't have money, is something you must take as a lesson and turn the story around.

Think of how to begin fighting your way out in the world as an important, successful person that the world would depend on positively. Nobody will know you better until you know yourself. Whatever the lessons of your life or how tough times might have been, if you don't reflect on them and create a new version of yourself, nobody will value any history about you.

I hate poverty. It has the power to make people lose recognition. Poverty can cause people to sit at the back door of life instead of at the front. But you were never meant to be at the back door. This is why you were placed on the surface of the earth, not underneath it, as a way of displaying you to the world. Circumstances that arise from poverty aim to hide your glory. Fight against it. Discover who you are. Nobody will know the good things you are made of, and for you, except yourself. You must recognize and achieve them in your life.

But some people in the world, because they don't care to understand their own history and learn positive lessons from it, live as though they are nobodies. They take the lessons of others and turn them into worries, running around talking about them without giving themselves a push to make the world notice them. Some go about complaining about others for their own wrongdoings. Some even blame their parents for not doing enough for them, leading them to suffer. Some focus on their family backgrounds, blaming them for witch-hunting or cursing their lives, and use this as an excuse for not succeeding. Stop thinking like that. Understand that whatever you see as life is you, and you can determine how it should be if you are willing to shape it beautifully. Nobody will do it for you. This is why life is independent for everyone, and you don't see anyone taking the place of another in creating happiness. No one will feel the pain you feel from suffering or poverty as deeply as you will. You are who you are, but you were not made to stay that way.

People are waiting to learn from your life lessons and how you succeeded so they can emulate you. If people should learn a good lesson from you, do positive things. The positive things will speak well of you and have an impact on the world, rather than just living recklessly. This is the lesson you need. People will be interested in hearing about you if you do positive things to succeed. If you did foolish things, nobody would want to keep hearing that story.

It is true that sometimes, when you start to engage in positive things, others will speak negatively about you. But stay true to yourself and keep pressing on, continuing to do positive things. Don't steal. Know yourself by learning to develop, which is a lifelong lesson you need to stick to. People may feel more comfortable hearing about your progress than the current status you may have now, where poverty is consuming you. Create your new world of success. In a world where such success is created, it will bring about compliments from people. I have never seen anyone give a greeting card of compliments to a poor man; instead, he receives a greeting card of insults. When your level changes, it becomes a life lesson that people want to speak about concerning you. People want to read about your experiences made of lessons. Think of this now! You can be a famous person despite what your condition may be like for now. But by the time you succeed, everybody will want to befriend you and bring you greeting cards. You can make a difference in the world despite your family background.

Don't let circumstances hold you captive and drag you into being nobody. Create a new lesson for yourself by identifying those things that may have been problems holding you down in the past and overcoming them. If nobody is succeeding in life in your family, make a difference in your family by ensuring your own success. If nobody in your family has gone to college or finished high school, make sure to finish high school and go to college, if possible. If nobody knows how to do business, make a difference by doing business. Success has nothing to do with your background if you strive to succeed. Those who used to see you as nobody will be the same people to bring you compliments.

Society only remembers those who do good things to lift it up. Do some good things to create happiness for yourself and make people share stories about whatever good you do. Know that God is good and always will be good. If He didn't create you to be good, you wouldn't have come to earth. If He didn't create you to live well, He wouldn't have brought you to this rich earth. Good things come from the hands of God only, which is why you must see yourself as a good being and not as a foolish one. Good deeds are what people remember. This is why you should never allow yourself to think that you can't make it in the world because of your present condition and start blaming God. You are an astute person created to help this world.

Create power in yourself now! There can be power within you if you start to picture that you were made to be good and to live well. Nothing is too hard for a man who wishes to be successful and takes steps that God will help him to succeed. Create economic power for your life. I want you to be positively famous. I want you to be respected rather than having poverty-power, which takes respect from people. Nobody will care to truly respect and love you if you are not focused on succeeding in your life. Be a mirror to your own life and learn to position yourself. If you don't stand rightly in the mirror of the world, you won't see yourself clearly in it. This world is a mirror. You are made to be displayed through the mirror of the world. But many people can't make any reflection in this mirror of earth. They are hidden by circumstances, especially poverty.

If you live in Africa and you aren't doing anything about changing your condition, know that in Africa, it is common that if you are poor when you get old, your family members, friends, community members, or society as a whole won't value you. Poverty can hide people and kill people soon. It can keep people in corners. And you weren't made to be cornered. You weren't made to be full of poverty and shame. You were rather made to be full of sheen. So, begin to shine now. Don't wait for another day or years to come. Set up the foundation of the kind of person you should be now!

I am concerned about your upliftment. See the value in learning to be successful as something that should be a testament to you. If you are successful, you will become famous as well. People will carry a positive lesson about you that is better to be told than the current one of how you are too lazy, poor, nobody, a criminal, a troublemaker, and so on. If you can't give yourself power, people will think that you were made to be the way you are and suggest that you will never make it to succeed or contribute to your society. Only insults will be heaped on you and your generation, as you were seen to be poor. Some people who know this about you will want to call you foolish without even valuing that God made you for a purpose.

If God, in His tremendous wisdom, used His holy and blessed hands, He isn't foolish when He did so, so why live foolishly on earth as though you are allowing the world to treat you anyhow? This life is about what you give it; the same it will give you. This is why in the book of Galatians 6:7 in the Bible, we are told that whatever a man sows is what he reaps. Make time for your good harvest if you can sow the seed for such a good harvest in the future. Focus on creating a positive lesson about yourself that should reflect the kind of person you are to the world. People will be forced to read about your lesson of success if you can create it now. People will be forced to read about your lesson about the many companies you will establish to create employment for people. Nobody wants to hear about how poor you are. People will celebrate you for what you are able to do and for being a help rather than where you might have been placed now. Help to create jobs by succeeding before the world can benefit from your efforts.

There is no good lesson in drugging yourself. No good lesson in cheating people. No good lesson in supporting bad ideas against your society. No good lesson in lying about or defaming people or being lazy. Nobody will celebrate that.

While in the process of creating a positive lesson about yourself, don't mind what people will say about you. Just focus on the future and remain steadfast. Be focused on your progress to make a life lesson that should reflect positively on the world.

If you are not successful now, nobody cares about that or will say positive things about your lack of success. If you don't have the means to spend money today because you are poor, nobody will see the need to put money into your pocket. It should make sense to you that you are your own power in this world if you can give yourself the positive power of learning to succeed. You are the way to your greatness, and you must make your way there now. Greatness isn't determined by how much talking, sleep, or laziness you can create. But this is possible if you can wake up, think about your life, and put up a fight for change. This is what people want to hear about you. If a bitter world is upon you now because of the bitterness of poverty, try to create a sweet world in the future from this bitter state. And it takes the power of persistence to create a better world for yourself. Push for it before it's too late.

Chapter 8

"If you align yourself with God and love, you will be beautifully tracing the path to your success on earth, as He will not deny it to you. This is because you did not come to earth by your own will—God brought you here."

– Frederick W. Sonpon

You Met Riches on Earth You Are Yet to See

Let's forget about the physical riches that are still on earth. I want you to see these physical riches as intended for the general well-being of everyone on earth—portraying that governments must create the means to benefit everyone. If the government in your land is not working, you can still succeed by bringing your talents or potential to light for yourself. These are the things you came with to earth, which are personal to you, meaning the riches of your potential or talents. Like the case of the earth's resources or riches, look at those who are making use of them. Look at those who are succeeding and making the earth great. Why give up? You met people on earth who might have gone through tough times before succeeding. You can emulate their examples. Those successful people, many I know, feared God for their lives. From their examples, learn to fear God too.

There is no good economy in this world until you can create that good economy for yourself. Open your minds in order to open the doors to your infinite riches that can never face depletion. Your talents won't cause global warming, nor can they be depleted by economic stagnation. Open your eyes and mind. It may be true that your eyes are good and open to seeing things around you physically. But you can have better eyes, seeing as a person who will picture the future, especially if you can recognize the fact that before you can have anything in your physical state, the receiving first takes place in the spiritual realm, which is even the basis of having a dream. Stop sitting in the territory of complainants. God knows the reason why you are still living: to prove that you are sitting on riches and must have an impact. The world is not hiding from you; it proves that you are blessed and can make use of the riches of the world if you wake up and learn a skill that will help you have a share. You are not buried in the ground yet; you are here to do good by positively displaying your values to the world.

Success is looking for people who can see it from afar and work towards it. It is not given to those who talk for nothing and never move to change their world. It is not looking for people who have small thoughts about themselves but for those who think big, use their thinking faculties, and know what to do with their lives. They stop standing on ground zero with their lives. Understand that success is not given to people with just physical eyes but to those with spiritual and better eyes who can dream and bring their dreams to light. Thinkers are not people with ordinary minds and eyes; they have big imaginations. Dreamers are not people with ordinary imaginations; they dream and ensure that the dream comes to pass. These are the characteristics you must have to stop daydreaming. You are one of the attributes of those who want to do better in this world. You can't be an ordinary person throughout your life. Greatness is not achieved by sitting and doing nothing to bring out your potential. You must develop a great thinking faculty that is different from the way you used to do things before. Adopt a new self that is focused and determined to be on top. By doing so, you have to put your body to work for you.

Laziness won't give you a thinking faculty or a place in this world. It only presses you against the world by making economic circumstances trouble you. So, be prepared to exercise your mind to achieve your next level of greatness. You must leave the world of the majority who are very ordinary, who might be complaining for nothing, crying, or frowning upon life, and instead enter the world of the few people who see life as a struggle and fight to get out of deadlocks. They know they must go through some hardships, out of which good things will come later in life. They know they must endure some pains before the sweet can come.

One day, I want you to deliver a victory speech on how you succeeded in a poverty-stricken condition. Make it seasoned. It should be full of smiles. A victor smiles. This is why you must know that victory is not tied to a complainer. Rather, victory is tied to those who see life as valuable and create a good life out of their hard times by making a struggle out of it.

They are the ones who stop complaining, crying, and frowning in life; they don't make themselves out to be anybody as if they were already in their graves. They know that existence is about rendering a service to mankind and their own lives. It is a reason for each of us to display the life we've got rather than acting depressed for no reason. This is why you should take note of this: each of us is at a stage of life. As you dance, others will, too. They create happiness rather than living in bitterness. They aren't natural sleepers; they are supporters of the world. They don't see things with ordinary eyes. Their thinking faculties enable them to see far into the realm of the spirit, not focusing on the little things based on their current state or status. Determination makes them wake up and fight for a change in their levels. This is the kind of person I want you to become. I want you to be in the business class of great people who also fear God and are becoming some of the best in the world, contributing positively. At that level of your life, your recognition will speak for itself. This is why I want you to strive for your upliftment rather than staying in your crying state, wishing for a good economy without working for it first.

I guess, at this point, what may be causing you not to progress is attributable to your thinking. Maybe you see yourself as a natural dependent on the world instead of seeing yourself as a supporter of the world. Just crack open the hidden treasures by thinking and bringing something from your spiritual world. Crack the hidden world of success before you. And it takes the kind of thinking and attitude that will develop the will to do this. A dream can crack such a hidden world. Even an idea can crack such a hidden world. Design the strategies now.

Can't you see the world you were born into, full of riches? This also belongs to you. It is not for special people, but you are part of those people. As long as you occupy a place on Earth or are located at a special point on Earth, you have the means to succeed. Nobody's name is on this part of the earth except God, who made it for everyone.

So, all the riches on earth are for us. They were made to make our lives happy and to enjoy them. God did this not because we worked for them to be here. No. He is simply a good God who did what He did for mankind. We were never made for the riches of the earth, but they were made for us. Together, we can enjoy them, and not only special people are meant to. You might think that since you are suffering, you are cursed and have no place here. You are not cursed. The lack of effort is the element of a curse. The evil that keeps you down is the real cursed element. Such a cursed element is not from God because He created you and me as good people, coming from His good and holy hands.

When you remain inactive, your life will stay static without attracting anything good. If you want good things to come into your life, you must move in the direction of whatever good is instead of sitting and doing nothing. If you move, your power of attraction will work for you. It is the way to make things happen for you. Remember, it is our movement toward greatness that brings things our way. The only power that can make faith work is for you to start believing in God and moving by worshipping Him. You can't sleep and expect to be blessed or respected by God. You can't sleep and expect to be paid for the work you haven't done.

You just need to locate yourself rather than dislocate yourself on the face of the earth. Be a part of those who are enjoying the riches of the earth because they believe that these were made for all of us. Until you take steps, you won't have a taste of any. This is why you should believe that not everyone in a country can be employed by the government. Don't wait for such employment. You must put life into yourself by joining the privileged few who enjoy the earth if you can find something to do and save to create your own business. Locate yourself positively in the world as an important person. Stop living in a subdued state and showcase your true self to enjoy the riches of the earth. You were never born to be a waste on earth, so you must bring out the glory of God upon you. If you respect yourself and learn to improve, others will give you the same respect. Life is how you make it, take it, and treat it. If you treat it well, life will treat you the same way. If you want love, you must cultivate love for yourself. If you want happiness, you must also nurture happiness.

What you need to understand here is that the gold, diamonds, crude oil, bauxite, uranium, etc., do not have anyone's name on them. When you dig for any of these by improving your life, there will always be room for you. They belong to the earth and are for everyone. However, these kinds of riches require ideas to bring them out for use in the world intended for human enjoyment. Don't put your hope in them too much, but instead, put your hope in the infinite riches of your potential or talents that you need to bring out to the world. The riches of the earth belong to everyone, but you can see a few people fighting to get almost all of them from the majority. However, no one can steal what is yours.

You were long ago made a marketable being because of the talents or potential you have. Start creating a trade for your life by bringing them out to the world. The world either needs your professional service to pay you for it, your music or talent as a footballer or athlete to create a brand for you or your books or story to help change the lives of others by bringing that story to the publishing world.

A friend of mine always told me something about the economy and spending money. If we were to go out and spend money, and I was allowed to begin spending, he always asked if any of our pictures were on the money we were spending, implying we shouldn't waste time spending it. He believed that money was made to be used and we should spend it freely. He was right to say that money was made to be used. If you don't have money, you won't have spending power. Some people make themselves poor, which is why they have no spending power. These kinds of people are like those who kill the economies of the world.

That friend of mine worked hard, but he spent money without budgeting himself. Today, the opportunity he had to make a huge amount of money is no longer available, and his spending habits have made him a suffering person. It's not that God didn't bless him with opportunities, but he misused them. No one knows what tomorrow will bring, which is why you must make use of today before tomorrow uses you for nothing, leading to economic struggles.

When a new regime came to power heading our institution, my friend was transferred from his director position and brought down to an officer position, and his salary was cut. The new government was facing difficult times, and workers' salaries were reduced slightly. He felt like more of a victim. The way his salary was reduced was inhumane, but what I want you to understand is that when opportunities come our way in life, we must make proper use of them because no one knows how they will escape us tomorrow. Opportunities come and go without notice. So, not every amount of money you receive must be used at once. Spend some and save some. By learning to save, you can use that amount for future investment. We mustn't waste because no one knows tomorrow.

But how can someone who doesn't have money because of poverty have the power to spend money in the world's economy? Imagine we are all in the world together, with some able to spend money economically and contribute to the world's economy, while others, with a negative mindset and nothing to contribute, remain extremely poor. Why should you be in that situation, too, when this world was made with riches for all of us, or when you were given potential or talents to develop? Can't you see that you eat every day, so you should be able to have better spending power every day? If you don't want to spend, you must close your mouth and stop eating. And if you stop eating, then get ready to be buried because it's like you're telling the world that you have no use anymore.

Even if you don't have money right now, understand that you aren't poor—it's just a matter of time. You must believe this about yourself. If you were truly poor, you wouldn't have the means to spend money because you'd be completely dependent on others for survival. The day those people stop supporting you, you might find yourself struggling. Even for ordinary people, if their employers stopped paying them due to a business downturn, they could face severe financial difficulties, possibly even hunger, because they would have no way of generating income. No company would want to hire in such a situation, meaning their income would dry up. Picture this scenario and consider changing your way of thinking or doing things. It's better to create your own pension scheme by working for yourself and investing some of your income than to rely solely on working for others. No matter how smart you are, you will eventually retire, but no one can retire you if you own your own business.

Why not create spending power beyond simply making money or earning a petty income? Spending and seeking money are what drive economies. Don't add to the number of people who lack the ability to spend money because they don't have skills or aren't working in an economy that generates income for their spending. Refusing to earn money to spend is like draining the vitality from your own life because such an act is akin to killing your own economy. Economies function when companies produce goods, which are supplied to businesses or suppliers; suppliers sell to wholesalers, wholesalers sell to retailers, and retailers sell to consumers. The final stage of utilizing the goods is with the consumer, who goes to the market to buy. If a consumer doesn't have money to spend, the production of that good won't occur. Thus, the consumer is essential in keeping the market functioning.

This is why spending money is crucial—it keeps businesses running by turning the wheels of the economy. If consumers don't buy, businesses can't function or survive. Don't become a natural business killer by refusing to work and earn money to spend in the economy.

My brother or sister refuses to be a beggar. Refuse to live in a place where no one in your family is succeeding. Refuse to be in a society where nothing works for you because you are poor. You are not cursed—that's why you are here on Earth. You are not cursed—that's why life is still within you, waiting for you to make an impact on others.

If you've lived your whole life without empowering yourself to contribute to the production, selling, or buying sectors, you need to change. Learning a skill can lead to employment, and in return, you'll have the means to purchase goods. Providing services and buying goods create the economy. If you don't want to earn money, you're effectively saying you're dead or that you want the world to suffer without economic activity. Contributing to the global economy relies on individual efforts to keep businesses running. Businesses can only thrive if there are income earners who also contribute to raising taxes for the government. Strive to be an income earner rather than living in poverty.

Don't be like those who see having money, or more of it, as a burden. These people often view money as evil, attributing it to the devil, and they judge those who earn money, even through honest means, in a negative light. Some see the wealthy as super-blessed by God. If God had a special list of people to bless, He might have included you on it for history to write about. You and your relatives are not listed among the poor in the Bible. Understand that seeking money to serve you is not evil, but the way you seek it—through good or bad deeds—determines the morality of your pursuit. How can you justify supporting acts of stealing from others to escape poverty or mediocrity? If you are educated yet corrupt, it's a sign of a deeper issue. If wealth was inherently bad, Father Abraham wouldn't have been a wealthy man, as the Bible tells us. King Solomon wouldn't have been so rich that he could build the house of God. Jesus wouldn't have died to save and create fulfilment for mankind, including delivering people from poverty. He restored all things to humanity that were once taken away by the devil. Adam and Eve suffered because they were taught a false doctrine instead of keeping God's teachings, which led them away from living in paradise. You must work to create a new version of yourself. See the revelation for your life and begin to walk in that glory in the near future. It is a shame to live in poverty all your life as if you are carrying a curse. The day I see you travelling to places, living in a good home, having spending power, and helping others because of your success, even heaven will celebrate you. Christ bore all these sufferings for us and brought us back into the power of God's goodness.

Ask yourself this: who produces all the goods on earth, those you see around you and those you consume? Did they fall from heaven? Everything you see on earth is the result of human invention. Look at ships, houses, planes, technology, and more—they are all human inventions. God was the first to show us what invention is about. He created the earth so that you and I could live a splendid life. You need to ask yourself, why are you consuming goods, and who produced them for your consumption? How are the clothes you wear every day made?

Aren't they inventions? What is your invention? Are you using your mind to create, or are you letting your mind use you? Don't join the ranks of those who let their minds control them instead of showcasing the power of their potential or talents.

You are part of the world's economy. The fact that you can eat, spend money, and travel means that you are part of the global economy. Even if you are poor or average, you are still part of the economy by learning to make money and spend it. Every little purchase you make has an impact on your regional economy. The sum of individual purchases contributes to the collective or national economy, driving it within a country. If you believe you are destined to remain poor forever, then stop eating because the food you eat is produced by thinkers and workers. The clothes you wear are developed by inventive people. You must have money to make purchases in the market.

Let me explain this to you one more time. Here's how the economy works relative to paying for goods and services. You can be a contributor to the economy, especially if you buy candy, for example. By purchasing candy, you contribute to the economy because you're buying from a seller. The candy was produced and left the producer's area before reaching the seller, and by buying it, you've created a demand that supports the producer and seller. Suppose you're part of a group of one hundred people buying from a particular candy company. In that case, you're helping keep that company in business, which in turn supports the economy and government through taxes. As a consumer, you are vital to producers and sellers because you are spending money by buying. Without money, sellers wouldn't be able to sell to you. This is why the lack of workers and consumers can kill economies. Don't allow yourself to stay in a position where you're not contributing. Learn to do something with your life now, and be either a worker or a buyer.

Open your eyes so you can meaningfully participate in the world's economy. Move away from the consuming and dependency side and reach the level of the producing side of your life to be able to spend money. By sitting idle, you won't be considered a producer or buyer. Staying at home without working means you won't have income to spend. Why live a life where you don't want to work? I don't think you would want to be naked or walk barefoot everywhere. The shoes or slippers you wear are made by companies that employ workers who need to be paid to produce more for consumers like you. People with ideas produce the clothes and slippers or shoes you wear, and companies are tasked with manufacturing them based on consumer demand. These items are made because people conceived ideas and passed them on to production companies, making them available as goods in the economy. You shouldn't see yourself as just a spectator in the economy. You are very important and would be even more important if you had good spending power.

You should, therefore, focus on developing an idea that allows you to produce something valuable. It's like creating your own world, one that you control if you can produce or work for yourself. Your world to rule starts with you. Put yourself together, and put your life together. Create a power within yourself to establish a new order where poverty no longer consumes you.

You can wield power better if you create a strong economy for your life. This is all about being someone who has spending power. Be someone who directs things or people in a positive way. Be a manager of your life. Don't let the world manage you by deciding what is good or not for you. Take your power in the world and direct it. But you will never give orders or manage people, whether in the world or in your home, if you make yourself a nobody, always broke and complaining every day. You'll never have a voice in your national economy if you have no ideas or money to contribute. If you are powerless because of a bad economy, you are voiceless. If you are voiceless, you become weak and can be treated poorly. Create financial power for your life. If you are successful, you can have a voice to command. You will be respected for who you are. When you gain economic respect, those who never knew you will take notice. Those who never served you will begin to serve you. Your family's history, which may have been ugly, will be told by others as a good story, making people want to befriend you and share the true story.

Why will this happen, and why will you make a good history? Because you have created a world for yourself that is powerful and worth celebrating. You have made a world from within, taking power from yourself. You have created a world, moving about in it and spending money. This is the power you need most—the power to spend. Don't let poverty limit you or take away your spending power as if you are suspended from the world's economy. Stop this, because as long as you can eat, since you are alive, you should be spending money. You can even wear clothes, which everyone—successful, poor, or average—must do. Therefore, you are part of the global economy, a segment that starts with you as part of a household.

Stop creating a world of poverty through laziness. Stop thinking you can't succeed by looking at those who are already successful, as if they were born with special privileges that you lack. Nobody is better than you until you make yourself better so others can see you as someone worth celebrating.

Until you learn to feature yourself in this world, nobody else will feature you. Be willing to work now before it's too late.

Outlook on Retirement

You have to try to develop yourself because retirement is inevitable. Whether you are educated or not, there are different classes of retirement that may force or require you to be packed away or cornered in life. Some of these do not depend on age but can occur unexpectedly. It is the uncertainty of life that requires you to always be prepared for any eventuality.

This is why you need to understand the different types of retirement. They are:

Age Retirement: This is the retirement that naturally confronts everyone due to age. Whether you like it or not, it will come because of the age factor. So, the question is, how do you prepare for retirement at your age?

Ailment Retirement: This type of retirement happens due to illness. When it occurs, it doesn't care about your qualifications, family background, or whether you are rich or poor. This is why you must work to prepare for it. It may happen to you, or it may happen to a close relative. What will you do about it? I remember the story of Mr. Pupu, a great engineer who had a beautiful house and lived lavishly. But then, a stroke hit him. The man, who was once the heart of his wife, found himself in a situation where his wife became evil in his life because he no longer had money. She turned his children against him; they no longer respected him, and they lived without regard for him. She often beat him and even scalded his back with hot water when he complained, which she didn't like since he was sick.

Circumstantial Retirement: This type of retirement happens due to circumstances—perhaps a condition of poverty. You could lose a business or a natural phenomenon like war or rainfall could cause it. If a war situation threatened you, what could you do? For me, the only option would be to escape to a safe area or a different country. This is why you must seek financial security. Don't let life retire you due to circumstances. Be prepared for any eventuality.

How to Promote Personal Value Addition

Personal Value Creation: This is the process of creating value in your life. You do this by learning something or engaging in positive ventures. It's about removing negativity from your life and focusing on adding value. You achieve this by gaining experience, learning from situations, or finding reasons to promote yourself. In this economic world, you must always strive to add value. Seek satisfaction and learn to obtain what you want through the concept of value addition.

You will not gain satisfaction in this world without understanding that it is an economic world in which you must fight to create your satisfaction. Only through work can you create the satisfaction you need economically. But beware that any of the retirements mentioned earlier could impact you. Life is such that situations can arise unexpectedly, and you must always be prepared for them. You must work and invest in your old age. This is something you cannot avoid.

Chapter 9

"You can't expect to receive anything from life if you haven't given something to it first."

– Frederick W. Sonpon

See Hardship As a Time for You to Work to Produce

Let this be emphatically clear: you and I weren't there when suffering was forced upon mankind by the creator of suffering—Satan. But it feels like we are inevitably affected by it. We are now in the world, suffocated or confronted by this suffering, and we must do whatever it takes to remove some of these negative influences from our lives. Therefore, to succeed in this world, you must first understand the spiritual problem and attack it with prayers. Everything of value or any dream that could help change our world comes from the spiritual realm. This is why the source of both good and suffering is derived from the spiritual realm.

Some people would say it is wrong to think of the spiritual side of life and connect it with the physical because they believe there is no such thing as a spiritual side. However, your sources of life are derived from the spiritual. Due to the effects of the spiritual, we are in trouble today.

You may be experiencing a difficult life or struggling to undo the problems that the spiritual side of life has created. You might be sensing trouble, feeling weighed down by it, confused by it, or facing some form of degradation because of it. The big question is no longer why people suffer, but rather, how can you overcome it? Because of the changes brought about by the spiritual affecting the physical, this condition has created poverty, which you should be more concerned about finding a way out of rather than complaining.

What is the way out of suffering? You must wake up and push for a change. It won't happen by daydreaming or simply waiting for it. You need to start working your way out of it. Push.

Do you realize this? Life will never change for you if you are not willing to learn from the past to bring about a difference in your current state. Seek a new life rather than clinging to an old one that leads nowhere. Success is made possible through first recognizing what will bring about change and understanding how it will be derived. Start participating actively in life now. No one will do it for you until you decide to.

Create both a positive and negative fear over life now. Negative fear, which cannot be managed, is the factor that is driving you away from success or keeping you on the path of failure. You may be burdened with poverty due to a lack of consciousness to learn and make a change. Until you can lift yourself up into power, you may remain stuck in a state of powerlessness. You cannot understand the value of success until you work to achieve it.

What to Do in Economic Hard Times

Let's talk about what to do during economic hard times. I want you to follow the story of a lime tree. During tough times, according to this story, the lime tree learns to produce fruits. The lime parable suggests that the tree cannot rely solely on rainwater to produce; instead, it learns to bear fruit during the sunny or dry season. The lime tree does not want to be seen as dependent on rainwater, which is why it produces during the sunny season. Understand that tough men don't perish during difficult times—they fight to make a difference and bring honour to their society.

Follow the lime story as a guide to change your life. This is all about putting power in yourself and never giving up, even when going through tough times. Difficulties will not leave humanity, but poverty can if you fight against it. Hard times are there to polish us in preparation for our period of growth. You must work your way out of these difficulties rather than sitting idly by. Stop daydreaming that life will get better by simply complaining.

Life may be difficult for you now, but you can overcome it and develop. Let the tough times confronting you motivate you to take the steps necessary to rise out of poverty. Create a season for poverty to end and prosperity to begin. Don't let poverty rule you as if you were destined to be cursed. Focus on God and trust in Him with your life. He didn't create you for an ugly reason. God didn't put poverty in power; you, as a human being, were put in power, not poverty. Restore yourself and your family's values. Start adding value to your life by removing poverty from your path.

Stop waiting for life to improve as if manna would fall from heaven. Create your own promised land now. Why are you carrying poverty upon your life? Stop it! Poverty is an element of the devil, meant to disprove God by making us suffer economically. See it as a curse. Poverty becomes a curse, especially if you do nothing to change your situation. It has the power to deface people naturally. You weren't meant to be defaced, and you should know that God made you in His own image and likeness to reflect His glory. God gave mankind the power to preside over the whole world, which belongs to you and me. This is why you are on solid ground and not placed beneath it. You must rule this world.

Remember, God made everyone and everything good, and we are complete in His creation. He rested from work after six days. Picture all that is happening in the world and recognize that God didn't create it for this reason. Now that the problems of suffering exist, you must acknowledge them and work to rise above them. Evil is ruling because a spirit being from the spiritual realm fell to earth and is teaching mankind how to promote evil. He is the source of evil, while God is the source of good. You must strive to follow the path of good. God didn't create us as evil beings or teach us evil. It would be a mistake to believe that. Take your stand; claim your power in the world. The world must not take power from you or against you because it was made for you and me. I am taking the power that God gave me to contribute to my life and the world. I want the world to benefit from my ideas. I am rising and choosing to live happily, not in lack and unhappiness. God says we must believe in Him and serve Him, which will allow us to enjoy the fruits of the land (Isaiah 1:19).

Like the lime tree, as you read about its production story, it produces during hard times. Why are you struggling during hard times? Be like the lime tree. This tree feels independently driven to make its own fruits without relying on rainwater. Similarly, during hard times, be productive instead of sitting and complaining. Embrace the concept of the lime tree and tailor your life accordingly.

The lime tree thrives in Africa, which I love so much. According to the lime tree, other lazy trees depend on rainwater to produce. But when the sun is out, and the weather is hot, that's when the lime tree has the power to produce fruit. It doesn't blame the lack of rainwater. The lime tree sees the dry season or sunny weather as tough times, but it doesn't wait; it produces fruit during those times. The lime tree is proud that no hard times can stop it from producing if it depends on rainwater.

In economic hard times, which I know will never leave the world, what are you doing about it? Understand that hard times will continue to confront humanity. But you must fight against them. God gives you the will. See hardship as a time of preparation for the next level ahead of you. Stop complaining and letting poverty limit you. Start embracing happiness by creating a better economic world.

Can you try to fight during hard times instead of giving in? You can't continue to stay down and expect to keep sinking. Understand that those who stay down are the ones drowning in life. But you weren't made to drown in frustrations. Take your stand; take your power. We belong to a winner, which is God. And you were made as a child of God (St. John 1:12). Imagine, you are made a child of God! Can't you celebrate this? This means you are carrying blessings upon blessings, not poverty. You carry joy, not complaints.

So, what are you doing with your life? Try to elevate your life now. You were made in the image of God, which means you don't belong to frustrations. You were made in the image of God, meaning you should shine. You were made in the image of God, meaning you should be on top of the world rather than being down and caught in odds. You were made in the image of God, meaning you should fight for your place of honour and not remain in dishonour. Take your power; take your stand. Take your stand, and take your win in life.

I can remember during the Liberian Civil War, which started in 1989 and lasted until 2003, life was not easy to live through the war years. My family and other comrades seriously struggled during that time. We struggled without giving up. I stopped in the fourth grade before the war started. My family and I left a mission and got to Monrovia. I was forced to attend some of the damaged public schools because of the hardship of the war, and my mom couldn't afford to send me to a private school. Despite all the hard times, my family and I didn't give up on life. We kept seeking improvement. We stayed focused until my six sisters, my brother, and I graduated from college. Only one of my sisters, Theodora, refused to complete college and dropped out. We are now each raising our own families.

We didn't sit idly by waiting for change to come. We knew we would not be living with our parents forever, so we took learning very seriously. We knew we wouldn't stay small and ignorant, and we pushed ourselves to grow. We also knew that our parents couldn't simply give us education by imagining it for us. As our parents worked hard for us, we also put in the effort. We pushed forward with a focus on the future, hoping for success. Today, by the grace of God, we made it through. The economic struggles are no longer as turbulent for us. We have become problem-solvers.

Focus on the fact that life is what you make of it. Plan with the goal of ending your struggle with poverty. Poverty can naturally retire people, but you must not sit on that natural retirement bench. Just as a car can reverse, you can reverse your poverty situation. End it now.

Nobody can give you more power than you can give yourself. Although life will be full of struggles, you must end the struggle with poverty. Believe that there is a time for everything, including the time for poverty to end. Let this be the time for your success to emerge by proving your value. The poverty you experienced in the early stages of your life should end with a better future ahead. Concentrate on fighting for change instead of keeping yourself chained to poverty.

Will you take the lesson from these struggles and fight to succeed? Become a thinker instead of allowing poverty to take root in your life. Poverty can corner and disgrace people; it is something you must fight against. Don't be like those who see poverty as an inevitable part of life. If you become a thinker, you will become wise, understand the world and the systems that promote poverty, and recognize why individuals may not succeed. Work to make yourself a success. Become creative, which will help you develop a strong work ethic. Let your productivity grow instead of being stifled by poverty. Consider what the Bible says in Ecclesiastes Chapter 9: "There is a time for everything under the sun." Let your time for ending poverty come now. If you are creative, you will never lack. Your progress will bring liveliness and happiness to your life. You can succeed. By the time you succeed and continue to multiply your life, you will be able to give to others, and success will continue to flow.

You may be in a part of the world where life is extremely difficult, especially if you are in or from Africa, where I am from. Remember, we are in the same world as the developed world—

Europe and America. It's not a different world in those continents; they are here in the same world with us. So, if you don't get tough now to succeed out of the dead situation you may be in, you will have to accept the tough days of poverty that will grow even bigger.

Consider the stages of life; each stage has its challenges. But you should envision the growth period ahead of you beyond the challenges of poverty. By the time your age increases and you grow older, poverty should be removed from your path. One day, you will get old, which will bring about a natural retirement. Think about what you will be remembered for when that natural retirement comes.

However, I've noticed that having responsibility at a young age makes it difficult to recognize how those responsibilities grow over time. Every human being has the ability to grow, and as you grow, expenses also increase. If you were a boy, the things boys wear will cost differently when you become an adult or reach older age. Your clothes, food, environment, and associations will change. This is why you must change your poverty condition now before it continues to change you into a worthless being. Change it before it chains you and ruins your life. You are the one who must try to improve. You are the one who must get better because the world won't get better until you do. When you succeed, your success will contribute to a greater change in the world.

Think about what development means: people see it as a way of changing the physical world. The earth waits for people to improve it. If there is no school in your community, it won't fall from the sky. However, people who are empowered to learn and build will have the opportunity to construct the school. This is why education is so important. The more informed you become, the better your world will be.

This world doesn't have the power to develop on its own. It waits for people to create laws to govern it. It waits for people to form governments and for those governments to rule.

Be part of a group of people who work positively and think about what to do with our world. Nature is waiting for you to tell it what you desire. Make some faith-based actions. If you want to learn, start learning now. If you want to own the best vehicle in the future, start saving money now.

This physical world doesn't act on its own to improve. We all have to put life into it. We all have to put sense into it. We all have to invest our potentials or talents into making it work. We all have to create markets for it. We all have to paint it correctly, based on how we develop our characters and treat it. We must move to make everything move with the world. We must move to improve our economies. We must move to improve our governments. We must move to make our systems work better.

Let your personal system of getting a job based on what you learned work for you now. Make yourself a force instead of making your life a discourse. Make yourself a power of greatness instead of embracing poverty or letting it work against you. Make yourself an influential person. Make yourself a help to the world by the time you succeed. It takes pain and effort to make your life work the way it's supposed to. No amount of idle thinking will change your life. No amount of tears or complaints will make it happen, either. Stand tough now so you can stand up tomorrow. Stand on your feet and see what happens next.

Life can sometimes bend, especially if you aren't careful to observe how it can come with troubles. Some troubles may arise from laziness, which is self-imposed. Until you put effort into your body, you can't just pray for laziness to go away. You must make practical sacrifices to remove laziness.

Start to strengthen your rumpled self. Spiritually, God didn't create us to be rumpled; we were made straight like Him. But our characters, because of sins, are rumpled in shame. Until you learn to fight for yourself, nobody will fight for you.

I remember my grandmother, Tanneh, telling me that if I learned to be strong in body and serviceable, people would like me, and I wouldn't suffer in life. She said this because she believed that laziness is not something to practice. She compared laziness to folding one's life, causing it not to progress straight. So, what are you doing with your life? Don't be like those who only know how to sleep and do nothing. They never see the danger of poverty by learning to work skillfully. The addition of sleep upon sleep results in a harvest of great poverty. This happens because what you give to life is what life gives back to you. The Bible says in Galatians 6:7 that what you sow is what you reap.

Nature is something you must speak to with your mind, making calculations and putting your body to work, bringing to light the things held in the mind. If you don't tell nature what you want from this world, nature will assume you are okay with the way things are while age catches up with you. Nature is blind until you make it see you and begin to work for or with you. You have to straighten up your life now instead of letting it bend with or on you. You cannot continue to let poverty bend your forefathers, you, and your family. Don't let it silence your voice within your family and community. You must become someone respected by creating influence. Having poverty with you is the opposite of that. This is why you must fight it. Allowing it to persist in your life is a bending process. Take your power; take your win against it.

Be aware that certain troubles in life are self-created. Nobody will help you take your place and your pains in poverty. This is what poverty and its sickness do to people. If you are hungry because of a lack of food due to poverty, nobody will take your pain at that moment of hunger. No one can share your troubles, so don't expect others to shoulder them. If you want money to travel but lack the funds due to poverty, know that no one will easily take your place and shoulder your travel. If you empower yourself, life will maintain you in power because you determine your power on earth.

Poverty is bad because I was born into it, and it troubled me and my family. Poverty is a mind disease caused by the inactivity of the mind. Until the mind is educated about its dangers, it will persist. It can grow feathers, and you must fight to cut them off by not letting them grow. Get a gist of my story about what I did and continue to do against poverty. Where would I be today, coming from a poverty situation, if I hadn't taken the help and advice of my grandma and others around me?

We came to earth empty of ideas, which is why some people don't see the sense in lifting themselves by discovering them. You have to be infused with ideas or a dream from God before you can succeed.

Learn from my story. Imagine, my parents weren't well-educated and never had the proper means to raise a child, but they did their best. I wonder how I would have made it without God.

Many people have gone to the grave without opportunities. It's not that those who are alive are better than those who are dead and gone with their glorious ideas. It's sad to say, but neither my back nor front, relative to my family's economic history, was good either. If God had not been caring, my dream of becoming a world-renowned writer, as you can see today by reading this book, would not have been possible. If my grandparents had lacked a mindset for development and sat cowardly, doing nothing to turn my poor condition around, I might not have been discovered yet. This is how some people live, with no means of gaining help. I might not have been known in the world for what I now do if not for the grace of God upon me. I don't deserve it, but He is doing it right for me.

What are you doing with your life? I learned that when a person takes steps in life, nature will not deny them the power to succeed. Because what you give to life, life gives back to you. Perhaps nature made that agreement long ago for each of us to decide what we want to become, depending on how we see this world and believe in ourselves to work out our lives. It would have been a surprise if my grandparents had cried every day without doing anything about their own poverty and mine. It would have been a dream story to tell about my whole life. If they were foolish, they would have looked at their poverty and cried poor every day, not caring about helping to change our futures as their children and grandchildren for the better. But my grandparents knew the value of learning something for life. You can now see the result of their efforts in me. Today, I am a writer of the world. You could be someone special because of the inventive power you are endowed with.

Look at what they did with my life which I see as positive-minded people who didn't just focus on spending every penny they had despite their poverty, which was as big as a whole wide world of trouble.

Life is calling on you to try and score a goal of success. Can't you see others who are scoring good goals of success? Are they better than you? No, they can't be!

Some people remain poor because they are not sensitive to development, carrying muddy heads of negativity. Leave that negative thinking of harbouring poverty. This is the time to start creating a positive attitude within yourself. Just imagine how long you will continue behaving negatively or thinking negatively about your life, and has this ever brought you something good?

Don't be like those who are blind to nature and never care about doing anything to change their perpetual condition of poverty. They never care to take steps, and they never care about helping to change their children's futures.

Stop blaming your parents. Start doing something about your own life now. Stop living like a boy throughout your life. Make a change in your level instead of creating a chain around yourself. Pity my story and see what you can do. I will boast about my grandparents for what they did. They weren't like those who, because of their great poverty, never cared to plan or do anything for their children's future, including helping me, their grandchild. My grandparents made living sacrifices, hoping to give me a reward for the future. Although they are dead now that my life has grown, I know their souls appreciate that I am fighting life positively and don't remain in poverty. I guess they may be rejoicing wherever they are.

Learn to make sacrifices by being bitter against poverty. Seeing poverty creating bitterness against you, you must also be bitter against it. The bitterness to have against poverty is for you to fight against it. Look at your life today and say that you will change the condition of your life or your family's history of poverty. Make sacrifices and have an impact on society without sitting and complaining for nothing. Sacrifices polish us for the journey of success. Sacrifices fuel seriousness in us. They are not meant to make us give in or give up on life. Stop giving in or giving up, and stop saying that God cursed you. Sacrifices are your preparation for the success that lies ahead. Sacrifices are the fulcrums on which the pendulum of life continues to be balanced. Follow my grandparents' example. My grandfather, in particular, helped his family through petty fishing acts. Sometimes, after a whole day of fishing in a little Kru Canoe, he could catch only ten small fish. He did some commercial fishing by going to Greenville, Sinoe County, for about a month, fishing in such a manner just to buy some copies for us, his children and grandchildren.

I couldn't grow up and do nothing with my life despite the push they gave me. There is a parable that says: "If someone is washing your back, be able to help wash your front." While my grandparents were helping in their weak way, I knew I had to apply the necessary effort instead of giving up on life. Because they desired a change in our family's status, they took steps by pushing us to grow. They made sacrifices by sometimes denying themselves livelihoods.

You may wonder why they did that. The reason was simple: their focus was on making a good future for us. It's power. They looked at the future and pushed us into that future, knowing that going to school was the best way out. This is what you need. You need to push yourself, even if no one is there to help you. Stand up now! Be bitter about whatever problems or poverty act against you and push yourself. No woman who wants to deliver a baby will not push through the pain before the baby is delivered. This is all about you trying to gain your power by envisioning a better tomorrow, which won't come by falling from the sky. As the world gets tougher, meaning lives will suffer economically in time to come, don't look for better days from your government but see that in yourself. Until you get better, nothing will improve, including your personal economy. The world will improve economically only if people with good minds, which you should have for yourself, move to change their ways of life. People must move to put systems in place. People must move to make the right things happen. People must move to build the necessary castles of change needed by the world. You are part of the world, so try to do something about your situation so you can begin to impact the world.

Life is like a market good. If you don't take your goods to the market to show, nobody will know or see what you have. You are made a market full of goods because of the potential inside of you. Know this: it is possible to make your economy better, and by doing so, you will help someone else benefit from your success. Don't see impossibility in yourself as long as God is your power. Create possibilities by breaking the barriers of poverty and disgrace. Create possibilities to move mountains in your way. Nobody will level the mountain of poverty in your path until you desire to. Create possibilities to change the world. Create the possibility that you are your own power in this world and must begin to push into a future that should be glorious.

But I don't want to hear you thinking that you shouldn't be among those who will succeed or seeing you crying all day long, cornered by poverty, or constantly complaining and never attempting to make a change. Stop chaining yourself by viewing the world as a place for a privileged few and believing that you don't have a place in it or the power to push forward. Activate that inner spirit in you by taking control of your world. Make a difference now to have a future as a great person in the world. Let your obstacles be turned into testimonies. Wake up and silence the calls of poverty from ringing in your ears as the voice of your life. Let your obstacles be overcome, allowing you to succeed in life. Economic obstacles shouldn't pin you down. You can make it. See yourself as being alive to prove that you will succeed. Put life into yourself.

If you can't make it happen now for yourself by learning to improve, and you expect that others will do it for you, that is a bad belief. What makes you think that, since you were born, perhaps in difficulties, those people you hope will help you can't or won't still come to your aid? They may be delayed because they are not the ones God chose to help you. You are the only one who can bring a better change to your life, not other people, which is why you must put life into yourself.

Why should you wait for others to help you? God helped you when you were born and didn't die in your mother's womb. What help are you waiting for from mankind again? Know this: time is not waiting for you. This should prove to you that you are the one who owns your life, and the same life is waiting on the steps you will take to change it. Stop waiting for others before you get a passport to travel. Don't wait for others before you dream of changing your status. No. Push through now! You can't wait for someone else before you start thinking. You can't wait for someone else before you learn something about your life. You can't wait for someone else before you see yourself succeed. Stop waiting and wasting time.

This world needs you to play your part, not just sit around having no part to play. You exist here for a reason. This world is not without riches, so don't think you are not part of those who should enjoy the riches of the earth. This world is not waiting on you because you are lazy. It is waiting for you to take your part and enjoy the riches that are here. Take your share.

You may be delaying the world. Maybe you are the person who is supposed to establish the first vehicle that will learn to fly. This world needs your ideas to make it better. It is a world in trouble because of the actions of mankind. This world wants your service to help it function properly. It is only possible for you to help if you can create life in yourself. Create a sense of pity for yourself with the hope of making something good happen. Stop sitting on the bench with those who complain all day long. Stop waiting on your community, national government, or the economy of your nation. This world's economy is waiting for you to try and participate in it with your ideas. Governments will always have problems with insufficient revenue. They will not always be good for the people of the world. They will only help people, but not 100% to eradicate their problems. You can only create a good government for yourself. This is the government you should focus on by eradicating poverty and creating respect.

I remember my stepfather being a classroom teacher for about fifty years. Since I got to know him, he has complained about the bad system of government, especially the educational system, and the treatment of teachers by the government. He complained about the lack of basic teaching services and incentives for teachers. Since the 1980s, when I got to know him, he has been asking for change, and until now, nothing concrete has been done by the government to improve the conditions of classroom teachers in Liberia. There is no good pension system to make teachers feel happy when retiring. The only pension my stepfather can boast of now is that he invested in his children, who are now able to help him. This is one reason Africa will continue to experience brain drain.

Life requires each of us to serve ourselves before society will value serving us. In this concept of society serving you, what you do will raise a positive alarm about you, attracting attention. What you do will determine how society will look at you and value you. You can never be served if you don't put yourself in a position to be respected and served. Nobody will recognize you for who you are if you are out of recognition or do not bring yourself up from a place of no position or from darkness. Gain the power of learning to recognize yourself first.

Complaints can create tears, which you must stop. Complaints can cause heart attacks. Complaints can build up disappointment, cutting your life short. Complaints can create holes in the heart due to the stress they cause. Complaints can create traumas, also coming from stress, which may prevent the body from resting.

Go for your happiness. What creates happiness is what I call good thinking, which leads to good actions and brings about good returns of economic prosperity. Positive thinking will create a new economy for you.

Positive thinking creates joy in the heart, not stress. Thinking positively can bring smiles. Thinking and acting positively, working for your life, will bring money into your hands, enabling you to buy and support the economy. If you don't have buying power now, aim to have buying power in the near future.

Work with your head rather than just with your body. Joy will never come if you don't do what is necessary to make your life prosperous. It is in your prosperity that celebration will come. The celebration showcases glory if you seek it. This is what we are meant to have in proving what it means to live a life.

The purpose of God wanting to see you and me happy should be a reason for you to know that you have what it takes as a world defined.

Get this straight: this world isn't getting better without you. I say this because you were the only person who was supposed to create a plane that could move in water, I think we would never have succeeded, which is why you must see the world in yourself. Until you get better, the world won't improve. Your success will affect the overall world, and this will be seen in your progress. Why are you looking for improvement in the world outside when you should consider yourself as the true world? But see how terrible this world is, already facing turmoil because of sins that are causing mankind to be evil and making lives harder every day because our ways are pushing God away. Nobody wants to be a brother anymore due to our tribal, political, or economic statuses. Keep in mind that evil has taken over the world due to the fall of Satan, who also caused the fall of man. In the midst of this, God has not forgotten you. This is why you are still alive. If you make up your mind, you can survive in the midst of this terrible news about the fall of evil on earth. Be bold in being very prayerful, telling him that he didn't topple your government because the God who made you is still God in your life and is with you. Tell him that he didn't topple your economy. Tell him that your God is alive and has given you power over the world to succeed and that you are not the one Satan has toppled. Tell the world that it was made for you, not for a spirit being like Satan and its forces. Don't see yourself as powerless. Take your power by managing your economy as well. Understand that Satan can only be a god to you and control your life and economy if you accept that you are made to be as you are, not caring about God. Appreciate God for everything concerning your life. You can only gain ground on earth if you gain God. If you don't know the true God Almighty, you will feel the troubles of this world. Not because Satan is mightier than God, who has all power, but because your ways could be promoting him. You are not buried in the earth but placed on its surface, meaning you are made to be displayed in power. God gave us freedom and the power to rule our own world. I haven't seen anything in the Bible that says Satan was given power to rule this world. But the only thing I know is that mankind was given the power to rule it. Stop letting Satan topple your world and your economy. Believe in God, and start controlling your world instead of letting the world control you.

Work while praying to God that Satan doesn't have to rule you and your economy. Agents of Satan don't have to either.

It takes the power of prayer to fight him. Praying takes faith, and faith requires work, not just sitting and believing. Even Jesus Christ didn't come to earth just to tell people that he was the Son of God without a mission. Nobody is born without a reason. But he worked out the faith of a new generational gospel and died to save mankind. He was an example of this and brought back the goodness of God toward mankind. Until you can work out your success, you will never work out of nothing if you don't work out something.

Use your struggle as a means to fight your obstacles, not to see yourself die from them. Be a winner against obstacles. As you may know, winners can endure pain, meaning they can take blows. But they don't endure pain as a way of accepting loss. Stop enduring the pain of poverty only to see yourself die in it. Winners don't focus on today and give in to frustration. Winners look at the future and empower themselves to achieve it through skilled work habits. Winners see the bigger picture of life and strive to be champions rather than being overcome. Have a winning spirit and a mind developed with hope that doesn't give up.

Poverty versus a controversial democracy/pure democracy in form be aware that the world has changed because of the actions of mankind. This is why I want you to understand a key governance issue of the world. If you don't understand the governance system in the world, especially in my country, you may not grasp the reason why people are poor and might have been victims of another system or leadership in your country.

I wonder why my country (Liberia) is poor, whereas the country is rich. There are many reasons for this. Despite the huge poverty confronting my country, it is a nation rich in natural resources. It has diamonds, gold, iron ore, etc. Beginning in the sixties, it was the leading producer of iron ore and rubber latex in Africa. Instead of using the enormous riches of the nation to help develop the people, these resources have been used by rulers to create a more impoverished society, as the people are kept down and suppressed.

Poverty, looking at the nature of things in Liberia, can be systemic. It is created both by individual laziness, a very suppressive political system, and the educational system. Poverty is devilish. It has a power that causes it to expand from a lesser level to a larger level, can consume an entire population, and causes underdevelopment as well. This is what is happening to my country in West Africa. For almost 200 years, a nation with about five million people has been one of the poorest in Africa and even the world despite its vast natural resources. In the sixties and eighties, Liberia was the leading producer of iron ore and rubber latex in Africa.

This small country in West Africa, called Liberia, was founded by freed slaves from the United States of America in 1822. It gained its independence in 1847. It practised a form of government called democracy. For about 140 years, our leaders continued to promote democracy, leading to the establishment of a form of pure democracy. The system of rule at the time did not allow the majority of the citizens to participate in the political process and the economic life of the state. To further dehumanize the indigenous people, rulers of those days established and promoted the system in a way that prevented the creation of a good learning atmosphere that could have served as a basis for developing the society, transitioning the nation from dark days to light in the world. What was so bogus was that a native child was banned from attending schools with the children of freed slaves, or native children were coerced into presenting themselves as if they were freed slaves by changing their names, which those who did were accommodated and enjoyed similar privileges as the freed slaves in power. History notes that those founders came from a suppressive culture in America and decided to practice suppression against their indigenous people. As a result, infighting became common and further promoted poverty.

This culture of controversial democracy promotes suppression and dehumanizes ordinary people until a coup is held that slightly breaks the barrier of suppression. But the former oppressor, meaning America, allowed the suppressed freed slaves to promote a culture where laziness and corruption became the order of the day. In the culture I come from, it is not just the individual to blame for poverty. Instead, it became a systemic structure orchestrated against the entire population, and the promoter of this so-called form of democracy pampers the rulers, who engage in practices that keep the country down rather than improve the lives of the people.

In the first place, there is no such thing as pure democracy in the world, as some scholars call it. What I see is what I call controversial democracy. This democracy favours the developed world, which introduced it, rather than favouring the country that practices it. This creates an imbalanced society in the country that practices it.

Democracy should not include a concept called pure democracy. The underlying motive of pure democracy is to break down human society. The general reason behind pure democracy is to remove God's influence from individual life and make the individual a supreme being over the majority through some form of power system or economic means. There is a power behind promoting pure democracy, controlled by a universal concept of power that attempts to eliminate God the Almighty. For any system, as I see, the concept of pure democracy, which tries to undo human values or remove God from human life, is a devilish concept. It is not that democracy itself is bad, but that its pure concept must be avoided. It is the ulterior motive of this governing system that gives rights to individuals without control, and it is catastrophic, as it does not have a break or stop with its implementation, and it is not workable through advocacy and non-governmental organizations. It is a system that promotes looseness in society. Because of its motive, it will continue to dehumanize, and that will create shockwaves—something very detrimental to its survival and mankind's survival would continue to be threatened.

Understand that I do not mean democracy in general is bad. No. But there is a concept of pure democracy that doesn't value helping but is imposed on and tries to control those it is imposed on, creating a new culture detrimental to their well-being. I must tell you about this because many countries in the world practice democracy and the negative side of such democracy they are practicing instead.

We must all be careful with the issue of democracy. A democracy that allows universal freedom and controls the leadership of a nation is a bad democracy. This type of democracy must be dealt with because it promotes capitalism and leads to the promotion of greed.

Some facets of this controversial/pure democracy are:
1. It allows our rulers to corrupt and go lay down in the enslaver's home with their stolen money, and they are never punished for the perpetuation of such evil. The reason this is done is that, as these rulers steal and sit in America, they are able to spend their stolen money by promoting economic policies that favour American producers.
2. It makes people poorer than if it had the ability to create systems and programs that would favour improving the lives of the ordinary or majority.
3. It creates systems that seem to be accountability-promoting systems, whereas they favour the ruler more than the people because they are full of manipulations.
4. This promotes a culture of dependency on foreign aid and grants rather than learning to produce by creating economic efficiency.
5. Economic aid and grants are given to the country, and the providers follow the money without proper accountability to prove whether the nation is doing well through its lending or service operations.
6. It promotes the interests of individual Americans who want to do business within the system over the rulers back home to the place of its implementation.
7. It creates a superpower tendency in the world. Therefore, if an American's business interests are not

protected, the ruler falls into a political problem with America.

8. It talks about the rights of the individual more than the promotion of collective rights that should supersede the individual's rights in establishing a more civilized world, not a loose one. It makes Americans and Europeans enforcers of gender equity and focuses on breaking down the individual and his culture by giving the rights of a community to the state. In this case, the people become controlled by the state instead of the people controlling the state.

9. It is a system that tries to do away with God by instilling a culture of individualism based on self-promotion rather than collective promotion. Because of this, an individual can decide to be gay or lesbian, which is something that should be promoted more overall because it is the individual's right to promote. The question is, how does one determine the order of such a society that should have laws to promote if everyone lives anyhow?

In such a culture, there will always be a wider gap between the poor and the rich. It is full of controversy because when the system seems to fall apart, it is full of political demonstrations or agitations. This can sometimes lead the nation to stagnation or more economic difficulties rather than progress.

What I believe is that a pure democracy should allow a free flow of things. But it shouldn't be imposed on the people by breaking down their systems and human dignity. This should be the determination of a pure democracy that allows valuing the people and their culture. It should work in a way that won't damage their human dignity by respecting the views expressed through their constitutions. A culture of rights with such a system shouldn't be imposed.

If you find yourself in such a controversial democratic system, you need to think and act positively to change your level.

The intention of such a system that doesn't listen and accept what is right by letting the people themselves decide on its tenets is a problem for human existence. Any system that lacks human development but is more cohesive about self-actualization is a bad system. Today, there are more poor people in my country because of the way our leaders, created by this system, behave, and they are never punished for the wrongs they continue to perpetrate against the state. They corrupt and find safe havens in America, and these same individual leaders continue to move through the corridors of power by returning over and over when they are broken down, or their money is depleted, just to have a share again of the state resources. They leave their safe havens trying to control the political order by entering politics, and the governments protect them in the place where their money is put into banks.

Chapter 10

"I may feed you with food and this knowledge, but the one who truly gains nourishment is you."

– Frederick W. Sonpon

Nobody Fights Better Than a Person Who Has a Dream

You have a great fight to contend with because life is about a struggle. You must realize that life is somehow already like a chain on people, held spiritually by an invisible hand. Sufferings came into the world from the unknown, and we are born into suffering. So, it is like a natural chain you must fight to break apart. It is as though it is tiring for people to lock them up. You must, therefore, be ready to fight continuously to remove whatever poverty chain is holding you back.

Do you sometimes ask yourself this question, meaning to know why you are suffering or why the same is brought upon you? Your own power doesn't create some of the sufferings of this world; they are like curses on people we are born into and might have travelled from those of old. Adam and Eve were the ones who brought sin, which travelled to our world today. You are not the source of sins. You are just born into it. You must use your spiritual fight to deal with some of the problems of sins and those that men create.

Some of the poverty problems are spiritual and require spiritual steps of prayers and fasting before removing them. So, if there was no good in you, nobody would want to fight you. But the creature Satan is fighting against the good of God concerning you and me. One of the things he uses to fight people is poverty. When poverty is around, he knows that people may sometimes become involved in criminal activities, trying to fight for survival.

You were made to be who you are but not made to be as you are. This is why you must stop thinking that you were never made to succeed in this world, either. Take that from your mind. Just apply some effort and see if God will not show Himself forth through your efforts.

Figure it out now that there must be a reason and get to know where such a reason for suffering is coming from, why poverty is reigning so greatly in the world, and why the world is not even decisive about eradicating it. It is the same way global warming has become lip service. There are too many people in poverty in the world compared to those who are rich, and you have to remove yourself from the list of those poor people. It is because of the good inside of you; know that this is the reason nature is refusing to let you rise. If there were no good in you, suffering wouldn't have been your portion to confront the forces of evil. Can't you figure this out yet?

Think about this: Satan wasn't with God to have you in His image and likeness. Rather, we are made in the image of God Himself for the good of the same God. Being in the image of God is a reason Satan is doing everything possible to disprove the value of God relating to the life of mankind.

Sometimes I try asking myself the question of why this Satan individual can't go back to heaven to God Himself and fight Him. If he thinks he has power, he needs to prove it by going back to God and taking Him from power. But he is not able to go back because there is no power in him to do so. His end is inevitable.

Each of us is a value of God, which is not for nothing that got us to be on earth. It is the purpose inside your creation you must pursue in life and stop sitting and complaining for nothing. You have some virtues. Until you can discover the good in or about you, nobody will discover such good about you and your world. Create the good for your appreciation that I believe you deserve so that it may start blowing the wind when you have it with you. Fight for the good since you know now that God made you a good person, and that is the reason you came from His good hands. Nothing good that God creates is without a good reason. Tell the world that you are somebody special who was made in the image of God and that your God is not a dead God. Live for the good of life rather than for the status of nothing in life.

Know that everyone is fighting to live a good life because they want to experience good. We are chasing something good, which is the reason for our services; we fight to be educated, and when we are educated, we show that good in service to mankind. It is time for you to step into the good world that lies ahead of you.

If good weren't tied to the life of mankind, nobody would have had the ability to seek the need for rendering service in this world through the education you get. And the source of everything, including knowledge, comes from God. Nothing good comes from the hands of Satanic people.

This is why you must tell life that you will chase after your good by depending on God, who will then prove such a good status by bringing it out into the world. I have never seen a person striving for a good future if there is nothing good about it that exists. Until you can make a good order of your life from your lowly state for the good, you may just be placed at the backdoor of your life. Bring out your good by making a discovery of your life to the world. Something good is hidden about each of us; this is the reason you and I have the talents and potential that God gave us. It is those elements of good He wants you to bring to light. In the book of St. Matthew 5:14, Christ proved that by saying that you are the light of the world and a city set on a hill that cannot be hidden. He called you a light and a city. Being a city, He says that you are a type of city that sits on top of a hill that all surroundings can see. By being on a hill as a city and a light, it means you must show forth the good of your life so that the world—referring to its people—can feel this about you, especially if you are willing to accept Him as Lord and Savior.

Bringing the good in you out will lead to you receiving compliments from people. You carry good, and I carry good from God as well, which is why you and I are not dead yet. We are still on the surface of the earth, not meaningless people, because we have the power to display the good of God in our lives to the world. You have good, and that is why nature is fighting against you to appear dull and irrelevant. Be of a bold spirit to tell the world that you are an image of God, so you must live a good life.

Establish such a world of success now. Success brings about a different world that is good for people, which you have to attain and show to the world. That world of success is not in your current state until you can create it. It has its own culture and principles, which makes it different from those who live in the world of the majority and are never discovered. You have to follow its principles in order to make it work. It is not ordinary to think that by sitting, a good world of success will just come to you. You have to wake up and work it out. Understand that until a seed is buried to grow, no germination or fruit will come. Circumstances of poverty and others show your seed of greatness the time of being buried yet. You are being polished for the good that lies ahead of you to show up to the world.

Bury your head in something now rather than letting poverty bury you. If you reach the level of success which I wish for you, you will have more power in the world and help contribute positively and economically. This world is not looking for inactive and non-contributors. It is a world of power, and you must give yourself power. If you say you don't want to succeed, it means you are telling the world that it should die in poverty. It is a mindset of dependency you may want to keep promoting if you keep hiding your glory and not succeeding.

See the value in your success and learn to harness it for the world. If you are successful, the financial stress you are facing now will go away. If you are successful, you can help many people you see around you. If you are successful, you can travel to places with the financial power to do so. If you are successful, you will do things that will create more happiness for you than being stressed out due to poverty crippling your economy. Limitations will no longer be your problem by the time you are successful. Enter that world of success now by planting a seed for your success.

Let your success speak to the world about being recognized and respected. Stop pampering poverty. It is like a fire that can burn people's lives. Stop letting such a useless fire keep burning you. If you don't fight it now, you will see it spreading its wings or squeezing you, making you feel trapped, as economic conditions will continue pressing against you just to keep you down. It creates burdens on people, like weights that prevent your true self from showing up to the world. Think about this now! Consider that you are on the surface of the earth meant for display. You are not hidden in the earth or buried underneath it yet, meaning you must show the good you have to the world before you are old and gone.

Poverty stress is detrimental, and you must fight to eliminate poverty. It can cause abnormal thinking, insults, sleep, food consumption, places to sleep, influences, and more. It can lead to sicknesses that you should be able to deal with easily but can grow and later affect you. It can cause family confusion. It is a divider. Don't let it divide your life and the lives of your family members. You may be planning a family in the future, but you shouldn't expect that poverty should be what you pass on to that family as if it were an inheritance. Don't make it a gift for life. Why would you want to be born in poverty and die in poverty? In fact, nobody is born in poverty because we all are endowed with potential or talents, which are our riches from God. Until you tap into them, they will remain hidden riches, undiscovered. If you don't plan your way up, expect to have an endless plan for going down unnoticed until you find yourself in that status as age catches up with you. Know that financial problems are like pressing elements.

Fight it in the morning, as poverty is a disease. Fight it at night with prayer. Fight it in the daytime by putting your body to work. Fight it with fasting and actions of faith, praying against it. Fight until there is no fight left by bringing in compliments. You have to do so now. Stop looking for redeemers elsewhere other than depending on God and yourself. You must stop looking for people to praise you or people who will help you before you think about achieving success. Many people in the world don't know their way out spiritually and physically; they are, by nature, blind. Stop looking up to men. If you want a better world for yourself or for all, you should be the one to start the world of such with your life by setting up whatever foundation is needed. Just imagine the whole world you see with many people; it started with a single man—Adam. He was later put to sleep, and unknowingly to him, a helpmate (Eve) was created. It was from their birth that the growth of our lives became possible. The Bible says so. Having Adam and Eve mate is a reason other humans exist, showing forth the goodness of God, as mankind was made with the power of reproduction and production, allowing them to fill the world with humans.

Value the concept of your multiplication on earth. We were born into this. You were made to produce value; this is why you are born and still alive. You are still alive, not because you are better than those who are gone.

Learn to produce now. Your production can be in the service you render to humanity, which should be paid for. Your production can be in your education to help others. Together, we can change this world.

What you should know is this: you are part of the cycle of reproduction and production. Your mind and body should produce value, meaning ideas and goods should come out of you where the world will benefit. If you were to have a child and train that child well, he or she will continue the pattern of good training. But many people are not trained to have their good characters show up to the world yet. Wake up now. We are a store of values with ideas that can change this world, and by doing so, we can have a great impact. This is why you must respect the upbringing of children and develop by planning for future generations.

Children who are given care are a good thing because they are the propagation of society's growth. They carry powers of greatness inside. Value your service. Your service can contribute to raising good children in this world. Be able to reproduce as well as to produce economically. It is like presenting a picture of production to understand that success is born from the mind. If you don't work to have a child by doing the things that will bring the child, the child won't be born just like that.

Here is the way out for you to really get started in helping your life. Understand that changing your way of life depends on you fighting against poverty with your life. Force your body while your mind initiates the process of work. When I was a boy, I always thought that to be successful; I needed to keep putting my hope in mankind and government until I learned my lesson well. Since I was born and became a man, I have taken part in eight public elections, voting for my officials and helping to conduct some of the elections. Some were presidential elections, while the rest were for representatives and senators. Today, we are still looking for solutions for our state of Liberia economically and politically, hoping for a good government by continuing to vote. Despite the many elections held, there are still no good roads, and government institutions are in poor condition.

All these years I have voted, I believed that the government would be the source of my personal prosperity, which is why I kept voting, waiting for a change. I thought that by electing these leaders, they would end my personal poverty if I sat idly without doing anything with my life. I thought they could make a difference for the country since democracy was introduced to us by the United States. However, my curiosity remains unsatisfied because most of the governments and legislators I helped elect have often been exposed to corruption. None have been able to create and promote tangible laws for lifting ordinary lives in the country. Every day is just a hustle and tussle, as they make meaningless noise.

None really know the importance of how the laws that would make lives better off should be made. They don't know that good laws should be the basis for changing people's conditions. They don't know that laws are needed to support the development of scholars, especially young people, to keep them basic and productive for society. There are no means of building or setting up a future foundation where knowledge will be translated persistently to the younger generations coming after, the older ones, thus creating a transition to changing lives in the country. However, corruption is a growing feature.

Laws are needed to create service programs, especially for young people who should make or have an impact on creating a productive society through obtaining a good education with the help of the state, transitioning the population based on stages. Laws are needed to create a friendly business environment that should focus mainly on young people taking part in or rendering services to instil financial discipline in them and make them productive corporate business elites or raise middle-income earners and producers through institutions. Laws are needed to shift the banking sector of the economy to the manufacturing sector, thus creating corporate ventures to generate more jobs and goods for export by bringing in foreign dollars. Laws are needed to create service and market zones, linking the transport sector as well. Laws are needed to ensure good electricity distribution so that services are provided in such a way that the people will feel the value of a functioning government. Laws are needed to create an export-based economy with a focus on helping domestic producers achieve returns and produce more. The agro-sector economy needs laws to keep farmers producing, providing opportunities, and becoming competitive, especially if they can benefit from their production through programs that will keep them competitive and allow them to export their goods for foreign income in return.

Because I want to see a functioning society for my nation, Liberia, to make agro-producers more productive, young managers or Liberians should be raised or trained in this sector, especially those coming out of high schools, to assist farmers in learning to better plan and create harvests. This could be done to promote productivity by starting with these high school graduates, whose services should be rendered in such a way that they are shifted into productive lives by first learning to serve the state. By such means, scholarships and other important programs could be developed with the hope of seeing them serve humanity. It will help reduce poverty. This could have national and international bearings on our state and on them. This can also be a basis to determine the transition of young leaders who will develop by being raised and guided; they will be scouted from as low a level as high school, and before reaching adulthood, they might have understood how the state works, including the economy in promoting production. But this is not the case these days. Young people who don't know how to even run their own lives because they are struggling on their own are becoming legislators as well. When they take power, because they are not groomed to understand the service-to-nation program they were to develop into, they become corrupt and self-centred. They become the voices of the people and break down Liberian society.

And while these laws that will promote production and services to the state, penalties should be prescribed or created as well to stamp out corruption practices in building a vibrant nation and responsible citizenries. Every good nation must value young people. These young people should be developed to understand the pattern of national development.

Change and even development are not something that can be obtained on a silver platter. It is a gradual process. But this is not the case these days with my country because government jobs are like the only things people want in Liberia. The private sector is dead. And governments in succession aren't as focused on developing programs that can alleviate poverty and keep young people focused and productive, which would lead to national development and prosperity.

The worst part is that since my country came out of a fourteen-year civil war in 2003, the things that were the main reasons for the war are being promoted more than ever before. The youth population is abandoned. Even retirement programs are poor, creating a brain drain situation. Imagine rebel leaders flooding the corridors of power, determining the survival of the state through them. This is one-factor causing high corruption. But let this be a clarion call to Liberians that we must correct the ills of our society by correcting our lives and striving for success first. Nations are built by people, and the people should be made to carry developed minds. There is no way that foreign persons will develop our nation better than we could by taking full ownership of our survival and development. But we are making our country and people more dependent on foreign aid, foreign businesses, and individuals.

The economic corruption of our leaders promotes other nations by leaving their own country to live in foreign countries. These vices are some of the key promoters of poverty.

There is a growing culture of democracy that is not really improving but rather raising a culture of looseness. It projects weak leadership rather than strong leadership for our country. It promotes a culture of hooliganism, as drug abuse is increasing daily and killing mostly our young people. This is why, as Liberians or if you are from a country in Africa, we must change the order of the world. A bad side of democracy is promoting looseness, as crimes are increasing daily among young people, who should be the backbone of society.

Be a contributor to change. A nation can turn into a failed state if there are no systems, people are poor, and its institutions are bad. Any nation that doesn't promote young people mostly will become a recycling state because trouble will not leave its shores. Practically, Liberian culture is becoming a loose culture. Disrespect and killing are hugely promoted by young people. It is becoming common for young people and older ones to abuse each other on the streets and at community levels. Society no longer frowns on this because of loose leadership, which creates its own loose culture.

I see this as one of the major reasons why poverty is rampant in my country. Additionally, the lack of self-financial discipline due to a bad educational system with an outlandish style of learning is causing poverty, and people aren't earnest in the public sector, which is believed to be the backbone of society.

Stop trusting in men and their systems without learning to develop yourself. Men will lie and steal from you because of their systems. Men will want to betray your trust. Men will even take away the little available resources for themselves, the few who are in power.

The state-run economy system in any nation, if you don't trust it, could take away what belongs to you, the ordinary person. Increases in taxes, thus causing high inflation, are salient markers of evil promotion within an economy against the ordinary. Men will promote economic strangulation, focusing not on lifting the lives of all but on satisfying the few elites. Individual development should be valued by us. When people develop instead of remaining very poor, they can have voices that collectively lead to better change for their states, compared to having many poor people who are suppressed by leaders and create national dependency. Create your economic power. So, stop trusting in men and their governments without thinking of setting up your personal government of success. See a good government in you to learn to improve yourself. The better you become, the more your success will contribute to others' success, creating a bigger success that will have value in your country.

Here is the causation or the way in which the economy's expansion is worked out. If there are programs to develop the people, the better the citizens of such a nation would see development as personal and try to be on top, which will drive national development. The more people who are developed, the more this will drive the course of national livelihoods overall, proving that nations you see developed today have their development based on the people. They are the ones who own businesses or institutions to create employment.

It is not something magical to know that every economy starts with an individual. If a small village with about ten people does not work, you will see that such a village will suffer from many things that are very detrimental to their lives, such as increasing hunger. This is the reason you, as an individual, are the basis of the start of every economy. From an individual-level economy, there is the family-level economy, which is composed of groups of individuals. It grows from that point to the community or national-level economy, thus determining the healthiness or unhealthy situation of the entire economy of a nation. So, you are part and parcel of the economy of your state, meaning a power within your nation's economy, especially if you stop being broke all the time and learn to develop and have the capacity to spend money. You must strive to join the list of producing people or the working class so you can make purchases as a way of promoting economic growth through sales.

The wealthier people in a country contribute to raising the nation; this has power in return, based on promoting infrastructure development as well, because they become the backbone of that nation, paying huge taxes that the government will use to cater to developmental projects. No poor person can pay taxes. So, if the government were to keep raising a poor culture of people, there would be no national development because nobody would pay taxes. Development is tied to the people. They should be developed before there can be an effect of bringing about infrastructure development to celebrate. Any successful person wants to own a good home, and success is mainly tied to growing businesses. Therefore, a developed person will want to live a good life, showing physical success. Any successful person wants to live up to a good standard. You would not want to remain a primitive person throughout your life once you become successful. It would be a change of level. And when the level changes, it has its own way of presenting a person whose level has changed.

Follow this example: if you were a villager and, luckily, you went to school or learned something that is marketing you, or from which you are earning income, you won't want to keep living like a villager, probably lacking economic muscle. You will have accrued some economic power right there. Or, if you had no opportunity and, luckily, an opportunity is given to you, where you left poverty, you won't want to refuse to leave poverty behind. You will feel like a new person with money and the ability to spend. The cycle of economic limitation would have been destroyed.

If you lived in a muddy house before and became successful from the skill you acquired, creating some money for your life, you would rather want to live in a concrete house, well-furnished, in the future. If you never used to have a shower but then learned to use one, you would have changed from continuing to use an outdoor bathroom. Every human's transition has its own style. Such a transition would force you to adapt to a new trend. You would be placed at a different level, with a different way of doing things and different influences, because your life might have changed and become no longer ordinary. That is a forceful transition you would have to adapt to due to such an economic change you made possible.

For example, suppose a mother and father were to have three children within a village, making the family size about five. Those children were well taken care of and educated and began working, earning good incomes. In that case, you should picture that the life of that family will change, no longer living primitively or being confronted by huge poverty. The family will gain significant power—educational power, followed by influential power. When there is economic power, society will benefit as well. They could become business gurus and create jobs for others within their society. This is what we call life.

So, if we had many economically developed families who are considered developed because they are positive thinkers, due to their positive steps for improvement, their efforts would add value to creating a wealthy society. It would help to break the cycle of poverty in families and society because everyone would be developed. It would help to develop a national vision. That is how today's developed world is made to be developed.

Stop thinking primitively or having negative thoughts about improving yourself or having money as something evil. That poverty confronting your world now is bad. Fight positively to have money because money is meant to serve people, not the other way around. If you think having money is bad, just sit down and do nothing, letting poverty consume you. God forbid!

Be positive now. How do you think people can pay for goods and services within an economy without you having money to do so? Every economy involves people rendering services and getting paid for what they do. If having money is bad, why use money? Why should a state make it a medium of exchange? Generally, money is for transactions and investments. If having money is bad, nobody should learn anything, and we should just remain primitive.

As you might know, the first humans driven away from God left His presence with nothing but the riches of their heads. You have the same power of knowledge to use and change your world.

Knowing the Types of Money

Money can be in various forms. It can be paper or a coin. It can be invisible, neither paper nor coin, but the same can operate behind the scenes in making the economy work. In short, it is not only seen in coin or paper form. It can be in an invisible form, acting behind the scenes within an economy due to various transactions that take place from one institution and country to another. This is why you can see people selling shares, which is not about physical money. Money transactions that seem invisible, or security instruments, are monies that operate invisibly. Even mobile money systems, wire transfers, services for services, etc., are examples of money operating invisibly or behind the scenes to work and grow the economy of a state. Until you understand the concept of money and its attached values, you may not wish to develop and become a rich person. Because people don't know what money can do to improve life, they see money as an evil instrument. It is the lack of management of money that can cause some people to make money and then lose it again and again.

I remember the barter system (where people used to exchange goods for goods or services for services, as we know about) is gone. We are in modern times where money is used, moving the wheels of the economy more effectively than barter trade, which was a bit slower in transaction purposes. However, we can still see a bit of a speedy barter trade system based on how the exchange process takes place, especially like banking transactions, and it is not as prevalent as it used to be with barter trade, such as goods for goods and services for services.

This is a reason for you never to see money and holding money or having much of it as evil. If you work for your money, it is not bad to have much of it from your work. Some work can make you rich, so will you attribute the money to something bad to have? It is the medium of exchange where transactions can take place within any economy. You need it in a church or religious centre for transaction purposes. You must have it if you live in an urban or rural area. You must have it even if you live in a village. It can be used to travel. It can be used to pay for goods and services. This is why it is called the medium of exchange. So, why should you hate the act of making money and becoming rich as a burden of life? Even the religious materials you see printed are made through money. This book you are reading was made by spending money.

You are a valuable person who should not struggle to have money by seeing money as devilish. If there is no good in you, you won't live for the good of society and won't have money to spend. If there is no good in you, you would have been discarded in life. If there is no good in you, you can't have an attribute of change to think of. Since you are still alive, this should make sense to you that you have a contribution to make to the world. You are in the world and still alive because the world needs you most. Empower yourself now because employers need you!

The concept of perfection is real. It was a reason for perfection existing with mankind, for which mankind was a close friend of God. It was a reason for perfection to promote mankind being created in the image of God. It shows that mankind is not really different from God because of carrying His nature or character. It is a reason for perfection to prove the existence of good in creation. If God had not created good in the perfection of His creation, He wouldn't have rested on the seventh day after His work in six days.

We must, therefore, strive to become perfect. It is a reason every individual strives to seek good out of life to prove there is an existence of a nature of perfection or good ahead of us that we must reach. It is about having some perfection or expertise in something to prove good, which makes life feel worth living when one achieves whatever is good or perfect in practice and performance. We are to strive for the good and perfection of everything in nature by looking up to God, who will make us reach the stage He sees as perfect. We must not see ourselves as good by thinking we are good and perfect in our work without acknowledging God as the source of such good and perfection. Good is the source of perfection, and perfection has a final end which brings relevance and beautification by God and nature, seeing us as valuable. This is why no one or nature should turn your perfect nature, as God created you as good, into nothing. Strive to reach your point of good and perfection so that mankind will see your good deeds or works and glorify your God in nature (St. Matthew 5:16).

So, nothing should make you feel like you can't fight to eradicate poverty from your life by achieving economic good and reaching your final end of perfection. Spiritually, you are designed as good and perfect and physically as well. Because you were created good and perfect, God gives you the power to rule a world that was made good and perfect. You may not be perfect spiritually because of the nature of sin, but you can strive to be good and perfect. You can be perfect in something you have learned that can prove a change and relevance in your life.

The world wants a perfect government. It also wants a perfect economy and to stop global warming. It does so with the hope of obtaining a good and perfect end of the Earth by living free of everything evil. It is the relevance the world is seeking and thinks this is obtainable without God. It is a lie. Only in God can we obtain a good and perfect end of everything.

Refute those who say that nothing is perfect and nothing can be sought as perfect. We all in this world are striving for the good and perfect world of everything. This is why you must strive to see change come. Strive to remove poverty by bringing about a good and perfect economy. Erase the negative thinking that you can't achieve goodness and perfection with knowledge and prosperity just that you must attribute this to God to obtain, rather than attributing your state of good and perfection solely to yourself. This is the pride in the world, thinking that by scientific advancement, we can make our world a better place without attributing such power to God.

This is a reason for seeking the good and perfection of greatness; we strive to become who we want to be in this world. The opposite of not waking up to seek good and perfection is domination by evil and suffering. This is why if you sit without doing anything to change your economic condition, the result of doing nothing will be economic difficulty. Therefore, picture the nature of good and its perfection as a direction to follow before obtaining it. Be the best you can be by working it out.

Chapter 11

"Until you elevate yourself to the power of success, you'll never truly understand its value as something to possess. Take action, and opportunities will naturally align in your favor. Become the world you've always wished to see—create it now, instead of letting the world shape itself for you!"

– Frederick W. Sonpon

The Way You Think Will Cause Poverty to You

One of my senior comrades happened to be a big brother, though we graduated from the university together. He graduated before me. The two of us are currently rendering our services working with the National Elections Commission. We were temporarily assigned to Grand Gedeh County in 2020. Our task generally was to conduct a by-election. There was a conversation when he said something. He said the world is unfair because he saw that the majority of people are poor while a few are rich and even extremely rich. So, he wanted to know why the overly rich couldn't help the poor. Our conversation was based on Jeff Bezos. He heard a story that Jeff had divorced his wife, and during that time, he gave her a total of $32 billion as her resettlement to move on with her life since he had left her in their relationship. So, this big brother said, why can a man have so much money and just pay that amount out without remorse to a single individual? Because of this, he said the world is unfair. So, he said the world is not fair. But I told him the world is a fair world created by God for His purpose. But the actions of mankind are causing the world to appear as unfair in nature. I further said that although Jeff got his money and can decide how to use it, it shouldn't be the basis for determining that the world is unfair. I said Jeff worked hard for his money so he could decide how to handle the foreclosure of his relationship by spending whatever he wanted to end the relationship. He refuted my view and maintained the notion that the world was unfair. But we all just laughed over his expression.

I countered this notion of his. I said the world is fairly created by God in that way. Therefore, I told him that we must see the world in us if we are to be seen as fair. Again, I said that if the world weren't fair, God wouldn't have rested from its creation when He got to work to create all things. Because God made everything perfect, He made us stewards over the world. I told him further that he needed to stop blaming people like Jeff for spending his money the way he wanted to. Jeff is not in a different world other than the same world we are in. He came from nowhere before he developed his life and became exceedingly rich today. Cultivate such a spirit in you to learn from his example.

You are made to be who you are but not made to be as you are. If poverty is troubling your life, you weren't made to be that way. Change the situation because you were never made to be that way; you were born into a world that has everything to make your life splendid. We are here to mind God's business of life and the properties of the earth. As mission agents, we didn't come to suffocate by losing our relevance, nor did poverty take a toll on our lives imposed either by ourselves or other humans through the systems of the world created by the same humans. It is an agreement between us and God for us to live a good life, and He doesn't want to see you suffocate. It is a motive for which He didn't make the world ungovernable despite mankind's sins. So, don't see the world as a place of disgrace to your life. See it as a place where you should showcase your power of greatness rather than letting other powers of degradation take over your life and try to blame God by saying that the world is unfair. Besides that, God gave us talents or potentials that can also make us show up in riches as individuals full of blessings, apart from the physical resources or riches on earth which are here for us to enjoy. If the riches of earth will be depleted, know this: your talent will not be depleted in you. It will not cause global warming or face depletion. He had created all things for every one of us to live our lives splendidly. You belong to a good God who placed you in a life of gain. He had a plan for each of us only to come and live happily while taking care of His business on earth. Carry such a notion so you don't think that you just came to earth created by God only to suffer. No. That is not the motive of your existence.

What you should keep at the back of your mind in life is that you have a mission on earth you must complete. Every mission has a timeframe. Every mission also has a pay. Furthermore, every mission has a purpose. It must have a final result to prove its completion. This is because we are on a mission, including you, and the reason you don't have a source in yourself to exist on earth is that your source is in God. This is why you don't have a source in you, and this world has yet to have a lasting solution for all things. Our political systems and economies can collapse. A mission in source is an agreement between the person who sends you on the mission and yourself. It is a process that must lead to a purpose of accomplishment. The bargain you have with God on the mission is that He paid you already in advance by having this earth for you to enjoy.

If you fail to complete your mission on earth and live in happiness when the time comes, you will be gone from earth, either in old age, and you will have to report back to God who brought you here. If your source is spiritual—from the infinite power—your end will be as infinite as well—either positively or negatively. So, be careful how you treat the life in you and deal with others in the world. Believe in yourself. Believe that you are carrying God inside you (1 John 4:4). Anyone who carries Him of that nature shouldn't see themselves carrying frustration, poverty, and sicknesses. If somebody were to tell me that I am like my father, meaning there is something unique about me or the other way around, as my father in characteristics. Our Father, God, is unique, and He made us unique for His purpose. It is the faith you must have over this life you have. This is why you should focus on how you can leave a positive mark on the world. You were never made to live anyhow. It is a basis of causing us to live anyhow; you see forces of darkness—or Satan and his infections upon mankind and through their systems—changing the world negatively.

What you need to understand here, from the whole creation process, is that God didn't make the world for Himself, meaning that He was to live here physically. He did it for human beings—us who have flesh and blood inside us. He didn't make earth for spirit beings who can't be seen with the naked eye. You don't have to sit back and let Satan drag you into suffering and do nothing about it. God is a spirit being but not a human being; He works through us by His spirit. He is invisible and works in people by His spirit to create attachment with us and by recreating us into relevance, which He knew He had created before should have the first humans be of such nature. Because He is not flesh and blood, He gave us the earth to live here as a place for us, the human beings, to display His wonders upon us.

He knew the earth was a place for mankind—having flesh and blood—where no other being was given the power to rule earth except human beings. This concept of power is meant for you, too. Imagine, God Himself, after His creation, didn't come to stay on earth, except humans with flesh and blood did. This should be a reason for you to understand that, because of the love He had for mankind, as you read that He made us in His own likeness (Genesis 1:26), He created a world for mankind to have the power to display in good, doing His ways here too. He hasn't given angels the power to own their own heaven apart from the heaven He is from biblically. But for mankind, He gave us a whole earth to live here and enjoy it. So, give yourself power here because earth is your home and the place to show forth your relevance. Here, you are to show power as a living being and not as a dead being by letting circumstances, especially poverty with its power, turn you into a subject.

You see, here is the problem with the world, which continues to suffer. The actions of men, who now don't see their existence in God but see it in their power through science and others, are the ones determining either the positive or bad side of life across the world, causing poverty or prosperity. This is why you must take positive action to turn your world around positively. So, the world is a gift to mankind. We didn't ask for it, but God just created it and brought us into it to enjoy.

As you read about Jeff Bezos, his power of creativity put him on top of his world. Put your mind to work so that your body will feel that value. After every job, the result must show up. Stop sitting and complaining. It is from work that people are paid.

Think of the case of Jeff Bezos. Use him as an example. He was once poor and worked to make his money by putting his ideas to work for him. His ideas came from his mind. He was not sitting and complaining before he put his ideas into action. He had to put himself in a thinking mode before he was able to develop something that made his world what it is today. He didn't do anything wrong before getting rich, unlike some people who want to be rich but kill or corrupt others before achieving such. He didn't find a diamond to trade before gaining his riches. However, the riches within him, relative to his talents or potential, were showcased through thinking and working. Something simple he did with his mind changed his world. He has been involved in selling goods (books and others) on the internet.

Because of his success, he has the power to decide how to spend his own money. But what would have been wrong with him, as I told my big brother or comrade, would be if he had spent his money to impoverish others or to kill or corrupt people. In that case, I could say that he might have spent his money wrongly. He earns his own money and spends it the way he wants to.

If you want to get rich through work, God will not stop you. Even nobody will want to stop you if you decide to put your ideas to work for you. What I want you to draw from the analysis of Berso's case is that you have the power to get rich like him. God will not stop you if you want to have money and take care of your life. Because He is a God who loves good for us, He wants us to have faith, and that faith should work. You have the power to make money just as Jeff does. This is a reason you have talents within you, created by God just to change your level. Turn those talents or potentials into physical goods that will be on the market soon. Goods and services are the basis for having a market and creating trade. People go to markets to buy and trade. Money is what enables them to buy. It keeps companies in business. It keeps employers on the job. This is about seeking a good life.

Your talents or potential are the hidden riches you have. You have to create faith and means for them to show up by thinking of them from within you first. You are naturally made as a marketplace with goods. It is the translation of ideas that makes the world and economies work. Talents or potentials are invisible powers of ideas that can be converted into products. Like the book you are reading, I thought it out. This is turned into a product after thinking it through. A publishing company collected the idea and turned it into a project like you are reading now. The final stage, as you see the book in your hand, is made a finished good by bringing about satisfaction through creation for the purpose of utility. You can be the best you want to be if you work for the best of such nature without just imagining it.

Your potentials or talents, therefore, are goods for your market to start. They can be turned into services. Just bring them out to the world by tapping into them. You will see them work for you and bring about economic satisfaction if you start thinking positively. You can begin to use your thinking if you first make up your mind to grow. If you start thinking positively about yourself, you will start to develop ideas, and those ideas are the talents or potentials that must become products to bring to the world. Thinking is like having a dream of an object to bring to the world. Nobody is better than you until you start believing in yourself. Watch the mentality you carry about yourself, the world, and others. It could either be killing your power or will, not allowing you to wake up and push to the place of your achievements by creating such a world. Your problem could be that you look at others and think they are more blessed than you and believe you were cursed to be the way you are now. Why would you think like that when God gave you five senses, and those who are succeeding also have the same five senses as you? Start pushing into your greatness. Time is not for you to wait on your nature or people, complaining without end.

Some reasons why you may not yet succeed could be the following:
- You don't see the power of God upon you and fail to recognize that you were made in the image of God, which you must showcase in success reflective of such an image;
- You may be crying over life and never give yourself a push;
- You lack faith in yourself to succeed despite your poverty;
- You lack faith in the things you will do to change yourself by not utilizing your potential or talents;
- You don't do anything to generate income and depend on others whom you think should help you before you can make it;
- You may not know how to spend money wisely;
- You are wasteful with your time, money, and life;

- You don't learn to save money and consume everything that comes into your hands;
- You spend almost all your income without leaving a portion for investment;
- You might be dividing your little income on foolish things or maintaining many troubling relationships that cause you financial stress; consider cutting down those relationships instead of having many. This is basic economics you need to understand.
- You are not willing to start thinking about your life to improve it; you may be lazy and not see the value in changing your condition. You are not willing to be positive about your life;
- You may see life as something made for your suffering while others prosper. Maybe you are holding such a perception;
- You are not willing to be part of the list of improved or successful people because you have a different picture of what making money is and never consider having it or plenty; you are carrying such a negative mindset.
- You overlook yourself;
- You may be a person who depends on performing juju, trusting in bad spirits;
- You see others who are succeeding and overlook their successes, thinking they obtained them through magic or evil practices, or you think they are more blessed than you. You accept your situation as it is and blame God for not making you rich;
- You don't pray over your life as a basis for having good dreams come forth. You act as if you are already dead because you believe success is magical and not attainable for everyone, so you don't see value in success and don't follow the examples of successful people;
- You have a negative mentality and don't accept that you can be successful or embrace those who have succeeded.

You term their successes as foolishness and attribute their achievements to evil practices, seeing them as unfair ventures;
- You are just daydreaming and never take steps to make things happen for you;
- Maybe you tried to succeed but faced obstacles and never wished to try again; you might have tried and failed and given up on life;
- Maybe you are influenced by negative factors that have broken you down, leading you to think you will never succeed.

As long as you carry such a mentality about yourself and society, it burdens you with negativity, creating poverty within you. If you can't change your mentality, you won't get anywhere with your life. You'll end up creating a life of dependency, full of complaints and setbacks. You can never be the head of a family without money to support their needs and feel comfortable about it. What is the logic in becoming the head of such a family if you can't support them?

Nothing lasts forever, so you must change your level now. If your today is bad, make way for your tomorrow to be good and splendid. Success is like travelling to a different arena. You can never be a traveller if you don't seek the money needed to prepare your travel documents. You can never be a renter if you aren't earning income to pay for your rent. And sometimes, if you don't work, age will bring a different story, forcing you to accept whatever condition unfolds. Age can force people to begin shouldering personal problems, meaning that whether you have money or not, responsibility will come. This is one of the things about age having no mercy on people. Some people who never cared to try to succeed but only rushed when they noticed age passing by them end up resorting to evil practices. Many African men delay themselves, and by the time they reach a certain age and see life has failed them, they turn to evil practices after wasting their productive years. Your problem of poverty might be due to wastefulness, which you need to address. You are made rich by God, and that is why you can do something with your hands, potentially bringing in some income. You can build on this.

I feel that those who should have seen power in themselves to succeed from the beginning but didn't accept to live in poverty and, as their poverty grows, turn to evil. They can be people who see others succeeding and view their successes as magic or evil. They might castigate successful people, saying things they shouldn't. You have life in you, and that person succeeding has the same life. He or she is not better than you. The person's head is working, and with God's help, a return is coming, changing that person's life. You can put your mind and life to work.

Don't you know that life is like a clock that can get late? If you don't do what you are supposed to do during the daytime before night comes, you may regret it. Just as your body transitions from infancy, let your mind transition to maturity and success rather than living in poverty for the rest of your life. Your hands, eyes, nose, feet, senses, and others are in proper working order, so why not utilize them? Some people may not be as you are to feel the power of God's correctness about them, but they try to improve themselves. They don't complain from morning until night.

They try to create powers within themselves. Understand this: those who see themselves as powerful work to empower themselves even more. The power of influence mostly lies in being on top of the world as an economic giant. Stop letting the world sit on top of you as if you are already dead. No. Rather, if you accept seeing the world sit on top of you, it will keep squeezing you, causing you pain, and degrading you to nothing. Invisibly, some people are naturally found beneath the earth instead of on the surface. This is why they seem like dead people who have no part to play on earth.

The thing about poverty-power is that if you were small while living, you could be as small in power as well. But as you grow older, it also grows in power and impact. It can multiply in trouble as responsibilities develop. If you never took care of yourself and you grew up starting a family by force, just know that your troubles with poverty will multiply. It is never too late to fight it now so you can bring happiness to your generation. Help yourself and help the world improve.

Be bitter about not sleeping much and being hungry, as always. Be bitter about not being able to help your precious family now because poverty is stopping you. Don't be like some people who get old in their parents' houses because of laziness. They expect their parents to support them forever and never take responsibility for learning to be independent despite their age. Be bitter about people mistreating your family, calling you all sorts of names because of poverty. Be bitter about not begging or letting that change in the days to come. Be bitter about not having money now but having money in the future, even making a successful trip abroad. Be bitter in understanding that poverty is a lion that must be killed and buried from your life and your family's. You are the determinant of your world, which you must design now. Picture a good world by creating it. Nobody will put you in power by having such a world of success until you put yourself in power.

See what I am doing against poverty: I am fighting it in the morning. I am also fighting poverty at night, thinking rather than letting myself sleep too much. I am fighting poverty even better during the day by working with my body instead of wasting time complaining or doing foolish things that yield no profit. I am fighting poverty the most during my quiet time, even when I go places, with my pen to write a new story to market, thinking it through, and taking the necessary steps to bring the story to light for marketing to begin. I am fighting poverty with my mouth frowning at it until my mind will not rest. I am fighting poverty with my eyes, picturing those who will come around me and embrace poverty but pushing them away or encouraging them to help fight it, too.

Ask me why I am fighting poverty this way. I have to do so because it had power over me when I was a little boy, and there were no parents to help me. I had to wear tattered clothes. All these things happened before God helped me have the opportunity to go to school and learn something that changed my story. As people helped me, I pushed myself, too. Your day to start your fight could be today. It is never too late to try and rid yourself of poverty now. Don't let poverty hold you back from your youth and possibly into your adult years. Stop carrying poverty into your old age.

Harness the Power of Your Mind

There is no greater power in the world than the power of working with your mind, causing it to work for your success. Create a positive power in your mind so you own the world instead of letting the world own you and treat you poorly. Stop creating negative powers of letting trouble and a lack of success occupy your mind, causing you to live as if you are nobody on earth. Stop creating poverty-power by letting your body not shine because you don't have money all the time. Stop creating confusion power when you know your mind should be occupied with positive ideas. Inaugurate your mind now for the future.

Let me tell you this: poverty can make people harbour hatred within their minds when poverty problems become too much to bear. Let your mind get well, and let it create business ventures for you. Stop creating poverty-power, as your mind should be full of happiness rather than stress. Stop creating poverty-power by complaining about survival when your mind should be fresh to always create positive influences that keep you healthy. Stop creating poverty-power by getting weak and believing you cannot succeed and have an influence in this world. Don't let it make you feel cursed when your mind should be working to create smiles on your face and in your world.

Terminate such a negative force from occupying your life. Your ruling power should also include financial power, which will bring you happiness.

God makes your mind rule, which never gets old, and lets your body rule in glory by how you treat it. You can work to empower your mind and yourself. Without empowering your mind, your body will not gain any power of importance other than the power of poverty it will promote. Your society will also not gain any power of importance if you are down.

This whole life we live is controlled by the mind. Your mind allows you to enter the invisible. And the invisible is controlled by God. The infusion of good from the invisible can lead to having a dream or idea that works for you.

Look at the motors around you. They are all controlled by their engines, which were invented by people who thought them up. They were created to make life happier. Think of your mind now to create something or provide a marketable service to change your world. Your mind is the engine of your body, connected to the head.

Because of the power of making the mind work, obtaining knowledge is essential. This book tries to give you knowledge by removing any oddities in not thinking positively about your life. It aims to give you the power to succeed.

You see, God has already given you the power to be great if only you recognize that power and start to develop it. However, you are not God to remain the same as you were yesterday, today, or forever. Stop being in the old self that makes you feel like nobody. You are not God to remain in that state. You have the power to change, too. He is a God who is good and perfect and does not need to change. He is who He is—good and perfect forever—not like you and me, who strive for our good. Therefore, you must have a sense of a changed mind, one that brings success. Never settle for keeping your old, purposeless mind.

From the day I discovered that there was a different power, very ugly, such as poverty-power, I have tried fighting against it. Don't let such a power conquer you forever. You should now be aware that you should be dressed for success. Success on. Successful people live lives of residing in palaces, and unsuccessful people live in detriment. Success won't come just like that because it has the power to enter into a new man, a man of a new mind and a new self to promote. It can't enter a person who is just accepting to be as old, of old doing, who is thinking negatively. Put on your new mind, your new self now, before you are dressed for success to have.

You can't ever put a generator on by just putting oil inside and expecting that it would just start by itself. Until you switch it on, it will not be a generator producing electricity. You have a light of God inside of you to start to electrify your whole life (Matthew 5:14). You are not made just as a light but also as a special city sitting on top of a hill. Christ says this about you and me.

So you see! You can't ever dream of becoming successful by just imagining the dream. You can't ever get married without having a relationship and planning the marriage, either. You can never be a champion by just sitting without training yourself. You can never be educated by just imagining the type of book you want to learn to become a professional person. You can't ever travel without having a passport. You can't ever have a baby without having a relationship and mating. Every dream must have a plan, and every plan must come with strategies.

Your mind is your engine that will make you do anything with your body; it should always be healthy to come up with ideas from inside it. It is the source of any action unto the body. It is the programming part of you. Therefore, try to program it with positive ideas. Try to infuse good thoughts about how you can make it. Terminate poverty before it terminates you soonest. This is what poverty can do. It makes you feel as though you are tied at the back with your hands placed there invisibly.

Don't let your body control your mind. Many people are like this, where circumstances are controlling their worlds. They can overwork themselves or their sexual habits, and others can control their beings. But let your mind control your body to think positively. Why do I say this? The reason is that some people never think of doing anything for themselves because their bodies are controlling them. Some can live in their petty state for years without changing their levels. Some can even do things before they think as if they were moving machines that must be pressed on before getting to move. How can you be a grown-up and just sit, doing nothing about your life while you are getting old? Age is not waiting for you. What age does is that it is wasting you despite waiting for a long time and not knowing what to do with your life? Age will never ask your opinion before catching up with you. It will never seek you to decide how you want it to come and treat you. It is a stubborn element that has a very big power that nobody can stop. It is packing you to the grave gradually if you don't know. As a very powerful element, when it reaches its full level, you will see yourself losing power and having nothing to do with your body because your strength will have sagged. By then, you'll be at your packing-off point, soon to be dumped away into death, which is a matter of old age. You and I will have to return to the earth as dust, meaning the same way we came from the dust. This is a reason you should work to leave a mark on the world. Do something.

You can be as old as Father Abraham, but please understand that you will still be forced to leave Earth one day, and you were never made to remain here forever. Age is a factor pushing us to our final destinies, soon to enter the graves, as being gone from the world of service. This is why you must know the importance of your soul, too, because this becomes the accountability part of your going to meet God to give a report on how you lived your life on earth after you have accomplished your mission. God made you a landlord, and you were to treat your life properly, depending on Him. You are just a manageable being of your life and the earth. But these properties of you and the earth belong to God. This is a reason you don't have the absolute power to reverse old age and time.

Start to play your part on earth appropriately rather than living without a purpose. Stop sitting and accepting to be suppressed for nothing and have nothing to offer your own life and the earth as a whole. If you overthrow poverty, success will become the new element that will cause you to stand awake. Stop making yourself a substance and instead make yourself a value or someone who is great. See the values you are made up of and prove that you are created in the image of God. Create a power to shine in the world. Trade your talents with the world. Stop sitting idly by doing nothing. You weren't made to sit supinely on earth but to work. You are meant to manage this earth instead of letting the earth manage you. You must walk your way through the earth.

What I want to know from you is, if you will be there waiting that long without improving. See this as an act of promoting shame.

Chapter 12

"If you look around you, you would see that the world is a garden of roses."

– Anonymous

Engage in Hands-On Activities

It is only your head that can direct your being in this world, not just your body. As your head directs your being, your hands will get to work as well. This does not mean you are better than those who don't have hands; this is why you make use of your hands. Your hands can have power if your mind can direct that power to them. You may be a prayerfully powerful person, depending on faith, but actions must accompany your faith. God can hear prayers, but He can better see actions of faith if you mix your prayers with actions. Faith prayer can only be powerful in directing God's attention to you until you take steps based on your faith prayer.

If you prayed for a job or business to be established, you have to act. This is why the faith-prayer must involve some tangible action. Never should you hope in a vacuum, praying for things to fall into place without effort. This is why, if you read the Bible, you will come across the story of the mustard seed (Matthew), where Christ said that anyone whose faith is as small as a mustard seed can speak to a mountain and that it will be removed. Poverty is also a mountain you must develop faith against to remove it from your way before your true self can emerge. Stop cherishing it. Notice how it can start as a hill before it becomes a mountain based on its intensity, which I know can be very dangerous. So, the start of your success could be in a small seed you plant or a small step you take. It becomes a medium of blessing for you. Start to reject poverty. When poverty troubles you, it is like diminishing God within you, including your potential for making a true impact in the world. You were placed on the surface of the earth, and poverty should not soil you down. It is dangerous and can take people down early to the grave. You are on the surface of the earth, not underneath it, so do not let poverty soil you and hide the values you are made of.

You need to ask yourself, since you left high school or college, what have you been doing to change your situation of poverty that may be consuming you? Ask yourself if childishness has been holding you back. Let your age defy poverty like Bill Gates, who started thinking about his future at age 12. Let your age defy poverty like David, who was anointed to be king at age seven. Let your age overcome frustrations, teach you to depend on yourself, and push forward rather than backward. Let your age, which for so long has labelled you as poor, change so that you can be called a rich person who helps others. Stop allowing poverty to bring you shame. It is time to schedule the end of poverty in your life through work. Do not let poverty continue to schedule itself in your life perpetually. Graduate from it now because there is a time for everything under the sun. Bring in your days of blessing and prosperity.

I know many young men and women who can sit from morning to night, complaining and taking harmful substances into their bodies. They do this to escape their worries. Some accept degrading names without caring to make changes in their lives or become successful. Instead of valuing themselves, they remain naturally dependent and carry no values. Their heads are not used to thinking of changing their lives because they feel life is too hard.

I have never seen a farmer who expects a harvest without clearing and planting. Life is not magic; you cannot expect to succeed without putting in effort. Sweat must come from hard work to achieve success. If you push yourself, blessings and opportunities will follow. They are like standing away from you until you get into the arena where they will show up.

One of the major effects of poverty in my life was the smell of sweat on my body, especially from my armpits, while I was still in high school. I couldn't afford cologne because even food was scarce. Sometimes, I had to use lime fruits under my arms to kill the odour. A lime became my means of destroying odours.

Some days, I wondered why this was happening. I realized it was because poverty was present. At that time, praying and fasting alone couldn't change my situation until I made efforts against poverty. I couldn't afford a roll-on or cologne, so I had to live with the smell of sweat, proving how much poverty was holding me back. Eventually, I became a real man who acknowledged the issue and fought against it before a change came.

You need to fight your own poverty, too. If you don't understand your past struggles, you will never find your way to progress or greatness. Whatever great future you want, you must start working for it today. Stop sitting idly. Learn to push yourself in life rather than complaining. If you push yourself to succeed, money will come to you, and you will have the power to spend and enjoy life. But stop allowing poverty to hide you in this world. Schedule poverty out of your life, and do not let it continue perpetually. The book of Ecclesiastes, Chapter 9, says there is a time for everything under the sun. So, let the time for your poverty end now and bring in your time of success. Balance your life rather than letting poverty create an imbalance.

See blessings, opportunities, wonders, and miracles as gifts from God. They come from an invisible power source, which is God Himself on His throne. You must receive your blessings too. If you were meant to be nothing, you would have been erased from the earth. But this is not the case. God activates blessings, and people must seek Him through prayers and praises. Simply believing in God is not enough; you need to act. If you sing to and for His glory, blessings will follow. They come from the mind of God to those who keep faith and work out their faith. Those who sit idly will not receive them. Not everyone in the world is a Christian, and not everyone who goes to church will be blessed. Let your worship of God be different. Make yourself different by not sitting and complaining. This is why not everyone in a church is holy, and not everyone in a church can be a pastor or teacher. Your blessings are unique to you. Until you learn to push yourself, nothing good will come to you.

Imagination and faith alone are not enough; action must accompany faith. We should not imagine God to be distant or think that one must cry blood before He hears us. You were not present when God decided to bless us in the world. If you want God to bless you, you must act in prayer for Him to act on your behalf. You cannot just sit idly without a plan to succeed. You are not an unknown soldier or statue. You must move. You were made to have power and use that power for the benefit of your life and the world. Your life needs improvement. Stop living in an ugly state of having nothing to show. Create your own world and build your own capital. Jesus said you are a city set on a hill that cannot be hidden (Matthew 5:14). Build that city by changing your level. Go for your transition and rise up.

Know that nothing good comes from sitting idly. Work is what brings a return, and companies do not pay people who have nothing to offer. Payroll is not made for those who offer nothing.

Consider the Children of Israel coming out of Egypt. They did not sit and expect the Promised Land to fall from heaven. They were not idle; they learned and took steps to make the promise come true. This shows that God believes in work. He created the world in six days, not by daydreaming.

The Children of Israel were not told that their Promised Land would fall from the sky. Physical matters require physical action. They prayed, took sacrificial steps, and suffered pain, abandoning their properties in a foreign land. They remained steadfast and determined because they wanted freedom and a good life. They established themselves on purpose when they arrived at the Promised Land by fighting wars to conquer and find peace, without giving up on God. It did not happen in Egypt; they had to take steps. It was not by imagination; they succeeded by taking tangible actions.

Even if your grandparents or parents did not fight for your success, you have the power to do so now. You can work to create financial freedom and change your family's status. Value work because it is about your life and how you should live abundantly. It is about stopping people from calling you poor and showing your worth. Money can bring friends, influence, and even prolong life with good health. Money can solve various problems and provide power. When you are poor, people complain and insult you.

You have been resting in poverty since you were born, but when will be the time for you to work and then take a good rest or even have a good vacation?

God has made all things good on earth, which He doesn't have to recreate. He completed His good work about you, your family, and the entire human race. What you need to know now is to recognize this for your life and push yourself out of the deadlock. Dead people are those who don't move, but our God can move and make things happen. And you are not dead by letting problems hold you down as if you are dead. He is not a piece of stick or wood that is dead somehow, either. He is not an immovable mountain. He moves because He is alive.

My God is not a god that is dead and static in a will or has eyes but is unable to shake, move, see, or comprehend like false gods. False gods are just false and dead to themselves. This is why He can perpetually perform miracles, meant to prove that He is a living God, telling the world of fellowship, not abandoned and that He is on His throne as a living God. This is why His Holy Spirit is still alive to help people remain alive, doing wonders, healing, and performing miracles in His name. So, people who go to Him must see themselves as living gods, work as living people, and experience goodness, but not as dead people. They must move for their blessings to show up and exercise their values from them. This is about life. Life is a living thing that moves to and fro. You can't sit with it.

I know who God is; He is alive and will remain alive forever. When I was dead in my youth days, as poverty was like a giant, nothing was working, and nobody knew the values I had to show to the world yet, He was there with me to make my life start to work out for the future that was to come in my today. When nobody could say a good thing about me because of my poverty, He remained the power to change my level. Stop keeping Him static as if He is far away from mankind. God is near you; it is a reason He says that we have overcome the devil, and greater is He that is in us than he that is in the world (speaking about His Spirit), which is meant to help Christians. Before there can be people to call victors, they must have been victimized.

Start thinking about your life now rather than taking poverty's blow against your life for nothing. Think of how God Himself, who made all things, moved before He could create those things He created, especially like. He did this by making you so you can create something, too. He was not sleeping when He made the heavens and the earth. He worked for six days. The Bible told me that He walked in the deep while the world was only watered before the waters of the earth could have dried off and later brought about land for you and me to inhabit today. He worked just to make us survive. He worked just to provide a living earth for us to exist in and do His business. He didn't make us for complaining purposes.

When ugly things confront your world, take them with a spiritual blow because nothing evil can come from God. Evil is from the devil and its agents. Apply some prayer power before the physical power can work.

Create your own six days of thinking to bring about a work period and for pay to later come from your work. If you give time to value, you will have time for a positive return. Go into your closet and design the six-day program of what you want for your life. Design the ways in which whatever you dream about will work out later for you. Create your own six days of working out whatever ideas you will come up with from thinking, and make sure you see that thing you think in a physical state to enjoy. Get to work and see if God will not get to you. Get up and get out, and see if opportunities won't come to you. Get out and see if connections will not come. Get up and get out, and see if those things that should make your life better off will not come your way. Get up and get out and see if you won't have a job doing. Life is like a machine you must turn on. If you don't put life in you, nature will take life out of you.

This is a practical life situation: you can never wish to get married without looking for the woman or man you want. You can never want to wear a tailored suit without sewing it. Imagination without action doesn't bring about growth. You must work out your imagination of being somebody great, not just by sitting and imagining it. There is no worth in this. But what brings about growth from imagination is that you must plant a seed of your imagination before the harvest stage comes, and before the later storage point of the harvest, which is based on supernatural glorification where enjoyment is made to be here, will be possible, bringing about attractions to the world upon you and who you really are to be seen and praised by others.

Get this other fact: you can never make a business of selling goods and expect to sit at home with your goods without entering the marketplace with them. You can never own a company without producing goods and expect the company to still be in business. What a company does is produce goods and take them to the marketplace. This is possible by taking the necessary steps to showcase the goods for the market, which will bring about a sale. You are made up of goods—referring to talents or potential, which ideas are staying inside of you, and you must bring them to earth to create a market that benefits your physical self. You have to trade them off. Just look around; everything around you is a product of an idea from invention. Also, you have space to make your product and sell whatever product you have to the world. Perhaps you have space to provide a service if you can learn to provide it. But you will never have space if you sit in poverty complaining. It makes people wander for nothing. No value is in this either. It is an act of pushing you aside in the world. See that also as pushing you off the earth because limitation will become your portion as complaints fill your life, making you die soon.

Many people are blaming God for their lives. You don't have to blame Him. Take your place by knowing your space on earth to succeed, just as others are doing. This is the reason you are here on the same earth where other people are staying and succeeding. He is not far from you until you can change your ways; then you will see Him in your life, giving you whatever you need as a change. Let God come into you to take control by starting a new life or being new (I Corinthians 5:17). If that happens, you will no longer be the same human being—ordinary, crying over hunger, without a purpose or will, and blind about your future, where you used to be without hope, complaining without knowing your way out. The new person you need to be now is a person of power and force to change things around. Instead, you will become a hopeful person rather than a hopeless person, carrying no faith.

You can make God sit within and work with you wherever you go. You can make God work in your hands to prove your relevance to the world. You can make God stand up and protect you wherever you go, showcasing the values inside of you. You can make God speak through your mouth by turning your impossible speech situation into a great situation, making you one of the best speakers in the world. God spoke through Moses, who thought that he couldn't make it. God spoke through His Son Jesus without Him attending any academic school or university other than visiting the priests to know what they were teaching the world and learning to correct them. So, having faith in success is not about attending a university to learn how to have it.

You can make God demonstrate His power in bringing your talents out. God is the source of every good, and He is who you need. The word that has been written in the Bible needs to be put inside your mind, deciding your case, giving you a sense of your being, teaching you self-actualization, and preparing your heart to express your way to success. So, whatever it is, you will have to make sense of valuing your life first and not giving up on life. If you follow His word, it is like you don't want to develop, or you feel as if you were never made to succeed, which means you don't want to put life in you. If you value that God is with you, it means you will be carrying Him, and He will continue to live within you by His Spirit empowering you. This will end your struggle by having the word of His power to speak against your situation and for a change in your situation. Because the word of God is God, it brings life and light inside the soul and directs the body on earth to function appropriately (St. John 1:1-4). He made us as His chosen people very peculiar by the grace of Christ. Let these words, as you read above, enter you and occupy your mind. Say to God that you will make it because you will be strong. Say that He is able to change your situation. Say to God that you will succeed without giving up. Say to God on your occasion that nothing is impossible through Him. When the word is inside of you, it means God is inside of you, and you have a sword (Ephesians 6:17) to use as your power to fight against circumstances or unseen battles and win against them. You will no longer think that He is not close to you, as if He is far away and can't hear you.

Circumstances poverty brings can make people think that God is far from mankind and that we have to struggle strongly before He would come to help us. You were not there to ask Him why He was getting to work to create, but He did it. You were not there to ask Him why He was creating the world before you were born, but He did it. So, knock on your chest and say to the world that you are carrying God inside of you, so poverty must get out of your way.

When you stand with the word, it means God is standing for and with you. This is how I see Him to be; His words, which I am learning to read, are the ones I am reading inside of me. So, I need to be able to read the words daily and at night. Put them inside you to have some health and start thinking good about your life, meaning that you are a power in the world. Concentrate on them. Meditate on the word because it has the creation and recreation ability to make you change levels. That is where your power is concentrated, which will lead to a change in your level. You are the temple of God to remove any tempering practices or conditions that can hold people down but to be removed from your way (II Corinthians 6:16).

Don't be ashamed to say that God is your power. Don't be ashamed also to say to the world that you will make it in life. Just imagine you are in your little corner of poverty, which nobody knows about now. This doesn't mean you have no value. You shall one day be in a high state of life, and the world will know about you. Don't be discouraged thinking that the world is looking at you and doesn't wish to help you. By the time your God speaks for you, others in the world might want you not to speak about God or want you to join all sorts of societies because you might have succeeded. Join me in speaking about God's goodness rather than waiting for mankind.

I want you to see the presence of God in you to suggest that the presence of trouble should go away from you. As long as you carry God inside of you, know that you are more than a conqueror, having untouchable power. Anyone who has God inside of them must be seen as unlimited, as a light carrier, full of radiance and power, and not accepting any shame because of their birth. You carry sufficiency in everything. It is the faith you should develop. You carry a spirit of excellence because you came from the holy hands of God, who put you on this earth for His purpose. It is the boast you should make of your life. You carry untouchable power to know that obstacles may come, but they won't bring you down forever. They may try to bend you, but you won't fall.

Fight to rise. When this is achieved, you will be made to eat with queens and kings (I Peter 2:6). Picture this from the spirit realm and work towards such a status. You are like a city set on a hill that cannot be hidden (St. Matthew 5:14). This means you are a beacon for the people around you. Just bring God close within you. When He is present within you, you are going to be a light, and darkness won't have room to exist anymore by confronting your world and keeping you down forever. Poverty's darkness will no longer take over your life, because it will be replaced by God's change, turning your struggle into victory. Nobody will comprehend your lifting, not believing in you. They might have thought evil of you because of the poverty they saw earlier and poured insults at you, but they will stop doing so and begin celebrating your glory.

Nothing creates darkness like poverty does. Poverty's darkness will go away if you stop being lazy. Out of poverty comes prosperity that will overflow as abundance. Gain that power now. Stop limiting yourself; take your place, claim your power, and bring your blessings close. God has an interest in you, which is why you are still living. Despite your age, God is able to make your life flourish. God was not crying before making you, which is why you are still good to see you live a life of fulfilment rather than living in pain.

My little faith confession, which I valued so much and learned to say to myself, is this: 'God made me. He is the eyes I can see with. He is the breath I have to be who I am today. He is the business I do in life. He is my travel around the world without limitation. I was born to be without financial limitations because I am precious to God. If anybody steps on me, my God will step against that person.' I confess these as a way of always giving myself hope. I walk with these simple statements or words, hoping in God and without complaining. These confessions help me keep hope alive.

So, you see! You must give yourself hope and live before things happen to you. I don't need to be as holy beyond words before I know who my God is to me. I don't need to be an apostle before I know who my God is that is blessing me. It is in your belief that things will happen for you. This is why before a prayer is made, you must first of all believe that what you will pray for has already come through before you take off to pray. If you tell the world that you are somebody great, you won't miss out on this because you have believed. Next, you must take a physical step for what you believe to come to pass for you. God is saying the same thing to you: to know that you are here on earth for a purpose, just as He made it possible for you. He is willing to push you up rather than seeing you being pushed down for nothing because of poverty or other circumstances. You belong up; there is a reason you have not fallen down into the grave yet.

Some things happened to me that I want to explain to you. My wife encouraged me to succeed in business as well. I can remember the pieces of advice my wife, Anna Sonpon, gave me, which have now manifested into great rewards. Here is how the story goes: we were renting a single-bedroom apartment while having kids. After some time, we started building our two-bedroom house. It was taking so long to try to complete our house. We were really struggling. But one day, she told me how we needed to move into our house and begin a business in the environment where the house was being built. We found it hard to complete the little house. But because she wanted us to stop paying rent, she said we should go and stay in the unfinished house. Though we had zinc on the house, by the time we were to move to our new house, as she told me, we could find a place to start a business there. Luckily for us, we moved to our new community and stayed in our incomplete house. The floor was not even cemented. After we got in, we looked for some money to start the business. At least we were not paying house rent anymore, which was something good to celebrate. We first paid for six months of the store's rent at a cost of one hundred United States Dollars per month. We started the business without having money to put goods inside the store, so we started selling in front of the store on a table first. I took the business very seriously, so when I went to work, by the time it was 4:00, I ran back to the spot to help my wife with the business. I did that every time, and even on my two-day break, I sat at the business site doing business.

We started by selling on a little table in front of the store without going inside because we did not have the money to buy many goods to sell inside. But the faith we kept was that we knew we were now doing business seated in front of a store we were renting. We were determined to do business with the hope that we would gradually make it by entering inside after some time, as long as we were serious about doing business there. We just kept our focus and determination on the business.

And truly, because of the determination and decisive steps taken, our faith continued to work. Now, I truly appreciate my wife for the decision she made to let us stay in the community where we had our incomplete house and start a business. I knew that we were working for ourselves. Well, after about three years of selling in front of the store, we finally moved inside, where we started putting more goods inside as we were making some profits from the little-by-little sales that were forthcoming. Each time I received a paycheck, we would reinvest the money into the business. We did this until we reached the full capacity of running a store without even going to a bank for credit. Our cash flow is good.

What I want you to learn from this is that our weapon of warfare was not carnal against the pouring down of poverty because we kept our focus on what we wanted to achieve, and we achieved it. It was difficult to achieve this, but persistence and trust in God were the weapons against poverty when starting our business.

Many individuals or women who were selling on the same road had negative things to say about our business. Some mocked us and said that we were foolish because they saw that we were paying store rent without entering inside at the time we were planning to fill it with goods.

There are things we did that helped us build up the cash to put goods inside the store. Just to put the goods inside our store, we had to deny ourselves many things, such as eating good food. We even continued to eat bunny fish for our soup. We stopped buying clothes for a while. In short, we cut down on costs. We did this in many areas of our lives just because we wanted to meet our target of doing business.

You must know who you are, and you must take steps to know where you want to go in life. Check your past poverty to move forward into the success you expect in the future by working it out. Just be focused and persistent with what you do. Don't mind what people say about you for the little things you do. Success doesn't require you to do big things before you achieve it. Just the little things you do or the little steps you take will build up to becoming part of achieving the success you expect to have in the future.

Our house wasn't completed and furnished either when we moved in. The floors in the rooms were bare. Yet, we started the business without giving in to frustrations. The seed of faith was planted as far as we were concerned as we took the steps to work for ourselves.

There is nothing too hard that you can't achieve in this world. Just look up to God and work hard and skillfully. Develop the faith you need for any battle of life to win against it. At the time, our faith started working out while we were looking up to God for a change in our level. Today, the store has reached its full capacity of being a fully operational store. And what this business has done is that my family life has changed. The financial stress of working for nothing and without realizing I was working because of the national economy is gone. I now see the salary as an added advantage that I make while adding more value to my family while my wife runs the business. I don't cry about my salary any longer, and it will come for a month. Anytime salary came, that was it. The reason is that I am removed from the desperate state of relying so much on salary, and I am at my power stage, making money to support my family. I knew my family was going to stop living in a manageable state. My family is now at the full potential level of managing what we keep making and hoping to go to a greater level. Imagine, for twenty years and more, I couldn't save a dime from my salary until recently, when my wife and I started to save because of the improvement in the business.

When insufficiency is strong, no savings will come. And salary will always be insufficient. This is why you need to open your eyes and be productive. Find someone you can trust to do business with. If the salary you make is little, you will not save because your expenses may be high, and the paycheck alone can't solve your many problems.

I got to understand from a business perspective that life is a sacrifice. This is why nothing big will happen in the life of a person who will not make a sacrifice. Just keep focused on the little things when you start up your own business. You must do this because nothing good comes so easily.

Life is a step forward, and you must have faith to always pray to God. If you believe in God and yourself, work out your faith. I came to understand that no amount of prayer without faith being worked out will yield results so easily for physical manifestation. Spiritually, you could pray for things, and they might manifest, leading you to have a thought or dream to achieve. But you have to plan from the dream your prayer might have developed. By taking such a step forward, it is as if you are bringing from your spiritual side into your physical side the manifestation of your gift from God, which is the dream. For this reason, you must join your prayer with faith, and join your faith with work or action, and join your action with determination and sincerity. The result of keeping those things will be a positive outcome. You can put that to work now.

Nothing is too hard that you can't achieve. You were made in the image of God, so you carry a creative power. Just take some steps and see what will happen next.

Let's be practical about keeping faith. I want you and I to perform a test of faith wherever you are right now. It goes like this: let's see if two people—meaning you and someone else— are in a church praying at the same time. One person will pray, while after prayer, another will take steps to achieve whatever both of you prayed for. One thing I know is that the person who prays and sits without doing anything or exercising faith will make the word not work. But the one who prays and takes steps by working out the thing prayed for will have a result better than the one who just prays without taking any physical steps over what was prayed for.

This is why when you think you want a good future, which might be perceived, you have to take steps for that future.

Father Abraham exercised his faith when he decided to sacrifice his only son. He further exercised his faith when he left his father's house by listening to

The order of God. Faith is like a seed planted, and action is the nurturing part of faith. This is why you must understand that between the two people, the one who goes out after praying to exercise faith will have a better result and live longer than the one who prayed and sat without further action.

Only the steps taken will prove the result of faith. It is like you were to plant a seed and didn't water it to grow. Your action is like watering your faith. If you believe that you will build a house, you must take steps to make that house be built. You must look for money. You must contract workers. You must buy materials. I mean, there are many things you will have to do just to build the house. It is what I call the success lifecycle you must follow if you want a good future.

This is what many people whom I see leading the church do to their members on the issue of faith. You can only activate faith by praying, but you can make faith work through action. Many of these modern church leaders create a feeling in their members that God will provide without allowing the members to exercise their faith. It is detrimental. God Himself worked for six days before He created all things in heaven and earth, meaning we must work before we get what we want out of life. It is the little things you do that God will continue to bless and build up, eventually leading to greater things and expected success. Stop praying and fasting as if it is a magical exercise that will bring success. It is not that praying and fasting are wrong; they are only meant to water the spiritual grounds for your lifting until you take a physical step towards achieving what you expect. Learn from the story of the people of Israel. Before the people of Israel could reach their Promised Land, they were first in captivity, a place of their lowly selves. They still gained the power of being polished for a change of level before they were able to embark on the journey to the Promised Land. Your Promised Land is distant, and until you take steps to travel there, you will remain with just a big dream and no achievement. Having a dream means God is sending a good thing from your Promised Land spiritually. Everyone of us who has faith in God has individual Promised Lands because we are seeds of Abraham. God told him that He was going to make him the father of many nations. It is the faith you must have, believing that you are part of Abraham's family. Because he worked out his faith, such faith will also work for you. There are many Promised Lands around us, but many don't see them yet. Christ placed us at a level where Promised Lands are available. This is why we are told that we are the lights of the world and a city set on a hill that cannot be hidden (Matthew 5:14). God is not far from you entering your Promised Land. Faith has already taken you there.

Just have faith now. Copy this: the Israelites moved before seeing the place of promise or blessings, which meant they didn't sit idly, hoping for the promise, but sought a way to achieve it. For example, if you promised a woman that you would marry her, though the confession is made, you must work out the steps that will lead to the woman becoming your wife. Pursuing the woman is an act of working out your faith in getting her, as you earlier believed and pronounced her as your future wife. If you say you want to be educated and have a job, you have to work it out. Believing you will have the education is one thing while taking steps towards achieving it is another. Obtaining an education and securing a job is yet another process. So, you see! To believe that you will marry that woman in the future is just faith until you take steps to meet the requirements. If you say you will travel outside your country, it is one thing, and when you take steps to find the money and obtain the documents needed, it is another thing, too. Believing, talking about it, and taking steps are different actions you must take to have a successful future. Watch out also for the little things you do. They could become the grounds for your Promised Land to begin. See your current position as the start of your greater self to come if you can start moving now. The challenges you may face on the way to your Promised Land, such as insults and pains, are experiences to endure while keeping your focus on the direction of your success. Keep pushing through. You will definitely reach the top of your dreams. Today, my wife and I don't worry about money despite having reached the stage of being physically rich. We believe that we are spiritually rich and are still working on the physical aspect. We don't stress ourselves about what we will eat or wear. Financial stability, with God's help, is our portion now, and we are experiencing it. We don't worry when it's time to pay school fees for our children. By the grace of God, we are going up and up. You must gain power before you can give someone else economic power. Fight to achieve your financial power. Until you decide what is good for your life, nobody will decide what is good for you. Take your life into your own hands instead of letting conditions control you. Don't let the world create power against you. If you take your life into your own hands, no one will diminish your worth by creating power against you. This is what I noticed about poverty. If poverty is present, it can make you feel like you are without life. It can make you feel dejected over life. But let me say this on the opposite side: if you have money, you feel like you are on top of the world. You feel very joyous in life. You don't worry about tomorrow's economy anymore. You don't worry about school fees for your children because you will have the money to spend.

Understanding the Cycle of Success Causation Success starts with a small seed that grows gradually into something great. Conversely, poverty also begins as a small seed or low state before multiplying into significant poverty that affects the whole. Success can first start with an individual's mindset. When the mind contemplates something to do, plans are expected to follow to achieve it. Also, when you are successful in your mind by thinking positively about something to achieve, caused by the way you see life and think about it, you will see a need to wake up and push. It is this push that will eventually expand into success in the future. A high level of success can lead to impacting others. I want you to see how the stages of success connect and grow. For example, if a few people succeed due to your help, it will affect your society because those people are expected to also help others. This is why success needs to be multiplied. If your society is successful, it means many others contributed to that success. In short, individual successes can lead to broader success, potentially becoming national success. Success creates a flow. Expansions of individual success, along with government power, can result in national success. When this happens, people will leave inheritances for their children, destroying the cycle of poverty and making society great. You were made to be who you are but not made to stay as you are. See the society you want to change within yourself. People, when developed, will also lead to infrastructure development. If a nation decides to focus solely on infrastructure development without developing its people, it is likely that the people, if not developed, may become angry and destroy those infrastructures. I saw this happening during the fourteen years of civil war in my country, Liberia. People destroyed buildings belonging to businesses and government officials they couldn't kill. Infrastructures such as dams and important companies across the country were destroyed. Illiteracy coupled with poverty is a disease. This is why development is often seen as focusing on the people. Development studies look at development from the standpoint of developing people first, which will later lead to infrastructure development or both working in tandem. Without the people, no companies or institutions will function effectively. People should be developed first, and such development would be spread out. My country was one of the highest exporters of iron ore and rubber latex from the 1960s to the 1980s. Its Gross Domestic Product (GDP) and Gross National Product (GNP) were comparable to Japan's. However, Liberia suffered from inadequate education due to a suppressive leadership system at the time. Consequently, leadership succession did not prioritize education, and foreign nationals with their education occupied lucrative positions. Their economic growth benefited them more than the people who needed education to occupy managerial and other key posts. Thus, the nation experienced growth without true development despite a healthy GDP. This is why it is crucial to improve your mind as a priority to fully participate in the body politic and economic life of a country. Learn something because your development should be based on what will come to light, allowing you to flourish physically. Your mind holds untapped riches until you bring them to light. You must instil the power to make your mind work effectively before it functions properly. Think of this.

This world will be a world full of hunger and disasters, which nobody can reverse by going to God to ask why things have to be this way. Poverty now exists in the world, and you can't change it, but you can pray against yours and work by removing the same from your way. Just know this: God put you in power to fight for your good. In fact, where were you in history when Satan the evil entered the world and created hunger and confusion by toppling mankind from power? This problem exists, and no man can change the situation except God, to whom we must look up. We have been told, and some of us have studied about this and know, that this world is not as God originally made it anymore because a fallen creature is occupying it, whose agents are operating through systems controlled by the same mankind affected spiritually by them. Satan is described as a thief in the world in the Bible (St. John 10:10). And he is still a thief and killer. God will punish him. But as he exists now, you can't kill him by your prayers. You can only control his powers from affecting you now through prayers.

These powers of evil agents are taking hold of mankind, starting from the mind. Understand this: nobody should tell you that God created this world just because He wanted to promote evil upon it. No. Our Almighty God is never a being that is evil. He is the source of good things. And He wants good for your life, which is the reason you are still here on earth. You didn't come just to eat and drink and die later on without fulfilling your purpose. You must also have an impact on the society you live in.

Here is the reason why I am opting for your success. Before you can go further, I want you to ask yourself this: where were you when the whole world became dark from the early creation before God spoke that there should be light, and there was light? Where were you before there was electricity until studies brought about this improvement in the world? Where were you before movable objects like ships and the first flying plane called a torpedo started to operate as inventions of mankind? Where were you when barter trade was a subject that kept the real market structure down or made the economy inefficient, but this was later changed? Where were you when nobody knew about technology until humans studied it, leading to the creation of technology? Where were you when there was no such thing as an industrial revolution? These came about because of ideas. They are human intuitions that brought about some liberations for humans to live better. These are the powers of the mind. Create your liberation now by making proper use of your mind! And your liberation for success is not a subject of a struggle that must start by sleeping or sitting idly with foolishness, doing nothing for your life and complaining throughout. Any change you need starts with your mind first before the real struggle in the body becomes possible. Cause an extinction of poverty now! Exert some effort to change the level. And for the exertion for your success liberation to be possible, you should work it out. You can't have liberation without a struggle for it. Even the children of Israel fought for their liberation from Egypt by going to their promised land. They worked for this liberation. They fought wars upon wars before whatever promise perceived spiritually came to fruition. Even the nations of the past fought for their liberation before gaining independence. When will your liberation from poverty come? Have you started to fight for this since you were born? Are you making any difference in the society you live in?

I can see excellence made possible with your creation. Feel confident to know this: you are still breathing and moving about, meaning you must create a life with the success possible. You are placed in your redemptive arena by God with mankind, which you must acknowledge before the difference will show up.

Good minds bring about good inventions. Good minds create good societies. Good minds build good infrastructure by making their dwellings comfortable. This is what a person of good mind must be willing to grow from poverty to reach even the highest level. He or she doesn't have to be sitting idle. See the good within and bring that good out to the world. Make sure to do something about bringing that good within you out to the world instead of sitting with the good within. You are made for display, not to be distressed and live distressfully.

What may demand you for success is about defining your true self and nature. You must demand a change by stepping out and defining whatever success should make way for you by seeking the path. You can wake up and work to prove to the world that you are a living person, especially if you create power within you to start doing greater things than sitting and complaining about life. No matter what you do with your life on earth, you must know that this life isn't supposed to be taken lightly or treated anyhow. What has been wrong with life? You can learn a lesson from the past and never allow yourself to be the same forever. Because you can make a change is the reason you were born to grow and never to remain the same. To better show that you have power will prove how important you see yourself in the world.

Understanding the phases or stages of tomorrow:

• Tomorrow is a day or years ahead to wait for. It's a living thing everybody wishes to acquire for a good life. I see it as a living thing because nobody approaches it without strength or making any preparations.

• If you don't take tomorrow as a living thing to fight for, you may be fought against by that tomorrow if you are not prepared for it.

Stages or phases of tomorrow: Every success has a base or initial stage. It is the concept of a better tomorrow everyone wishes to have. Look at tomorrow as a standing entity spiritually. It is up to you to picture and design whatever tomorrow you may be looking at. Do you want a good tomorrow or not? If you want such a good tomorrow, you must go through a process that begins with a dream or idea.

1. A dream phase or stage of tomorrow—is the part of tomorrow related to having a dream or thinking of something to do. This stage serves as the source of motivation and strength that must be stirred up; it is a

dream phase of this kind that can make our people help us learn something for our lives. A process of letting a child go to learn something or attend school is about a part of success at a dream stage perceived that would lead to this.

2. A foundational phase or stage of tomorrow—is the planting of a seed from a dream held. It is a planning stage where setting up goals and strategies must be developed and built upon.

3. An in-process or step-taking phase or stage of tomorrow—is the stage of tomorrow based on taking steps to reach the top of whatever good tomorrow you seek.

4. The harvest phase or stage of tomorrow—is the part of tomorrow where you have achieved your dream after making some efforts through the steps and strategies you took.

5. The satisfaction or enjoyment phase or stage of tomorrow—is the part of tomorrow where you see your dream before your eyes or with it being achieved, requiring you to now rest and feel the power of your dream by the result or benefit made possible, which satisfies your life because you have achieved the dream of a good tomorrow. It is no longer an expectation but a tangible element to be touched physically.

6. Impact phase or stage of tomorrow—is a stage or part of tomorrow that says, after achieving your dream, you should focus on having an impact with your achievement.

Remember, every tomorrow has a stage, you don't just jump into a tomorrow expecting it to be glorious. You have to follow the stages if you envision a change of level and for such to be incubated.

God created a good tomorrow for each of us, He gives each person the ability to think or have a dream. The dream or thinking of something to develop upon is the basis for action. He allows us to pass through stages. This is where you must know that, for you to be successful and hope for a better tomorrow, it is a process, and God needs this for you. Tomorrow exists because life is a process. But many people don't want to observe and pass through the stages of life. Some are aware of this, while others just sit there blaming people for their lives without pushing themselves.

Chapter 13

"The world is made for everyone, but it is only opened to thinking to becoming or successful people."

– Frederick W. Sonpon

Discipline Yourself to Build Good Character and Wealth

Big nations or small nations, their people and systems are promoting corruption in various forms around the world, which is also causing more poverty. And the thing about corruption is that it depends on its scale, with the amount of money stolen reflecting its nature. It could be terrible or not. In big nations, they carry out big corruptions, while small nations carry out small corruptions.

In Africa, lobbying openly through legislators is considered corruption, while in the USA, the same action isn't considered corruption. So, corruption has forms and strategies that can make it either a civilized element or not.

Well, no matter what you do, know that those who build wealth aren't ordinary people because they don't do ordinary things for their greatness. Just don't corrupt and kill people for wealth creation. I will always say that the first wealth for you to build is to start with building a good character. The reason being, there were people who were successful and had money, but later on, their wealth was diminished to shame because of the way they acquired their wealth. Like the case of those who promoted drugs before achieving success and ended up killing people because they wanted money.

But let's read about a guy from the USA and his story. I read the story about Enron in the USA. It was a company headed by Manager Fastow. Despite managing a company that became very competitive in the business world, his actions were meant for evil. The figures he presented were derived from fake financial profitability statements. He robbed the company and destroyed the trust of investors. He fooled investors by making himself rich at the detriment of those investors by producing fake financial statements. He deceived the business world by creating false profitability data that was presented and placed on the stock exchange by the Security Exchange Commission (SEC) of the USA. His actions were meant to deceive investors and the business world by falsifying the financial records of his company. In the end, this made investors consider withdrawing their investments. Enron, as a company, went bankrupt.

The story went like this: he presented a false picture of profitability. He made the company's shares be captured on the US Stock Exchange for a good number of years, presenting it as a good business, while inside, he was stealing from the company, and the company didn't know he was stealing until it was discovered after an audit by Arthur Andersen, an audit firm that proved this.

He reported creating false financial data, which was presented on the US stock exchange. His numbers were deceiving. And this action benefited Fastow the most. Fastow became rich from stealing, while investors were deceived. But with all the money Fastow had, he was sent to jail.

Since then, he can't help himself out of jail. His character has gone down the drain, and his money can't save him from this.

When character is lost, you lose everything valuable about life. It is like salt to food. This world is experiencing difficulties because of one of the major factors—corruption. Corruption is causing this. This is what poverty is also trying to do by making you broke and stealing your joy.

This is why you must know that character is the best riches to have and offer to the world for your return. So, it is better to build a good name while getting rich than to build a bad name or be involved in criminality before acquiring wealth.

Father Abraham, Job, and others in Biblical history got rich not through evil practices. Abraham reared animals. He and even Solomon worked earnestly to earn their riches.

You are who you are, but not made to be as you are without a purpose either. Therefore, the first step to walking into the field of success with certainty is to work on your character. It is necessary for you to build up your character to reach places that others won't if you practice good character. Do so because your character is your first business to have. You must cultivate a good character because success is about building a different world with different principles. From this perspective, those who want to or have success must live up to the standard of that success as if they are in a new world.

Because of success, if you used to eat unhealthy food, you will no longer eat those kinds of food because of the new world of success you have entered by following its standards. If you used to sleep in a dirty place or on the street due to poverty, you will no longer make it there. It is about a change. This means that when your position changes, your level must change.

Know that defamed and corrupted minds will only sit on the fence of the good world, far from reaching its goodness. Lazy people will be spectators on the economic field of life, like those who play football where some players are made to sit on the bench while others watch the game. Don't let this be your portion; learn to work for your life. If you never knew anything but learned, or if you were uneducated but became a business-minded person, this is not bad. You must know that there are things you will have done, and keep following the pattern to reach your great level. You must have a different mindset, different personalities, and some principles. It comes with different ways as well.

Every business person follows the discipline of doing business, which are things you must also learn to tailor to yourself before you can really make business and be successful with it.

I want you to own your world, which is possible if you can create your own business. To be truly successful in business is not an ordinary act. The rule starts with you first learning discipline, character, understanding how to manage money, or having financial discipline. If you are someone who loves to spend every penny you make without saving some to invest in the future, it becomes almost impossible to see you develop and maintain such development. There are people who can be successful but, due to lack of financial discipline, can end up out of business or jobs and become very broke. You will need to change this attitude before you can climb the ladder of success.

Discipline yourself now! After disciplining your mouth, your ability to use money, work on other parts of your character. Work on your thoughts and your friendship level. Have this self-discipline in you first. If you learn to control money instead of money controlling you, you will definitely do well in the world.

This world is abnormal until you make yourself better. In short, the world is not getting better until you make yourself better.

Know that success requires a different character from you and steps to take with it. It has a different atmosphere in which you need to create and be. You won't be ordinary without learning to increase wealth.

This is why you must put yourself in the arena by starting to build your character. The only character will carry you to the full level of possible success. Put yourself in a mental school, not as ordinary as you used to live your life, but based on a new self that pictures a big world ahead of you.

Here are some steps you must learn to exhibit before building a bigger picture of life that will get you up the ladder of success. This is about working on your character. For example:

- Value your life as your top priority.
- Learn to trust yourself and inspire others to trust you.
- Establish principles to guide your life.

- Build trust with others by managing responsibilities with integrity.
- Assess your current situation and think critically about how to improve it, especially to escape the cycle of poverty.
- Envision your personal growth by imagining a "city" in your mind, and focus on the concrete steps necessary to turn that vision into reality, staying persistent and focused.
- If you haven't started planning your life or developing a dream, begin now. Engage in meaningful work with your hands, treating it as a purposeful endeavor, not just a routine task. Avoid distractions from those who don't value growth or ambition. Don't settle like people who remain stagnant and refuse to think about improvement. Instead, learn to plan, think critically, and set schedules that foster change.
- If you are educated, carry a notebook and pen during quiet moments or when inspiration strikes, so you can capture your ideas and dreams.
- Develop and act on the ideas you generate, especially those that involve practical work. These ideas could be your key to personal development and overcoming poverty.
- Gain control over your financial life by mastering how you handle money, starting with saving, instead of letting money control you.
- Be passionate about your ideas and dreams, recognizing that they are the seeds of future success. Don't just sit on your dreams; bring them to light as gifts from God to develop and share.
- Persevere through hardships, maintaining focus on your goals. Don't give up when challenges arise. Keep moving forward as long as you've taken steps or are contemplating action.

- Don't rely on others to help you succeed. Find strength within yourself and push yourself forward.
- Understand that pursuing your dreams and ideas will involve challenges, but these difficulties will eventually pass. Stay tough and focused on your path, knowing that the process will shape your future.
- Be selective with your relationships. Surround yourself with people who share your ambition and desire for success, not those who waste time on unproductive activities. Avoid friendships with people who think negatively and resist self-improvement.
- Create a savings plan and invest consistently. Develop a performance strategy to track your business growth, so you can continually improve. Focus on refining strategies and ideas as you move forward, and implement a system to assess your progress over time as you pursue your dreams.

You must feel a sense of urgency about your life today and look toward your future with sharp focus and hope that it will be bright, without letting anything stop you from pursuing this goal. To truly succeed on the journey of life, you need to be someone who can see—not just with your physical eyes, but with insight and understanding. Stop closing the "eyes of your mind," as doing so is like closing the door to your dreams.

Let me explain how I feel about poverty, which I despise deeply. Because I hate poverty so much, I've become a rebel against it. I began fighting poverty by first reflecting on my life— where I was, where I am, and what I need to do each day to add value. Every day, I picture poverty as something dangerous, and I've made it my life's enemy, continually fighting to push it away.

Ask me why I see poverty as evil. One of the reasons I feel empowered to fight poverty is because I believe that God Almighty, who created me, is not poor, and He placed me in a rich world. This suggests that I am not meant to be poor.

There are other reasons why I fight against poverty. When I was younger, I often reflected on the difficult economic conditions of my past and regretted the struggles that came with poverty. From the moment I recognized how dangerous poverty is, I made a promise to myself, by God's grace, that I would continue fighting it. I will not rest until I find my way out of it. This is the mindset I have developed in my battle against poverty. Develop the same mindset. Don't let poverty strip away your true self. Don't let it leave a mark on your life. Don't let it make you believe that nothing good will ever happen for you.

I've learned from my past and I work on my present while focusing on my future because I want to be a great person. My past has become a history that drives me to change my condition of poverty. This is what it means to learn from one's past. Don't allow the history of poverty to repeat itself in your life. If your parents or guardians experienced it, don't let it persist against you.

Here are some reasons why I continue to fight against poverty:

- My father didn't care about me or offer any support, leading me to feel hated from the start.
- People insulted me, calling me a poor boy from a bad background.
- Some friends mocked me, saying I was a fool because I didn't know how to improve my situation.
- I wore tattered clothes and often walked barefoot.
- I watched my grandparents work on small farms that couldn't sustain our family, leaving us constantly struggling to survive throughout the year. Our farm produce never lasted long, and subsistence farming was difficult.
- I attended substandard elementary schools and never had the opportunity to go to a private high school or college.
- My parents never owned a home of their own.

- My grandparents didn't have a solid house either. Instead, we lived in a mud structure when I was in Niffu Town.

Are these not sufficient for me to frown against poverty and fight it? These were some of the reasons why I became a rebel against poverty. I didn't mind the condition of my life by giving in to frustration. I didn't keep myself as dead without doing anything that would have brought about a good future today. I knew I needed to fight and had hope that one day, God would get me out of the trouble of poverty. I didn't fold my hands. I didn't even give up on my life. So, I became a Rambo against poverty or, in making war against it, starting with my mind gaining some power through my senses, working first before my body got to work. Definitely, I would have died in poverty, looking at how my upbringing was, but God didn't make me die, for which I am still making it. Because I didn't die, I knew that I was born to be a winner. I became bitter about fighting poverty and unabated about this.

I learned from my deadly past or story that when a person is poor, nobody knows him or her easily or respects him or her either. Nobody will want to figure out what the future of that person is going to be like by helping you when confronted with this ugly poverty. Make a push now! You were made to be the person you are, but not made to be the way you are.

Get to know this: nobody will see the good in you without you bringing the good out or harnessing it. The only thing I know is that people will see your being nobody as a reason to start raining insults against you. Because of these insults being rained against you, sometimes you might try to give up on life.

Some people who may not value you will want to insult you by voicing their insults against you. They will want to do that so you can feel hurt. You must figure this out. Fight to obtain your good out of poverty instead of witnessing your troubled state by sitting and doing nothing for a change of level. Don't accept what people say about your life and live like nobody.

Poverty can eat people up like cancer inside the body. Fight it. Stop wasting your time and your life, and continue to put up with a fight.

To succeed in this world, you should first of all be able to wear the garment of a warrior against poverty with a focus on God and put up with determination. Stop wasting your time on things that have no value in your life. Take a weapon of seriousness against poverty. See it as an enemy you must fight and not part of God's making for your life. Start your fight during the day, at night-time, during evening hours, during your vacation at any place, and keep planning new things against it. Your second weapon is to be strong instead of being lazy. Have a thought for your life that you have to live well. Have a thought for your life that nobody will do it for you until you do it for yourself. Have a thought that in a few years to come; you must not be the same and in the same place. Change your position of poverty eating you up.

Some people's poverty can make them stay with the same jobs over and over without getting anything out of the jobs. Some people's poverty is such that they stay in relationships where their partners are not serious about life. Some people's poverty condition can be that they are wasteful. The description of poverty can be many.

How does your own look like? Have a good thought for your life that society needs you most or more than you may be in need of society, for which you must make a contribution to it. Stop taking from society what you have not given to society yet. Let your society receive from you instead. In this case, be a giver to succeed rather than being a receiver who would live as a dependent.

If you want to see a good country you are in, work to pay some taxes to your state. But if you don't develop, it means you are saying that your country must not have taxes paid to it and must not develop either. Create a buying situation by having a job and paying some taxes as well. Also, do business to pay some taxes. You can even render a service to society. This is about being impactful. This is the reason you must get to the level of financial power.

Your third weapon to fight poverty is having faith in yourself. See it as your biggest weapon for the fight. Have faith that nobody will change your life for you until you wake up and keep pushing yourself to succeed. Have faith in yourself to do something about your life without giving up. It is the biggest weapon in your arsenal to use and fight.

Your fourth weapon is to understand that pain will come through your fight but not to give up in the face of pain. Understand that for any good thing to happen, there will be pains involved. Be like a trainer who wants to win a championship and must endure pain while training. That trainer goes through tough times before reaping the reward of winning. Do not act like someone is weakening their resolve if you wish to become a winner or a champion. You should not approach your training for a race you want to win with a small child's mindset.

Your fifth weapon is to view money as a servant that should serve you in the future. By doing this, you will create money without complaining about life. First, if you are doing nothing, move to the stage of working for money. Once you have passed the making money stage, the next step is to move to the stage of creating money. This is when you will realize that business matters or that working for yourself is beneficial. You can never retire yourself. But if you work with institutions or other people, you will eventually be retired, regardless of how smart you are.

Picture money as an invisible power that requires steps to be taken, from thinking it out to making it happen. To start valuing money, you must have it to count it regularly. When you learn to count money, you will develop a sense of its value. Having a spirit of valuing money doesn't mean you should serve money; it means you should value it and learn to share it. If you want to develop a spirit of money, be able to count money for someone else and see if you can own money. Let someone leave some money with you and start counting it. Ask yourself how you would feel if that money were yours to use. Ask how you can increase money to invest with. While counting, think about how people should work for you and how you should be able to spend money travelling around the world.

Those who value themselves understand the importance of having money. For me, the smell of a bundle of hundreds or fifty U.S. dollars, especially when it comes straight from the bank or an ATM machine, can be quite pleasant. It motivates me to hold more to meet my needs and wants. I want money because I want to be a good buyer. Holding and spending money makes me feel important. Having money to spend can make me feel like I shouldn't be broke and should always have money to spend. When I am broke or lacking money, I don't accept temporary poverty easily. However, I don't cry for money because I made money seeking me rather than focusing excessively on looking for it. I know how to bring money to me.

For example, I create money by writing books that are sold worldwide. It's a way of saying money is looking for me because people around the world, on Amazon, buy my books and help me earn or create money by the grace of God.

In life, our talents are the things God can bless us through. If you work to bring out your talents, you will have money. If we sit idle, life remains stagnant. Life is a dynamic force that requires us to move with it, creating impacts that the world will recognize. Life produces results if you move with it. It is wise to say that you cannot play the game of life without being prepared. Life makes us prepare to play, but if you don't take positive actions, you won't feel that you are actively participating in life.

Spectators are around the field, but you were never meant to be just a spectator. You are on the field of life on earth, not around it. You cannot be on earth and not be ready to play, and you should not sit complaining or waiting for others to help you before you succeed.

Your fifth weapon is to envision victory and the crown of glory in your mind. By picturing a glorious future, you no longer believe in defeat. Despite the troubles that may confront you, you remain strong.

Life should be viewed as a winner living it. You belong to the class of living beings, not non-living things, and you should not sit idly like a non-living thing that can be controlled.

Before we were born, each of us was awarded a good life. We didn't create ourselves, but what we do with our lives reveals it. Goodness in life is hidden from those who don't know how to picture it in the spirit realm and who need to think or dream to bring it into reality. You may have talents, but if you don't know how to bring them to light, you could be sitting on untapped potential.

If you want a great reward based on how you seek to improve yourself, it will be offered to you. Life gives back what you put into it. As stated in Galatians 6:7, "Whatever you sow is what you will reap."

Picture the crown of glory ahead of you, visualize its size, beautify it, and create the power to bring it into the physical realm. Once you achieve this, maintain it if you develop the understanding that your future will be bright, work to reach that level. Lifting yourself will lead to glorification. If you are not willing to fight poverty, be prepared to suffer its effects. You must have a strong desire to overcome it and work tirelessly towards your dreams. Understand that you will need to enter a different world of success, one that is not ordinary and belongs to a few who can access and utilize life's storeroom. You must control the storeroom of enjoying life as a warrior with power.

Chapter 14

"Discipline yourself first and you will have success directed to you."
– Frederick W. Sonpon

Value What You Achieve Today

Your situation today may seem small or degrading based on the things you do or earn. You don't have to remain in a state of having little without planning for bigger things. Value the small beginnings as the start of the bigger ladder you are about to climb. Don't abuse your modest situation. Understand that rain starts with a single drop. Your small beginnings are like your days in elementary or high school before progressing to college and eventually landing a job. Make use of the little income you earn as your starting point for reaching the higher levels you aspire to.

Valuing your current small earnings doesn't mean you should become complacent or compare yourself to others, which can lead to jealousy. Manage your small income, learn to save, and invest a portion of it. Success is not just about how much you earn but about working for yourself rather than for others. Control your life because it is a gift from God for you to manage. Life is about how well you utilize the little you have, and learning to save and invest wisely will lead to true financial prosperity. Avoid spending all you make without a savings plan, and don't just save money in a bank without investing in productive ventures to grow your wealth.

I learned this lesson: life is not about making a lot of money before you start saving. I managed to buy a piece of land to build my house with a modest income after saving for it. I saved and invested in my book projects with a small income. I travelled to see other places and gain new ideas for my personal happiness and growth while earning a modest income. I also encouraged my wife to invest, and we ran a store selling foodstuffs and other items.

The problem for many people is a lack of financial discipline. I used to eat all I earned without a savings and investment plan until I changed my mindset and environment. Now, I see a bigger picture of life by working towards my goals. I don't value sleep so highly or complain about life.

In Africa, having support or an income can be challenging due to poor economic conditions and ineffective governments. The demands on families in Africa can be high, placing pressure on our modest incomes. However, you must strive to help yourself, as no one will lift your burdens of poverty for you. Empower yourself financially and create your own economic opportunities instead of relying on others. Strive to improve your situation so you can better help those who are less fortunate. Focus on your financial development, and once you reach financial empowerment, you will be able to empower others more effectively.

Learn from those who have succeeded in life. Reading books can help. To improve yourself, consider attending seminars and workshops and read motivational, biographical, and autobiographical books about successful people. Reading about great individuals can inspire creativity and problem-solving.

Value reading because it can enhance your life by learning from others' experiences. Reading opens up the world for you to learn about people and places.

If you are still struggling, remember that others have faced and overcome even greater challenges. Reading about their experiences can motivate you to persevere rather than give up. No one is better than you; you can shape your world based on how you approach it. I am a living witness to this. See your world as being in your hands and treat it accordingly.

I buy books every time to keep reading. Also, since my wife discovered herself and we made a plan together to create money for ourselves, we are working together selling in our store. This is helping me while I am still working, so I don't worry about when I will be paid at my workplace. When pay comes, I see it as an added advantage these days. It's not that I don't want the pay, but I see that I am climbing the ladder of success bit by bit. This is why I don't want you to remain dependent on a paycheck forever. Let the time of your paycheck be the foundation for a higher level where you create money from the money you save to establish your own business. Your economic strength should not be seen and proven by relying on a paycheck as the only way out. Have a big mindset towards the future to grow money. I have a bigger mind to learn to work for myself, doing business rather than working for people or institutions.

This was the mindset to grow money that my wife and I are working hard and harder to create, laying the foundation for making money. As I am working for the government, we are using the income to set up the foundation for a better tomorrow. It is fundamental to have a source of income.

Now we can determine how much to spend daily without worrying about money because it is serving us now. Our pockets never run dry of money. It may be a little, but we always have money available to solve problems or spend meaningfully through the grace of God. That's determination. Success brings about happiness, especially when you have money to deal with your economic problems. Investment can better help you reach the top. This is the power I want you to create for your life. I don't want you to keep living a life of limitation, which would cause you to be begging all the time. Don't be as foolish as those who see making money and being rich as bad because they have surrendered to the concept that having money is bad and brings trouble to life. If, as they think, having money brings trouble, why do poor and average people fight to work? You need to ask yourself this big question. If you look at various crime rates in the world, you will notice that most of these are committed because of people wanting money, and mostly, poverty-stricken places are confronted with or promote these kinds of things. Poverty can be the cause of many of these increasing crime rates in the world. Create spending power for your life now. Build a financial cradle. That determination to achieve financial success will help you travel to places with money and without worrying about how to have and spend money. Make your life one of the best within your region. This is why you must have economic power. Economic power is what you really need to get to places you haven't been to. Economic power is what you need to change situations around. Economic power is what you need to help others. So, make sure to have it. Stop thinking negatively that money is not good if someone works to have it, even in large amounts. Thinking this way is limiting your life. Look for money by achieving success, but make your success in God. Work earnestly and skillfully to create your wealth. He is the God of prosperity, and when you focus on Him, you will make a difference. Those of us who follow Him with our lives are never let down in shame. Glory upon glory becomes our portion. But if you build up your mind without reference to God and feel that you can make it on your own, you will continue to experience frustrations and economic difficulties or twists that will always confront you. This is why wealth without God is like chasing after the wind. Refuse to be poor and live in poverty. Refuse to remain in the same place of insignificance caused by poverty because this is bad. You see, this world is mostly controlled by people who feel they have money and don't want to see poor people. Learn to compete and make sure you rise. Refuse to see your family, and even extended family, living in extreme economic difficulties because nobody in your family has succeeded yet. Be concerned about striving to succeed and then making a difference in your family. Make your family have financial heroes and heroines. Start the foundation now. It is never too late to try. Age has nothing to do with success if you make an effort now. It is never too late to see yourself succeed despite difficulties, with poverty being the major cause of these challenges. You have the sword of the word of God you can use. It is also good that you seek knowledge. Knowledge is power. It is by seeking knowledge that you will open a new world of success in a better way. Imagine, Christ Jesus says in his word from his Father that if any man is in Him, such a person is a new creature (I Corinthians 5:17). You were born to be great, and this is why Christ wants you to get back on the road to show your greatness to the world, making you a new creature. The word 'new' suggests a spiritual rebirth. It is talking about your recreation. By this means, you will have done away with your old self. Your old self is one that doesn't know God, is self-prideful, boastful for nothing, an evil promoter, etc. But this is the change Christ envisioned for you.

Part of making you a new creature spiritually will manifest physically as a turnaround in your situation. Christ envisioned this long ago for you, which is why he came to die for the world and was resurrected. He didn't remain in the grave. Follow the word as you are told in I Corinthians 5:17. As a new creature described, it doesn't mean you will be turned into a devil—not belonging to this human world. The word is talking about a clear change through believing in Christ Jesus that should make everything around you work. Your character transformation, because of being accepted spiritually as part of the family of God, will place you into a different realm of life. Christ wants everything about you and your world to work for your good and the good of others. He wants you to succeed and enter your contributing stage—meaning having an impact on others. Know that you were made to be the person you are but not made to remain as who you are without having a purpose. Change your status, change your world. Though I am telling you to make money, understand that money is not all there is to live. You need God first, wisdom, and love. You also need people. You need people to be connected to or friendly with. Be more people-centered or connected. When there is no money, but people are in your life, money will definitely come your way from some of them who may want to lift you in life rather than bring you down. Connectivity with people is quite good if you want to succeed. You can create more connections if you have money. Money brings power with people following you. Just watch out for the friendships and know how to connect. It can also create influence by bringing about security from the same people learning to protect you if you learn to connect. Have money to spend and see what becomes of you tomorrow. Nobody should tell you not to have it. Just look at the opposite of not having money and how life can be. Those who come around you while you are in poverty may just be carrying different stories about you because of your poverty. The intensity of poverty-induced shame can be huge. I know what poverty can do to people and their societies. I am a living witness to this, as poverty ate at me from my youth days until my adulthood before a difference was made against it. It is this difference against poverty that you need to also make by undoing it from your life with strong determination. If you are poor, some people will want to call you a "for nothing" person just because you are in poverty. Some will want to curse you in your presence and behind your back. My parents were abused and termed "for nothing" poor people.

Don't Be Bitter Against Rich People

Stop being like those who say that money is of the devil, always bitter against getting rich and those who are wealthy. That is narrow-mindedness. Money is what makes an economy function. Many poor and average people say that money is evil because they create stress for themselves by chasing it. Some wake up early just to earn money and seek pay raises by going to work, and yet their expenses also increase, leaving them with nothing after subtracting their expenses. They are merely chasing satisfaction by working hard to have money to spend on what they want in life, but they are not concerned about finding the root of their poverty and learning to create their own wealth.

Negative working stress is not good for you. Learn to rest your body. If you learn to work for yourself, you can have more vacations and rest often. It's foolishness to view money as a devil's agent and chase after it for nothing. Money answers all things economically, in a sense of wisdom. This is why you must have it. But understand that it wasn't the devil who created mankind, who in turn created money for trade. It wasn't the devil who gave mankind the thought to improve the world through business interactions. No, the devil's will is to spoil the world so that nothing good happens here as a way of disproving God as the creator of all things who must be worshipped for His goodness. God's will is to see that good things happen, which is why He gives mankind ideas to make the world better.

The idea of money came from God for business interactions to be perfectly done within the world. Holding and having plenty of money is not evil. Erase such a notion from your mind. You should blame yourself for how you perceive and use money. If you misuse money, that's when you should attribute it to the devil. But God is the giver of all good things, including the idea to use money. Anything good that leads to mankind's improvement comes from God. He is the source of good, as you read earlier. This is why everyone seeks good, and you can't get good from the devil. The source is God. You must believe this because He created the good in His world and in everyone. You didn't create yourself or the world; He did.

What you should understand is that it's God's will for lives to improve, especially if mankind learns to discover their potential and change their ways. We were given the power to rule the world, and that power should suggest to you that you have the key to your upliftment. Creativity is within you, involved with the power of being part of those who rule the earth. Because you have the power of creativity, you have the potential and talents within you. To succeed, you have to tap into your creativity to get what you need from the spiritual realm by ordering things spiritually and physically to manifest. It is through dreams or thinking that you make an order from the spirit realm.

Money can give you power and solve problems. It is the medium of exchange for you to travel to places you might or might not have been. In short, it is what people use within their countries, regions, and the world at large to carry out transactions. People work for it for many reasons, including precautionary motives. You have money to take precautions against potential emergencies that might require spending. The transactional aspect of holding money is for business purposes. Investments are all about holding money.

Making money is something our parents or guardians saw the need for, ensuring that we learn something for our future lives. They sent us to school to learn something that would allow us to start enjoying life. If money were bad, you wouldn't have had the power to acquire a skill or learn something. You need money today, tomorrow, and for future generations.

Stop following the notion of those who say that money is evil. Those who steal, corrupt, or kill for money are the ones who are evil because of their motives for wanting to acquire it that way. Stop supporting those people who call money a substance of the devil. They can make themselves evil promoters by chasing money and doing wrong things to obtain it.

If you had money to spend on food or school fees for your children, would you say that you are promoting an act of the devil by having that money? No. Don't follow the mentality of those who attribute making money and having plenty of it to the devil. It is not an act of thinking smart, especially if you support such an idea. Just picture the world and understand that, as poor and average people, we all live here. But poor and average people struggle so much just to make money. Your struggle ends when your money problems end. You must have money to always satisfy your wants or needs. It is the power you need for your life, not the poverty-power that tries to deform your being.

Understand that money is never real until you can make it real. What makes it real is the power it has when used for transactions. You can either earn it or create it.

There is a way people can make money, while others may create money. You need to ask: How do people make money? It works like this: people can earn money based on the service they provide. People can provide a service if they are educated in the subject matter of that service. Many of those who work for money do so to survive, often by working with institutions or for other people. This is why people go to school to learn as professionals—to make money. Sometimes, these people work and work, and upon receiving their pay, they pay bills, accumulate huge debts, and struggle to get out of them because the money they make seems insufficient. They are just chasing it. Because they focus on making money, they strive for pay raises. They make life a constant chase for money. Some work hard but become wasteful, falling into huge debts and possibly passing those debts on to future generations. This should make you realize that money is never sufficient for those kinds of people. They are just looking for money to earn.

Here is why it's important for you to learn how to create money, which should be your primary focus. When you make money, you should move beyond the level of making money and reach the level of creating it. Creating money allows it to work for you, whether in front of your eyes or behind your back. It serves you, making you feel happy and comfortable because you always have money to spend. You will always have money to spend any time you want without worrying about how to get it because you are creating money, which will naturally come to you. Make money your servant rather than making your life a servant to money.

Move beyond the level of making money by advancing to the level of creating money. This is why you first need financial knowledge. You need to make money and then learn to create money. Working for or with people is an act of making money. But if you learn to save while working for others with the intention of starting your own business, you will begin to create money. If you learn to create money, money will find you wherever you are, and you won't have to run around looking for it. It should seek you out, allowing you to use it without stress. Another example of those who work for money is government workers. You don't have to create stress by chasing money. You don't have to corrupt people or kill them because of making money.

You can create money, and you don't have to work for it. Those who create money, for example, are those who invest their money. Investors have the power to spend more within an economy. They are the promoters of the economy. They create happiness for themselves and others by helping those in need. Instead of chasing money, money chases them because their services are valuable to the world. They have the spending power and don't worry about how to spend money because they have saved, invested, and now have plenty. However, for the poor or average person, there is much worry about getting a job and earning money. He or she sometimes can't sleep well because of the need to get up and go to work. He or she might be stressed but is forced to work for the institution because of the need for money.

This is why rich people have financial power—because they learn to create money. Poor and average people, however, chase money throughout their lives. They worry about retirement. Whether sick or healthy, they are forced to work for their money. Some average people strive to get master's degrees, PhDs, or BScs just to earn more money at their workplaces. It's not that learning is bad, but you need to understand the importance of money and learn to invest rather than work for money your entire life. Degree holders who seek pay raises by learning more may be better off than those who don't strive for anything. However, these degree holders and workers are always focused on learning more and working harder. Some even create conflicts at work just to get what they want.

It's good to keep learning, but one of the best ways to create money is to see it as an invisible power that can be generated through investments or foreign instruments. These don't require your physical presence to create them. They should work invisibly in the background through your investments. Don't be like some Liberian government officials who never invest their money. When they leave their jobs, they end up broke and become recycled politicians involved in criminal activities.

What I have observed in my seventeen years of making money working for my country's election commission is that many poor and average people working in government are often unsuccessful because they are wasteful. By the time they receive their paychecks, they have already spent what they earned. Many never wish to retire, holding onto their jobs and manipulating the governance system, which keeps the country stagnant.

Some Liberians I know who have only a high school education or are college dropouts are doing better financially because they have the mentality of creating money. In contrast, those with high degrees may keep working for their employers, constantly chasing money. As a degree holder, the lack of financial knowledge on how to create money could be very harmful to your life. You need to learn from wise people who understand the concept of making money. You could be a high school dropout and still learn to create money, which has nothing to do with your level of formal education. In fact, you could live better than someone with a PhD.

I know many master's and PhD holders whose knowledge seems to create more problems for them. They suffer instead of enjoying the knowledge they have obtained. Until you learn the discipline of making and creating money, you will constantly complain or chase after money like the wind.

I see this attitude creeping into many people worldwide. They work hard throughout their lives, making money, but they never have enough to meet their needs. As they age, life forces them to live desperately, having nothing to show for all their years of hard work. They see work as the source of survival, something they are always chasing. Some people, because of the struggle to make ends meet, die stressed. Some chase money so relentlessly that they have no rest because their problems outweigh what they earn. Understand this: as long as you work for others or institutions, becoming rich will not be easy. Others will determine your pay. You need to learn to pay yourself by working for yourself. Working for money can stress you out, especially when you're promoting others or institutions instead of your own interests. Working for others isn't bad, but you should eventually consider a change. If you spend your entire life working for others, you are merely making money. However, if you learn to work for yourself by starting a business, managing a corporation, or running a farm, you will be creating money. If you bring your talents or potential to light or create something that can be turned into a product, you will also be creating money. Focus on learning to create money rather than simply working for it. By creating money, you won't just use money; you'll also spend it. See money as a seed that can spread, which must be planted and nurtured to grow, eventually leading to a harvest stage where you can live gloriously, celebrated by others as you spend money. Otherwise, you risk living as a poor or average individual, relying on others for survival.

I remember the Bible telling me that King Solomon asked God for one thing: wisdom. He didn't ask for many things, just wisdom. You don't need many things to develop; perhaps you just need one idea to work with your hands or bring out your potential or talent, and your world will change. One thing I've noticed about success is that it can prevent you from stressing over how to obtain things, as having money allows you to buy what you need without worry. In contrast, poor and average people constantly worry about how to get money and how to spend the little they may have.

Having a winner's mindset by learning to create money is the right path for you. This is how I view my life. I don't worry about what I will eat because I am working to reach the stage of creating money. God is with me, providing me with a future that I am working towards. But when poverty was a part of my life, it felt like my hands were tied behind my back, like the walls of my life were falling in on me. Poverty troubled my parents and me, which is why I despise it and am fighting against it. I do this because I want to become my best by the grace of God. I want to rise above so that when I am up, I can help someone else rise economically. I want God to help you, too. Everyone should think about learning how to impact society by the time they succeed.

If you don't learn to work for yourself and only have a mentality of making money by working hard for others, you will be considered someone who works for money instead of letting money work for you. Keep in mind that your employer can determine how much to pay you. They can decide to end your employment at any time, and no one can change that. This could happen if the economy gets tough, forcing your employer to cut costs, and you could be the victim of this. Your employer could close the door to your source of income.

Employment by institutions without a plan to work for yourself in the future can be detrimental. What will happen to you and your family if your employer suddenly ends your employment during tough economic times? This is what some people face with wicked employers, leading to early death due to worry. You can make a change by learning to work for yourself. Determine your own economy rather than letting someone else determine it for you. If you create your own economy, you can decide when to work, when to be paid, and how to work. You can plan your vacation better. However, your employer may not be lenient if you miss work; they could cut your pay for missing a day. Or a future illness could lead to termination.

In my case, I learned how to create money. I started working on this journey almost nine years ago. I focus on generating money rather than simply working for it. For example, my wife and I run a business, and I also publish books worldwide. I can choose not to work for anyone and instead make money by selling my books, either online or through physical means.

This is what I want for you: to start a business for yourself. Stop working for others and develop a mindset that focuses on creating money. If you have this vision and put it into practice, you will be better equipped to help others and make a significant impact because you might become a money maker or creator. You could even gain recognition for your contributions to humanity.

There are many things you can do to learn how to create money. You could own a company for a reason, and when that happens, you'll be in a better position to help others. You can also create money if you are an inventor with a patent or copyright to a product you can sell.

However, the power of creating money lies in your ability to learn financial discipline. This should be the first lesson you must master before attempting to succeed. Next, you need financial training to learn how to invest money. The reason is that many people produce things but don't know how to market their inventions to the world. As a result, their ideas remain hidden, and no one benefits from their potential. Without financial discipline or the technical know-how to sell, they may find themselves trapped in poverty. What you need are marketing skills to make money work for you. Don't worry about making a little at first; focus on how you can grow it and improve your life.

Start by reducing costs. Eat simply, like dry rice with red oil and a little something inside it. You don't need to eat lavishly until you have succeeded. Don't let today's struggles ruin tomorrow's opportunities. I know that you may be eating simple food now, but the time will come when you can afford a more luxurious diet. When you have the financial means, you'll have the power to decide your diet. But when poverty controls you, you won't have that choice—nature will decide for you.

I fell into the trap of lacking financial discipline and not knowing how to market myself and my products. I ended up in the same position as an author I knew, one of the best writers in my country. Despite his education, he was very poor, and after his death, his family was left with nothing. His bank account was depleted before he passed away, with no investments to show for his efforts. His children now struggle on their own despite the greatness of their father.

Being smart in school doesn't mean you're wise in the world. It's one thing to have knowledge and another to know what to do with it. A wise person learns to do things that will make their life great and impactful. Unfortunately, this man's children now have to build their wealth from scratch without relying on any inheritance.

The children decided to make a change by thinking wisely. This is why you need God—He can make people wise.

Stop carrying a poverty mindset like so many poor and average people do. They create endless struggles by chasing money without properly planning for the future. The only way to become rich is not by working for money but by learning to create money by working for yourself. Be a producer and earn money from your products. You'll start creating money when you begin to produce, invent, or sell. Be like Jeff Bezos, who started by selling books and created Amazon. He wasn't a producer but learned to market the products of others, which made him a billionaire. It's about being talented.

What you should know is that while others may pay your salary, the best salary is one you determine by working for yourself. Start a business and make money grow. This is about employing yourself. When you employ yourself, no one can sack you during tough economic times, and no one can dictate your working hours or your pay. You can pay yourself overtime, and you won't face economic hardships like others.

Keep in mind that businesses may struggle, but once you overcome those challenges, your personal economy can thrive. The perfect economy is one you create for yourself by learning to work for yourself. While businesses may close down during hard times, your personal economy doesn't have to suffer if you can create and sustain it.

You may want to reshape your business during economic hardships by following God. He is above difficulties because He created this world and heaven. Nothing in them is beyond His control, so if you depend on Him, you will succeed.

What's wrong with the world's economy is often due to a lack of individual planning, government planning, and business managers failing to observe and adapt to economic changes. Economic hardships arise from poor coordination, static policies, and professional complacency. Governments that create excessive debt increase taxes to pay off debt, and fail to innovate can cause economic instability. Without foresight and proper planning, economic hardships can creep in.

As an individual, the start of any economy begins with being dynamic in your life. Your dynamism should involve learning new ideas and not sticking to outdated ones. Many businesses have failed because they didn't adapt to changing times. They continued to produce the same products without innovating to meet modern demands. Ideas must evolve over time, and so must our business and marketing strategies. Our banking and monetary systems should also be dynamic.

For example, my grandfather was a fisherman who was never educated, but he could look at the weather and predict what it would be like. He knew when it would rain, when the sun would shine, and other things that might happen during the day. He could observe the weather at night to know when the moon would rise, when the new month would start, and when tortoises would come ashore to lay their eggs. He learned this from his parents through careful observation, which guided them during the day.

Make some observations about the kind of future you want and work towards it. Stop clinging to old ideas and old ways of doing things. Look at the business world and adapt to new policies and trends. In short, be creative. Adopt a self-conscious approach if you plan to start your own business. Make the business and employees a part of your daily life. By being self-conscious, you won't just focus on the institution's growth but also on the well-being of the employees who manage its progress. Listen to your employees and consider their advice and wishes, which can bring dynamism to the institution and its product line. Many business owners fail because they don't care about their employees' well-being or listen to their input. They stick to old patterns without observing the economic landscape and how to reshape their business operations.

I want you to learn how to make money and then create money. Money has a good spirit if you learn to control it, work with it, create it, and let it work for you even when it's beyond your immediate reach. However, it can have a bad spirit if you let it control you—if you're constantly chasing money to satisfy your needs and wants without ever resting.

Money will not have a bad spirit if you don't believe that having it, especially in abundance, will bring bad luck or cause you to worry. Money has its own misfortunes if you spend your whole life chasing it, cheating people, or selling harmful substances. The desire you have for money can lead to either a positive or negative outcome, depending on how you pursue it.

What makes the act of making money bad is the intention behind it, particularly the way people seek it. Stop stealing or engaging in corrupt practices just because you want money. Stop using juju to harm people because you want money. In some parts of Africa, people perform juju rituals, even taking lives, to get rich. Becoming wealthy is a simple idea you need to understand. One crucial thing you could do to create money is to seek God's wisdom. Keep God and His word in your heart. Be persistent in the positive things you do. Maintain faith in yourself and never grow weary in pursuing your dreams. Be creative in your endeavours. Stay close to people rather than isolating yourself, as you can learn from others to improve your lifestyle.

Take the example of Jeff Bezos, the founder of Amazon, as a great role model. He didn't create his own products to sell. He simply had an idea that made him rich. He started his business by selling books online, which made him extremely wealthy. He utilized the internet to connect people with products.

Similarly, look at Mark Zuckerberg, the founder of Facebook. He simply connected people across the world. These were just ideas that Mark and Jeff implemented, which made them some of the richest people in the world. They didn't rob or kill people to succeed, unlike some in Africa and Asia. Some people in Africa go to juju priests to make traditional medicine, killing others in the process because they want money. Others perform juju to take someone's job. They chase luck rather than trust in God, whom they should rely on when seeking money.

Mark and Bezos didn't sell drugs to succeed. Because they are successful in their businesses, they pay more taxes to their government, which in turn helps improve the lives of others and the country, America. They didn't corrupt their societies.

You can never have a million dollars and keep it in a bag without investing it or putting it in the bank to make it grow. Invest money in productive ventures rather than just keeping it in the bank. For your safety, avoid holding large sums of money with you. Protect your money by investing it to avoid misusing it, or keep it secure if you have it for a specific purpose. Invest it in security systems, allowing it to grow and create your economic power. It must work beyond what you can see to expand. The power of creating more money lies in letting it work for you.

If you have dollars on you right now, you may feel either happiness or anxiety about spending it. Money has the power to satisfy your desires. However, if you have it in the bank, you might be tempted to withdraw it when a pressing need arises. But if your money is in bonds or real estate, you can't just withdraw it instantly to spend. If it's invested in a security system, you can't access it immediately. Similarly, if your money is in shares, you can't just spend it right away.

If you don't learn to work for yourself, life will work against you. Make money work for you instead of you working for money. If you only work for money, when old age comes, you won't be able to work anymore. This is the point where many academicians and professionals experience stress because they refuse to retire and leave the workplace. When you can't work for money anymore, you will start to struggle. This is one reason why many retired people suffer in old age despite their educational achievements.

Working for money can limit you financially. People may insult you, calling you all sorts of names because you are broke and have to work for them, allowing them to treat you poorly. Your cleverness might no longer help you due to age. But if you have your own business or corporation, people will work for you and create money for you even in your absence. Having money can bring stress, as people might take advantage of you. Create the power of money, primarily by making it able to generate more money for you rather than working for money.

You won't always be young or part of the working class, so you must prepare for old age. You need to start planning for future travels with your family to add value to your life. This is what we call living a good life—when you have money, you won't face economic limitations. Stop living with limitations and economic frustrations due to a lack of money.

Chapter|15

"You may become a burden to life if you suppress your conscience by enslaving yourself. If you don't recognize what's good for you and actively work to bring those good things into your life, your journey will reflect the effort you put in, and you won't find success."

– Frederick W. Sonpon

Investment Strategies: How to Grow Your Wealth

One of the greatest powers you need when you have God is economic power, and that comes from creating wealth. This is the point where many people don't know what to do with their lives. Life should be valued, and when you start to rise, make sure to stay up there and remain there. Don't rise and then fall again because of how you manage your life and finances. This is why you need the education provided in this book. You need to learn what you are about to study because when I went to college, I didn't acquire all these skills as a business student studying for my accounting profession. It was only after I graduated that I started learning these lessons. I had to leave college before I could see the bigger picture of what life was, how to make money, and how to create wealth.

I graduated from college with a business degree, but I didn't get a job in my profession or in what I learned to do in college. Life pushed me into a different field as a writer, and I started working in administration. This is why you need to be dynamic. Don't stick to a single idea of relying solely on a degree because life requires dynamism, and you must observe and act on what will market you.

Learn about money investment. One key thing about investing money is to have marketable skills, to assess the market around you, and to know how to sell your product. I suffered from this, which is why I want to advise you. I had a product I invented that I wanted to sell, but I didn't know how to proceed with it. I wanted to be a publisher, and I eventually started publishing books. I published my first book in the USA, but I didn't have the money to pay for marketing, and I couldn't develop the urge to market my own book. It took me seven long years after the book was published to start marketing it gradually. I thought the problem was with the publisher. The same thing happened when I published my second book in Nigeria. Instead of focusing on marketing the first book with the little money I had, I went ahead and published the second book while the first one wasn't earning any returns. I was eager for nothing, publishing books while no money was coming in. After publishing my second book, many people wanted copies, but I couldn't order more because I had spent the money I got from the first copies on personal expenses. I lacked a business mentality, failing to keep copies of the book in stock to continue in the business. It was a mistake to spend my business income because of the mindset I had at the time.

I wanted to make a change. I tried to double down by making a change and learned to invest the money from my book sales. Selling books was the means of my success, and I know how to sell them. I am working to get rich, so I am developing a new strategy on how to market products. I keep refining this idea and strategy over and over.

If you look at human life, we are meant to be displayed. That is why we are placed on the surface of the earth rather than underneath it. This is a reason for display; you must bring your talents out to the world. When you bring your talents out, you need to create a market by learning to sell your products, which stem from your talents.

I know I will reach the level I aspire to, becoming a rich person, and God will make it possible for me. To fulfil this, I need to keep pressing on and on. It is the mentality I carry within me.

But earlier, I was like a fool, despite having a degree in accounting and supposedly knowing better about marketing a product. It was as if the education I received in college was limited, not instilling the technical know-how required to handle products or market them. I had to revise my thinking before my life was transformed, allowing me to grasp the bigger picture of what it meant to create and make money.

I also learned one thing: if a person is creative and depends on God if one idea closes a door, they will be productive enough to develop another idea that opens new doors. If they are productive, they will be marketable. If they are marketable, they will be successful. And if they are successful, they will be impactful. Just be creative. This happens by learning to think positively. Whatever you want to achieve, keep practising in that field without giving up. Stop sleeping on the idea. Nurture it repeatedly. That idea will eventually make a way for you. It represents the display of your talents or potential, which will eventually manifest. These talents, turning into ideas, are the kinds of riches God gave you to bring into the world. They are infinite and cannot be depleted, unlike the riches of the world that can be fought over and diminished.

Start investing now. To begin investing money, you must consider the following:

- Have a source of income;
- Start saving a portion of that income;
- Train yourself by reducing your spending habits;
- Be willing to take risks with money when you want to invest;
- Start with the little you have and focus on the future with confidence;

- Create a savings plan while expanding your business gradually;

- Be mindful of your associates and cut down on costs related to social habits, etc.

You must grow big to do big things. It is in your greatness that the world will truly benefit from you by recognizing the importance of your existence. You were made to be who you are, but not to stay where you are. Change your level now! To successfully do business, you must leave your small level and rise to a higher level in the days to come. This is possible if you learn to invest. Investment is the key to making money grow. Practice making money grow in your hands instead of learning to spend money and letting it die.

Staying in Business: What to Keep Doing

If you want to do business, you must first and foremost put yourself in the mental attitude or arena of doing business. It is a culture, not something you can approach casually. Here are some things to consider:

- Be smart in the market while investing. To avoid being duped, watch out for criminals, especially regarding how you promote your business on social media networks or receive messages from clients. You must remain vigilant.
- Create a savings plan so your money can be used for further expansion, creating a subsidiary of your business, or extending its branches.
- Don't focus on selling a single product or having only one segment of business as you grow. You should learn to offer different products at the same location based on the nature of the business; consider opening different business lines.
- Watch out for deceivers and counterfeiters of your products.

- Obey business and tax laws.
- Regularly assess the market to understand how it is functioning before placing your money or strategizing on investing in a different product or adding a new branch to your business.
- Don't rely solely on a single business line. Learn to create diversity to keep cash flowing.
- Be cautious of the people you associate with and those who discuss your business with you because some could be either beneficial or harmful; you can learn from both.
- Learn from other businesspeople whom you confidently approach to discuss the economy.
- Avoid living flamboyantly with your business income; budget your business income to know what is allocated for which expenses, and spend it in line with business needs.
- Separate your personal expenses from your business expenses and activities.
- Stay focused and do not give in to business pressures.
- Don't allow your constant presence at the business site to disrupt activities or create problems.
- Don't be the kind of businessperson who blames the government or others for business slowdowns or failures. Instead, look for possibilities in your actions, study the economy, adapt, and act accordingly in your business.
- Learn to respect your customers by treating them as close friends and showing concern for how they feel about your business. Obtain feedback from them regularly.
- Stay informed about other businesses by checking the profitability trends across the economy and reading business news, agendas, or articles that could educate you further.

- Regularly appraise your business to test its strengths and weaknesses, as well as the strengths and weaknesses of your employees. This will help you decide whether to invest more or not.
- Learn to pay for services when people work for your business.
- Understand your business taxes well and stay current with paying your portion of taxes to the state.
- Train your business staff well or seek further education for yourself as an added advantage. This will help you succeed by repositioning and adapting in the future.
- Know your cash flow—determine how much is spent to grow the business and how much is coming in.
- Always aim to increase your assets rather than your liabilities and expenses. Know the difference between your expenses and income, and between your assets and liabilities in business.
- Be sensitive to market pressures—inflation, uncertainties, tax impositions, and seeking tax incentives.
- Keep track of business law and tax policies to stay within the confines of the law.
- Don't keep money around the business that isn't currently needed; instead, put it in the bank.
- Create a practical business strategy for the overall operation of the business as a standard key for every employee to follow, distinct from business policy or human resource policy. It should guide how employees are expected to behave in dealing with others, outlining what is acceptable and unacceptable practice while on the job or running the business.
- Learn to do good by supporting charities and churches while in business.

Spend Your Money Wisely

You will never graduate from poverty if you don't know how to spend money. A lack of knowledge on how to spend money can affect some people who inadvertently come into money but don't know how to grow it. They can squander or waste it because of the mentality of not knowing how to manage money they don't have.

Create a spending plan and test its power to avoid overspending. You can never grow big if you aren't big in your mind yet, and for you to grow, you must think big. Your spending size or growth shouldn't be the determinant of your success in business. You must not forget other things you need to know and do.

After you have learned how to create money, you must also learn how to spend it. This is important because some people who get opportunities or luck to manage money can squander those opportunities or waste what they didn't earn. Stop being like poor and average people. Some ordinary people make money and spend it loosely or excessively without the mindset of creating more money. They can mismanage and let opportunities slip away. They only know how to spend money. Spending money is not difficult, but earning it is, which is why you shouldn't be wasteful.

It's not that some people have never made money before or that luck hasn't come their way, but they let opportunities slip away, expecting that the same will come back again. They are just dreamers. Because of this, they may rush to spend or worry about how to make money. But the rich or successful people know how to make and create more money. Your act of making money should be for a season, and as time goes by, you must elevate yourself to the level of creating money. Poor people spend what they don't have loosely, while average people work to earn and then spend loosely as well.

This is what I want you to do: move from your small self to your big self. This is why you must hate poverty. It is better for you to take control of your life by creating money and investing in your personal economy, especially in your nation, than to let poverty take control of your life. Create spending power.

People who don't learn to own their personal economies are the ones whose country or others can determine their economies for them. Similarly, in my country, Liberia, many Liberians don't recognize the problems of their nation, which suffers so much and has many very poor people. The nation is taken over by foreigners who control the economy, essentially controlling even their livelihoods. This situation makes it very precarious, making it impossible for many to find better livelihoods because most of the government's spending, budget-wise, goes into the hands of foreign businesses. These businesses win big contracts in construction, agro-projects, services, export, import, etc. Even customs services are controlled by foreign businesses, leaving the nation poor. The government doesn't have a means of creating a middle class, especially by focusing on developing a better agro-sector economy. There is often a huge budget shortage or deficit.

This national situation means that government after government doesn't have much of a voice in the economy, and somehow politically, as well. Our government cries more for foreign aid and grants instead of investing domestically. There are more foreign individuals in the economy, so business importations and exportations aren't well regulated. The lack of domestic investment that should lead to more exports and bring in foreign currency is harming the economy, as the exchange rate is a major issue to contend with. Our government is more of a salary-paying entity that doesn't have the power to develop infrastructure on a wide scale. There are no price regulations in the economy, and no system controls foreign business people, especially regarding how much of their profits should remain in the economy and how much they can transfer out, controlling capital flight as well. In short, more money is transferred out than is brought in from export activities. This economic problem is causing the government to be unable even to determine the domestic rate against foreign currency.

This is the poverty that is promoted in the national economy of my country. When economic hard times hit, good economies of the world are affected, but they can reshape their economy by focusing on food production and reducing the costs of food and basic essentials.

We must work to eliminate this. We must promote Liberianization (a Liberian business concept of helping Liberians operate businesses with state support to keep them running) by creating incentives for Liberian business owners.

You will never graduate from poverty if you don't know how to spend money. A lack of knowledge on how to spend money can affect some people who inadvertently come into money but don't know how to grow it. They can squander or waste it because of the mentality of not knowing how to manage money they don't have.

Create a spending plan and test its power to avoid overspending. You can never grow big if you aren't big in your mind yet, and for you to grow, you must think big. Your spending size or growth shouldn't be the determinant of your success in business. You must not forget other things you need to know and do.

After you have learned how to create money, you must also learn how to spend it. This is important because some people who get opportunities or luck to manage money can squander those opportunities or waste what they didn't earn. Stop being like poor and average people. Some ordinary people make money and spend it loosely or excessively without the mindset of creating more money. They can mismanage and let opportunities slip away. They only know how to spend money. Spending money is not difficult, but earning it is, which is why you shouldn't be wasteful.

It's not that some people have never made money before or that luck hasn't come their way, but they let opportunities slip away, expecting that the same will come back again. They are just dreamers. Because of this, they may rush to spend or worry about how to make money. But the rich or successful people know how to make and create more money. Your act of making money should be for a season, and as time goes by, you must elevate yourself to the level of creating money. Poor people spend what they don't have loosely, while average people work to earn and then spend loosely as well.

This is what I want you to do: move from your small self to your big self. This is why you must hate poverty. It is better for you to take control of your life by creating money and investing in your personal economy, especially in your nation, than to let poverty take control of your life. Create spending power.

People who don't learn to own their personal economies are the ones whose country or others can determine their economies for them. Similarly, in my country, Liberia, many Liberians don't recognize the problems of their nation, which suffers so much and has many very poor people. The nation is taken over by foreigners who control the economy, essentially controlling even their livelihoods. This situation makes it very precarious, making it impossible for many to find better livelihoods because most of the government's spending, budget-wise, goes into the hands of foreign businesses. These businesses win big contracts in construction, agro-projects, services, export, import, etc. Even customs services are controlled by foreign businesses, leaving the nation poor. The government doesn't have a means of creating a middle class, especially by focusing on developing a better agro-sector economy. There is often a huge budget shortage or deficit.

This national situation means that government after government doesn't have much of a voice in the economy, and somehow politically, as well. Our government cries more for foreign aid and grants instead of investing domestically. There are more foreign individuals in the economy, so business importations and exportations aren't well regulated. The lack of domestic investment that should lead to more exports and bring in foreign currency is harming the economy, as the exchange rate is a major issue to contend with. Our government is more of a salary-paying entity that doesn't have the power to develop infrastructure on a wide scale. There are no price regulations in the economy, and no system controls foreign business people, especially regarding how much of their profits should remain in the economy and how much they can transfer out, controlling capital flight as well. In short, more money is transferred out than is brought in from export activities. This economic problem is causing the government to be unable even to determine the domestic rate against foreign currency.

This is the poverty that is promoted in the national economy of my country. When economic hard times hit, good economies of the world are affected, but they can reshape their economy by focusing on food production and reducing the costs of food and basic essentials.

We must work to eliminate this. We must promote Liberianization (a Liberian business concept of helping Liberians operate businesses with state support to keep them running) by creating incentives for Liberian business owners.

I travelled to Nigeria and read about wealthy Nigerians who became rich by engaging in business. They are not focused on getting public jobs before achieving success. They are focused on the private sector economy, creating their own wealth through fostering economic growth. We Liberians can do the same. Let this mindset start with you, the reader of this book, by learning to take ownership of your own economy.

You are made to be who you are, but not to remain where you are without fulfilling a purpose. This is a problem for many people around the world. A great number of people don't know how to create and manage money because they didn't receive financial education from a young age. Often, when poor and average people have money in their hands, they don't observe much about how to spend it—they just spend without planning. Because of this, they can hinder their own progress or limit themselves. For example, one hundred dollars that should be spent over two days by an ordinary person without financial awareness could be spent in seconds. Learn to plan your expenditures before going to the market to buy. This exercise is beneficial in helping you manage your spending. Never go above your spending limit when you have money; understand that money should be used wisely. Learn to create a savings plan and develop the habit of being able to invest in your future.

It is unfortunate if you have risen or are struggling to rise in life but now find yourself stagnant or declining, or your life is just in between. This could be due to various factors, such as living carelessly or failing to learn how to manage money properly. This is a problem you must address and overcome. Another factor could be poor financial health, which may be causing financial difficulties. For this reason, you need financial education.

Life can be predictable. Sometimes, it comes with certain standards you must meet and maintain to live well. As you grow older, economically speaking, understand that age comes with its own standards that you should be willing to uphold. You cannot grow old and continue working for others instead of working for yourself. Learn this: if you are advancing, ensure you maintain your standard of living and avoid falling back into the same trap of struggle and poverty. Maintain your economic growth by learning to manage yourself well. It would be unfortunate if, after achieving financial success, your lifestyle changes, and you start squandering all you have because of the way you choose to live.

Many people who become successful but still lack financial education can lose everything and tell themselves they were not born with riches, so if they lose their wealth, they are comfortable with that. I see this attitude as akin to a dog returning to its vomit. In short, you cannot succeed after struggling, and then you start to decline again. This is why you must learn how to invest and manage money. Don't be like those who throw away success because of things that cause them to change. These are some of the reasons poor and average people attribute the possession of more money to the devil or view it as a troubling thing. Some people who struggle to earn money spend it carelessly, and their needs continue to control them. Because of this, they never blame themselves for their struggles, which they view as detrimental. They see money as something devilish that they desperately seek. The way they spend money without observing their spending habits can cause it to disappear from their hands, with their many needs dragging them down, leading them to complain about having more money. They then experience stress again just to acquire more money. This is when they view money as the devil's property because they start to regret their actions. This can create so much worry about life. They never spend wisely, no matter how little income they have, so their lives are always stressful as they seek more money, especially the poor and average people.

Being poor is not a curse. However, if you do nothing to change that poverty, it becomes a curse in life.

What you need to understand about having more money is this: you should develop a mindset that focuses on learning what to do with money. Be productive with money and always seek to invest it. I want you to adopt a growing-money mentality. Do this because a life without the satisfaction of fulfilling one's wants and needs can be painful. Create a financially stress-free life concerning your future. Do it before it is too late.

Things to Observe When You Are Investing Money

- Watch that your social life is not too strong;
- Watch the clothes and food you buy;
- Watch the places you go;
- Don't compete with people who are above your level, thinking you can be in a money-spending race with them;

- Watch the things you put on your body apart from clothes and food;
- Watch that the way you give to charity or help people is done wisely;
- Don't follow what people say by spending your money indiscriminately or changing your investments wrongly;
- Learn to plan your spending habits;
- Have a saving mentality rather than an eating mentality;
- Don't gamble with your money while in business;

Another key way of having money and learning to spend it well is to create happiness; you must socialize a bit to create happiness for your life and keep yourself healthier. It is not because you want money that you should keep yourself unhappy or frown at spending money. Don't just save money without creating investments and having time to enjoy yourself. Step out of the confines of your life by going on trips to see other places and spend some money. This exercise can bring a newness to your spirit that could add value to your business or your life as a whole. As you visit new places, you may gain new ideas from people or see things that can help you better redesign your business strategies or start a new line of business when you return home because you might have seen other businesses or people with different good ideas you could learn from.

Have a money-serving mentality. Let money serve you instead of you serving money. And if you learn to create money, you will find that you will create a stress-free life. Money will chase you instead of you chasing money.

Reach the point in life where money comes to you without you seeking it. When you learn to invest, money can come to you even behind your back. People could be working for you while you have more time to spend with your family and enjoy your life.

This should be the primary reason for having money. You should do this because life is meant to be enjoyed, not to create stress by worrying about how to get and spend money. In the future, you may be retired from working for others. It doesn't matter how clever you are; you will eventually retire. So, the question is, where will you be with your life when you retire? What will you do if your retirement funds are lost due to the economy or social security system in the future? It is not ideal to work for others in old age when others should work for you by owning your own businesses.

One thing you need to understand about making and creating money is that money is to serve people, not for you to serve it. You should never enslave your life, working for others and for money. Learn to invest it as if it were working for yourself. If you work for yourself, you will have more time to spend with your family and create more happiness for yourself. You will have more time for leisure. As long as you are happy with good money, you will be healthier. Conversely, if you are unhappy because you are stressed about money or working for money, you will not be as healthy.

Find yourself among those who create money. You will have less time to worry about money and to spend it properly, including on leisure, compared to poor and average people who don't have it to spend and must worry about obtaining money through working. The poor and average people often struggle, creating stress over money. If an average person works for someone else and seeks a pay rise, they might try to please their bosses by working hard or being very serviceable, possibly working extra hours. While being hardworking is commendable, eventually, the body will not have the strength to work due to age. How will you manage to please your bosses when you are retired? By the time one reaches retirement, despite all the knowledge and strength acquired, it becomes clear that life has stages: a time to work hard and a time to prepare to step away due to old age.

Poor and average people can stress themselves out, always on the run for money. Though they view money as bad, many can engage in acts detrimental to their survival compared to rich people. It's a similar mentality that Liberians have about being rich. They love good lives, but they don't work for good lives before living them. They make their lives petty throughout. They don't have a rich mentality, so they can be content with a little. They don't have the mindset to make big money by starting businesses that could even employ people.

Because the rich can create money, they don't worry about paying their bills or forcing themselves to acquire money. They always have money to spend on important things. However, poor and average people can even cry or refuse to pay their bills or debts because their money is not always sufficient.

If you check the crime rates in the world, most of those crimes are committed by poor and average people, either instigated by them or in their environments. Some engage in crimes because of the need for money or stress from wanting money to pay bills. This is why many people complain that the world is hard to live in. Some of these poor and average people say that the world is not fair. The world is not hard to live in because God made the world rich for you and me. We didn't come with riches, but we met riches on earth. What we need to do to have a share of the earth's riches is to learn something and work to obtain it. If you have talents, you must practice to bring that talent out into the world. You can't be relaxed and expect to develop your talents. God will not deny any of us money or wealth if we work to obtain it.

I have experienced many people from America complaining about the American economy while in Africa. They spoke of how hard America is and wanted to return home if they could find a little job better than staying in America. It is a funny thing to me. While some were doing well, others, due to their spending habits or attitudes, were stranded. Some face child support problems, working just to pay bills. Many love social lives. I want to ask this question: while some are doing better and others are doing poorly, are they living in a different world than America? No. Many of their economic problems, especially the hardships many Liberians face in America, are due to their lifestyles. They don't control their spending and never learn from others' mistakes or invest their money wisely. Liberians want to live at a level, even if petty and sometimes compare themselves to successful people who worked hard for their money. They try to mimic the spending habits of those people without considering their own circumstances. They don't need to emulate others negatively.

How can a person experience extreme poverty and, when a little light shines on him financially, never focus on learning to spend money wisely? Liberians are like this. They never focus on their backgrounds to learn to grow money instead of spending it unwisely, despite not having much. Because of this, they struggle and complain about money from morning to night. They talk about their economic difficulties detrimentally. They are living in financial stress, controlled by foreign entities in their own economy, and continue the same behaviour away from their country, lacking control over their spending habits.

No people will develop by just sitting idly or being wasteful. No society will develop without people being conscious of their lives and helping their society improve. This is why you must put your mind to work for you. In everyone's mind, there lie potentials or talents that are personal riches of ideas yet to be tapped into. You and I are more than rich; we are endowed with these potentials by God. We have to bring them to light to enjoy this world, which is our own, rather than suffer due to our behaviour.

Understand this hard truth: when Adam and Eve, the first humans, sinned against God, they had only their heads as the power to change their world, not natural resources. Why did God allow this? Was it diamonds they had? You should also ask why God didn't destroy them immediately but gave them a second chance for survival. God had the power to do so, but He didn't. It shows how loving God is. He loved them still and wanted them to repent, giving them a second chance. The reason is simple: God was angry but knew they would survive and later seek repentance. This shows that God is very merciful. He knew that mankind wasn't the original source of sin but had learned it from an evil being (Satan). This is why everyone has a second chance for repentance, and only mankind, not fallen angels, was given the power of repentance. Adam and Eve were given a second chance for repentance, survival, and thinking about improving their world, making a difference, and rethinking their eternal future. See this force of God's forgiveness and tailor your greatness accordingly.

The issue of a second chance is why God didn't allow mankind to remain dead without finding a way out. He showed mankind mercy by avoiding various sacrifices, using Christ to save mankind once and for all.

Discover what is holding you back, whether laziness or poor money management and stop blaming others. See if you are lazy or have nothing to offer your own life. Don't blame the government or others. Many people are poor because of human factors. Some suppress others by keeping them in bondage, while individuals themselves create poverty through their lifestyle choices. The world was evenly made. The Western world was not created before the underdeveloped or developing world. Everything was made at the same time. This is why I expect us all to develop at the same level. However, human factors cause delays for some people across the globe. Fight to change your personal economy now.

Poor and average people can stress themselves out, always on the run for money. Though they view money as bad, many can engage in acts detrimental to their survival compared to rich people. It's a similar mentality that Liberians have about being rich. They love good lives, but they don't work for good lives before living them. They make their lives petty throughout.

They don't have a rich mentality, so they can be content with a little. They don't have the mindset to make big money by starting businesses that could even employ people.

Because the rich can create money, they don't worry about paying their bills or forcing themselves to acquire money. They always have money to spend on important things. However, poor and average people can even cry or refuse to pay their bills or debts because their money is not always sufficient.

If you check the crime rates in the world, most of those crimes are committed by poor and average people, either instigated by them or in their environments. Some engage in crimes because of the need for money or stress from wanting money to pay bills. This is why many people complain that the world is hard to live in. Some of these poor and average people say that the world is not fair. The world is not hard to live in because God made the world rich for you and me. We didn't come with riches, but we met riches on earth. What we need to do to have a share of the earth's riches is to learn something and work to obtain it. If you have talents, you must practice to bring that talent out into the world. You can't be relaxed and expect to develop your talents. God will not deny any of us money or wealth if we work to obtain it.

I have experienced many people from America complaining about the American economy while in Africa. They spoke of how hard America is and wanted to return home if they could find a little job better than staying in America. It is a funny thing to me. While some were doing well, others, due to their spending habits or attitudes, were stranded. Some face child support problems, working just to pay bills. Many love social lives. I want to ask this question: while some are doing better and others are doing poorly, are they living in a different world than America? No. Many of their economic problems, especially the hardships many Liberians face in America, are due to their lifestyles. They don't control their spending and never learn from others' mistakes or invest their money wisely. Liberians want to live at a level, even if petty and sometimes compare themselves to successful people who worked hard for their money. They try to mimic the spending habits of those people without considering their own circumstances. They don't need to emulate others negatively.

How can a person experience extreme poverty and, when a little light shines on him financially, never focus on learning to spend money wisely? Liberians are like this. They never focus on their backgrounds to learn to grow money instead of spending it unwisely, despite not having much. Because of this, they struggle and complain about money from morning to night. They talk about their economic difficulties detrimentally. They are living in financial stress, controlled by foreign entities in their own economy, and continue the same behaviour away from their country, lacking control over their spending habits.

No people will develop by just sitting idly or being wasteful. No society will develop without people being conscious of their lives and helping their society improve. This is why you must put your mind to work for you. In everyone's mind, there lie potentials or talents that are personal riches of ideas yet to be tapped into. You and I are more than rich; we are endowed with these potentials by God. We have to bring them to light to enjoy this world, which is our own, rather than suffer due to our behaviour.

Understand this hard truth: when Adam and Eve, the first humans, sinned against God, they had only their heads as the power to change their world, not natural resources. Why did God allow this? Was it diamonds they had? You should also ask why God didn't destroy them immediately but gave them a second chance for survival. God had the power to do so, but He didn't. It shows how loving God is. He loved them still and wanted them to repent, giving them a second chance. The reason is simple: God was angry but knew they would survive and later seek repentance. This shows that God is very merciful. He knew that mankind wasn't the original source of sin but had learned it from an evil being (Satan). This is why everyone has a second chance for repentance, and only mankind, not fallen angels, was given the power of repentance. Adam and Eve were given a second chance for repentance, survival, and thinking about improving their world, making a difference, and rethinking their eternal future. See this force of God's forgiveness and tailor your greatness accordingly.

The issue of a second chance is why God didn't allow mankind to remain dead without finding a way out. He showed mankind mercy by avoiding various sacrifices, using Christ to save mankind once and for all.

Discover what is holding you back, whether laziness or poor money management and stop blaming others. See if you are lazy or have nothing to offer your own life. Don't blame the government or others. Many people are poor because of human factors. Some suppress others by keeping them in bondage, while individuals themselves create poverty through their lifestyle choices. The world was evenly made. The Western world was not created before the underdeveloped or developing world. Everything was made at the same time. This is why I expect us all to develop at the same level. However, human factors cause delays for some people across the globe. Fight to change your personal economy now.

Be Mindful of Wealth Destroyers

To create wealth is a difficult thing, but to destroy wealth is easy. Therefore, there are factors that can destroy wealth which you need to study so you can guide your own life on how to invest. Some of the factors are:

1. A change in one's mentality along the way;
2. The change of business without observing the way out before doing so;
3. National struggle or bad economy;
4. Tax policy;

5. The lack of business dynamism;
6. Personal poor health;
7. A lack of self-motivation and employee motivation as well;
8. The lack of business morals and learning to improve on the product line;
9. Increasing business expenses and liabilities;
10. Natural disasters, etc.

In the midst of this uncertain world, you must be very careful how you manage your life and business as well. Things will happen naturally and unnaturally, which should be a basis for guiding you in the future to know exactly what to do with your life.

I can remember that African kings of those days were focused on having land as great wealth. Because of this, many men in Africa focused on having plenty of children by owning many concubines whose children could become their strength for making large farms. It was also the case that the era of landlords ended with the start of the industrial era. Currently, it is no longer the era of the Industrial Revolution but the Information Age. Because of this, nobody has to struggle much to become rich. You can stay anywhere in the world and be informed to start advancing yourself or bringing your talents to the world. Technology is a growing power in the information age. The power of the infinite riches of mankind supersedes the power of natural resources based on the land, which was turned into production by the Industrial Revolution. We have entered the era of infinite resources—based on the mind's usage, which is triggered by the information age and technology.

This is why technology was not based on tangible resources before it worked. It is based on the use of the mind. This kind of resource can't be depleted as natural resources can, which power is based on machinery. For example, Japan is the electronic giant of the world. While it took America over 200 years to develop its educational system, it took Japan just 40 years to do so with its educational system. It is for this reason that you don't need a large number of years to improve your talents—such resources can't be depleted.

Chapter 16

Stop Corruption Practices

Corruption is not only practised in public life. You can see corruption everywhere. I see corruption in business places, the transport sector, schools, public life, etc. But keep in mind that we should avoid practising corruption. No way will your society get to be good if your life isn't getting good either, and by learning to live within your means and avoid corruption. If you aren't going to be good, there is no way your government in your land will be good, especially if everybody is living anyhow or being corrupt.

We are the world, and our actions must determine what becomes of it. Human development will not happen for the majority if everybody lives without laws or somehow lacks respect for each other and their state or country. Nothing good will work out for the majority, either. Laws make people, and they must be respected to stamp out corruption practices. Corruption is one of the major factors creating political confusion and bitterness.

No way will a nation develop if the crooks keep having the chance to lead and keep developing. It is bad that the few corrupt people are the ones determining what should become of society. They don't have good intentions because they are corrupt. Bad things or corruption are factors that influence what underdeveloped and developing nations are today. This is troubling, especially in Africa, due to the bad institutions created by leaders. These kinds of leaders have nothing to offer their own people and country. I did not understand how the corruption—like I see its persistence—concerning my country being what it is today until I became a boy and started seeing the nature of this corruption getting wider and wider. Everywhere, corruption wells are being dug. If you go into churches, other religious centres, schools, or public transport services, corruption wells are getting deeper and deeper.

No matter what we do, whether by cheating people or circumventing our laws or if corruption is increasing in our societies, promoted by us or others, that is making our societies ungovernable, we should understand that we are here on earth for a season to try to do our best while we are still living. We will one day be accountable to God. But we must, first of all, be accountable to ourselves and our societies. Believe this because you didn't come on your own to earth; God brought you here for a reason of doing His business, for which you will have to report back to Him. The way we live our lives and with our fellow men will determine the accounting part of life, and we will have to report back to God on this. We are accountable to each other, which defines the characters we live on earth. Your character in the way you are living is the same as reporting to your fellow men before you to prove who you are to the world.

Why must you do your best to practice being good? The reason is simple. This is because every human being has a two-part fold—meaning having a spirit and soul, and the body—which are accountable elements belonging to God. Your character is a resource your fellow men need to value the person you are or not. Right on earth, we must account for God, men, and ourselves with our characters. If you can't even be accountable to yourself, life will have no meaning to you. You must respect yourself first. Because you are accountable to God and mankind, it is a reason you don't have the right to kill yourself. We must be accountable in public life. We must also be accountable in business. In your profession as an educated man or woman, you are accountable for your education, which is why your service in your education matters in helping to serve humanity. If you attempted to kill yourself or somebody because you might have chosen to live anyhow, not being accountable to mankind and yourself, the laws will hold you for living or acting anyhow. You are who you are but not made to be what you are, lacking a purpose.

You are made as a human being that is somehow accountable. And after this life on earth, we will account to God again, and our souls will stand in judgment of this. You didn't know where you originated from, so you will go back to your origin, which is in the care of God, who created you beyond your own understanding and made you who you are in this world.

Each part of life accounts for itself. This is a reason you don't have to be corrupt. Stop corruption against yourself. Stop corruption in your society. Stop corruption in public life. If you live anyhow on earth, you will be accountable to God concerning the way you live this life. Stop being corrupt in your success or how you do business. Your character will judge you with men and with God. Because you are also accountable to mankind, nobody can allow you to live anyhow in your community or by making yourself nude in your community and thinking that society doesn't have to bother you. The concept of living anyhow is whatever idea a pure democracy is concerned about— meaning to break down mankind's society and make us an element of control by the state. By this means, the government will have become the supreme power, and God will become nothing to mankind anymore. Not that having freedom is bad. No. But the modernity aspect that promotes a pure democracy intended to break down society—is promoting the devil, which wants to break down human society. Because if society is made to be lived anyhow, it means God is no longer respected. In this case, the devil is lifted. Mankind wasn't made to be without some level of restrictions either. There must be some restrictions so mankind will not just act anyhow. It was a concept of giving mankind some restrictions; Adam and Eve were told to avoid going to a part of the Garden of Eden and to eat a certain fruit. But because of the defiance in support of the lack of restrictions, they went and ate the fruit. God is the only one who is not restricted because He is supreme, but mankind is not because we didn't create ourselves.

You are accountable to God and the world of mankind. If you weren't accountable to the world, you wouldn't be alive, as found in the same world together with the rest of us.

Your success will depend on people who will make it happen. For example, if you invent a product, people will use it, and this will bring you returns from those who become your customers. If you live anyhow in life, know that your soul will be before the judgment seat of God to account for what you have been doing on earth. So, live your life as a respectable person in God. Live your life in private or public, the right way.

We were all born naturally as accountants to God and to men. Never dispute this fact; you are already hired as an accountant to God and to men. Be cognizant of this. This is why it is better to make a good name than a bad one for yourself and learn not to be corrupt. Judgment will be based on service, and service is based on profession, and profession is based on a particular character of a subject you learn to exhibit in the world.

We must see our societies in us. We must see our institutions in us and work to make them great. We must see values in ourselves and tailor those values to our societies. We must become good so our societies can start to be good as well. But I see much distrust in the private and public lives of those who lead people. I see corruption at various levels, which can be traced back to home practices that have grown larger.

I want to know if our parents are still teaching their children the right things to do. Are our schools helping to create people instead of fools? Are our religious institutions dying, unable to keep the values of promoting what Christ taught us by keeping our characters as examples, not as corrupt even in promoting lust, depriving the majority? I ask this most because many of our churches or religious centres these days seem to be self-centred, often headed by family members who only care about protecting their own well-being or wealth created through religious means instead of protecting the trust of Christ.

Some have built schools that graduate people who then work in private and public places but are very corrupt. If you go to church, you see corruption in how churches are managed as well. You can see internal fights over power or riches. If you go to a marketplace, you see corruption, too. If you enter public life, you see corruption, even among those who create national budgets; they use those means to infuse money into the budgets and then collect it through state-run systems without noticing their corruption. They use stolen money to develop other countries and deprive their own people of livelihoods. I saw a representative from the institution I worked with lobby and put money into the budget. When the budget passed, he came to the institution to collect what his committee had put into the budget through some programs designed to extract money from the system. Budget makers can design fraudulent programs, and when the budget passes, they carry out these bogus programs, collecting the money through them. Sometimes, institutions can shift budgets simply to spend money.

Maybe you haven't worked in any private or public institutions or government yet to understand the level of corruption. I know what it is like. There are some public individuals who don't care about making a name. I want you to help yourself so that when you start working in either the private or public sector, you can be one of the best, and society will depend on you to make a great change.

I know many people who have built mansions or condominiums or run private businesses after stealing from governments. They boast of their wealth. They present themselves as the voices of the people by engaging in politics just to maintain power, even though they are very corrupt. They even bluff in their communities as if they are good people, spending their money in various ways. These are the same people who are elected by the people and continue to bend the laws of their societies for personal interests. They do not want to see good things happen, and ordinary people see them as good despite their bad habits. They flaunt as if they are good, but in reality, they are not, spending their corrupt money on the same people they try to suppress.

What individual corruption is, which you need to watch out for, is very detrimental to your society and your life, and it can also be spiritual.

Examples of individual corruption being practised can probably be as follows:

- You don't believe in God (a great source of your destruction) and see yourself as your own creator or wealth creator.
- You take things that don't belong to you and do the same in practice at home.
- You encourage or support people to do things that aren't correct, or you are involved in those actions.
- You steal money that is not meant for you; this practice may reach a national level by making society worse.
- You practice evils by affecting people.
- You aren't trusted at all based on your profession, and people don't trust you.
- Maybe you go to work the hours you wish without working the hours that the institutions require. This means a person who learned as a professional accountant and, in practice, ended up stealing public money by fictitiously putting records together is also a rogue.
- You take people's property as your own.
- You sell things to people that aren't aren't correct.
- Maybe you and somebody entered into a business, and you failed to adhere to the rules or corrupted the terms just because you wanted more than the other person or chose to steal from that person.

- You lie to people to seek favour for yourself.
- You are just unable to speak the truth in your society.
- You encourage divisions for selfish gain or simply because you want that to be.
- You talk evil about others.
- You have a poor opinion of yourself, acting as though you are nobody and unable to help yourself or society while just sitting and complaining for nothing.
- You defame people just for your personal gain, serving as a conspirator.
- You mastermind killing people just because you want to take their rights for your personal gains or for money.
- You sell bad products or drugs to people, thinking you are making a living.
- You support those who want to bring society down.
- You teach people the wrong things just because you don't want them to know better, preferring to be seen as the best in your society by corrupting them with your foolish ideas.
- You are sexually disoriented.
- You use your position to do wrong things against people.
- You refuse to pay legal bills for your state.
- You refuse to pay taxes.
- You refuse to take care of your children, leaving them with their mothers or staying with other concubines without reason, just wanting to be foolish. You know the right things to do but refuse to do them.
- You see evil passing before your eyes and do nothing to stop it, etc.

What on-the-job corruption, whether in private or public life, entails is reflected in some of the things you read. What you need to understand here is that whatever is promoted at the private level or from home has the power to spread to the public level and affect the majority of people. If you see society, such as

Africa, as bad or Western nations suppressing poorer nations or Africa, it is because many individuals in Africa failed to understand what real change is, as they allowed their people to suffer. Africans have not learned from the past. They live their lives the same way as yesterday, today, and tomorrow as if they are not made to embrace change.

If a system suppressed me and I was able to figure this out, the next step I must take is to fight against it. Just as slavery ended in the world, some Africans are cultured and have not changed from the state their forefathers and mothers were affected by, learning to establish their own new world by emulating even those who suppressed them. Instead, they copied their suppressors' way of life and continued living the same way as if they were incapable of change. They keep blaming the suppressors. This is not right. If someone suppresses you, I believe there is something you can learn from that suppression and use to make your life better once you are freed from it.

Mental evil education can only be removed by another form of mental education. In Liberia, the cycle of corruption is increasing. Liberia tries to copy its founder—America's culture—rather than reform its own culture and learn from the positive aspects of its colonizers.

Corrupt individuals with their private lives, especially government officials, and their level of corruption promotions are growing wings.

Examples of promoting either private or public corruption include:

- Taking public properties like vehicles and buildings and incorrect tax disclosures, where taxpayers end up paying less tax due to your manipulation of the amount.
- Having the privilege to lead the majority but failing to do so properly because of selfish reasons.
- Taking public money through strategies designed by those you trained to manage state resources for your benefit.

- Using your power to exert undue influence on others because of your interests.
- Being in a private or public position and being sexually disoriented affects your society.
- Creating public budgets and hiding money within them just to steal.
- Collecting public resources for your personal use.
- Using public resources to educate your own family.
- Promoting gross incompetency in public life.
- Bringing in family members or friends who are unqualified for positions just because they are your acquaintances.
- Supporting state-run systems by undermining the laws of your land to please a few or for your own benefit.
- Failing to implement state policies that may counteract your corrupt actions because you want your interests to prevail.
- Being given a position where you are naturally incompetent to serve.
- Corrupting employment systems for personal interests without following proper practices.

Society needs you most because you live in a society, and you are obligated to learn how to help manage its survival and growth. Institutions need you because you may be part of them, and these institutions exist to make society better off. It is unbecoming to say that you are living in such a society and are unable to do anything positive other than being engaged in corrupt practices. You won't be a positive member of society by living your life like this. Rather, you should fight to create reputable values for yourself and help promote them within your society by building a good character. Your character is like salt to food. If you don't treat your character well, it could reflect poorly on who you are.

Societies are getting worse because people are getting worse. As long as these people are getting corrupted daily, their societies will also retrogress. Their actions may strangle the economy or government or lead to a shortage of appropriate taxes needed to support infrastructure and make the country better for everyone.

Until we all realize that societies are for the people and must be protected for the people, they will go nowhere for the people either. Many societies, like the world is now, that are economically strangled are a result of rampant corruption. Gradually, this corruption eats away at the society until it creates economic downturns.

Imagine if the entire world was made at the same time but some parts are more developed or advanced than others. What is the reason? Corruption is the cause of underdevelopment driven by greed. In societies full of corruption and with no fear of God, people will continue to suffer because corruption kills love for people and the country. Economies and governments will lose value as people may not respect them, and societies may promote their own looseness through corruption.

Don't ever help or practice taking what belongs to the majority for your personal gain. We are the world, so we must learn to protect what is for the majority. Our trade systems or company operations must be good. We must make this world a better place for everyone. However, practising corruption only satisfies a few by creating infighting and greater trouble for society.

This is why you must not sit idly without developing your life. You can better change society if you achieve economic development. People need services or food to survive, and by ensuring your survival, society will benefit. You must not allow poverty to take hold of you without having any power to show or exercise within your society. Fight to earn money in a positive way instead of sitting and complaining. If you have money, it will change your life. You are what you are, but you are not meant to be where you are. Until you work to make society better, make everyone live happily, and know that money is power, you must have it. Strive for success now.

I am talking about your success, which should be good at all levels, starting with you. Never live your life in a way that is detrimental to society. Your voice must be heard. Fight for your success now. Get up and get out. Don't wait for people to help you before you succeed. Nobody may want to give you money to start with, apart from the little you may be making, so you must make proper use of it. If you go to school to learn, it's about making money, so you must learn what you need to learn very well. Since you were born, you have been eating or using clothes, which shows that you can at least spend money or someone may be helping you. But that is insufficient. Develop your spending power and learn to give through it instead of remaining dependent and unsuccessful. If you fail to succeed, know that life will throw at you what you don't want.

If someone helps you, it means you have a greater chance to go beyond that level by learning to help yourself succeed now. Keep in mind that if someone or you are working for money, if you value it, you should learn to make more of it by improving your life. Great things can come from small beginnings, especially if you value and build upon them. Satisfaction does not come from having nothing.

Another thing you can do to grow from your current state is to cut down on costs, especially if you are making only a small income, and learn to save a portion of it and invest in the future. Your delay or attitude towards money and spending may be causing you poverty because you are wasting the little you make.

Don't be like others who are looking for big money and disregard the little they have. Use your little instead of letting it use you. Or, your delay in success could be due to your outlook on the world, meaning you don't see your power as a conqueror and don't push through. Whatever the case, know that you own your life and can decide how you want the world to be with you.

You have the power to make the world what it should be until you take action.

Now, wake up instead of wasting away in poverty! You need to wake up because the world is not waiting for you, nor is time. Now is your time to do something before night comes and you have no power to act. Start fighting for your place of honour now. Demand a change of your level by working for it. Wrestle with life to succeed. Today is the day to start fighting. Today is the day to think about what to do. Today is the day to plant the seed for your rise. Begin to dream now! Create the power for a shining tomorrow. Add to your today before tomorrow brightens.

I know you will succeed unstoppable. I know you will create a room out of your current poverty state or circumstances that make you feel you can't succeed but try your best now. Be like those who see change as good and work for it. People who want a change in their level learn from others and take the necessary steps. I know you will begin your change now. Whether you started long ago, are delaying, or have been lukewarm about succeeding, you will change momentum and start empowering yourself for the change in your story. Push through. Stop holding on to negative desires or feelings that tell you you won't make it. Remove negativity persistently. Cut it off. Even a fire eventually cools down, and you must work to extinguish the fire of your poverty.

As Christ told us, greater is He (God's spirit) that is in us than he (Satan's spirit or the spirit of this world) (I John 4:4), meaning you are a moving lion, part of the family of Judah. You are made as a conqueror. You carry some great features that nobody in the world or even within your family carries. This is to say because we have God in us and we are made like Him, it is reason to say that we are more than great people. Carry such a mindset in you that you are not a small person in this world. By the time you accept Christ as your Lord and Savior, you are made a new creature (I Corinthians 5:17) and do not have the ordinary spirit of man, which has no power to conquer situations until God's spirit acts upon that individual. Now, you are more than a conqueror who must do wonders in the world. Carry such a mindset or desire in you that you are not ordinary like others who have no faith in God and faith even in themselves and the things they do. Carry such thinking that you are power in the world that must give power to yourself now. Carry such a force within you that you can never be turned into a nobody person anymore. Carry such meditation daily, seeing power in you that you are moving forward but not backwards anymore. Say you will not remain static anymore because you have discovered your place of honour through God. See God in you that He created you, and you are carrying Him inside of you, with you in your body, in your actions, at your dwelling or location, at your workplace, at your social gatherings, in a hard economic country you may be in, and so on. Everything about you should show Him being with you to make you succeed in whatever you do. I don't carry negativity over my life. I don't even care how people see me as nobody, but I see myself as a great person. This is how you should see your life and fight to be at the level of recognition instead of giving up on life and staying perpetually in a place of lack of recognition. Never think of looking at your life as something that should make you doubt God. You have life, but you didn't make your life. You were rather made with life that should be controlled by you, determining how you should live on earth. Whatever decision of success you want is left to you. Think of this! Get to know that the God who gave you that life is not dead, and until He died, He created you for a good purpose, which you must showcase. And God can't die.

Don't forget that this world needs a turnaround, which involves you changing your ways. When you follow God, you are turning your world around from having evil and a lack of success. Turn from having evil or evil troubling your world by turning to God, who shall gradually change your life and world. He is the source of wisdom and knowledge.

If today is bringing you worry, let your tomorrow bring you happiness. Your everyday mustn't be the same forever, especially when poverty occupies, and you have nothing to do about it. Don't mind your location. Your location on any part of this planet earth shouldn't determine how you are to live. You should determine where you are to live and how it should look good, concerning your whole life radiating in the good of God, who made you for a reason. You are who you are made to be, but you were never made to be the way things are with you now, meaning not yielding a good purpose. This is the fight you must put up with: you belong to the family of God that should shine. You belong to God because He created you and put you in the world for the purpose of doing what you are to do for Him and live in expediency or excellence. In Revelation 5:10, which is in the Bible, Christ Jesus made us as kings and priests: and we shall reign on the earth. So, what are you waiting for to start reigning on earth? Say to yourself that you are on a mission for God, which you must implement with expediency, and that should be about your lifting. Say to yourself that you are located in God, and God is located in you, so you will make it. Say to yourself that Christ came to die for you in the world, and nothing like obstacles should hold you down anymore. Say to yourself that poverty was put to death by Christ on the Cross a long time ago, and poverty must not trouble your world anymore. This means you should carry a spirit within you that you are a winner. You can only be a winner if you believe in God and believe in yourself. Christ has taken you from your powerless phase and brought you into your power phase.

Think of this now! Charismatic Jesus did it for you and for me. Christ has done everything necessary for success for you and me; this is the reason you are made as a king and priest—carrying a holy characteristic of God and not as an ordinary being anymore, to believe about your existence now. This is why your head needs to be put in power and for your life to enjoy the power of God. You are a natural winner who Christ has made, so

He said if any man is in Him, he is a new creature (I Corinthians 5:17).

I can see such a victory coming for you now! Only your belief will change your world. Because what you think of yourself is what you will get for your life. Wake up! I wish you the best in your journey of life as you design a personage of destroying poverty now by becoming a great person in time to come, especially financially as well. See your society in you to do something about helping it to grow from deadness and for you to have your best out of life, or for you to improve rather than sitting doing nothing. You belong to a living class of people rather than being in the dead class of people who see their survival only in other people and never give themselves some push. You belong to the living people who must learn to do living things, live life to the fullest, live without comparison of being called foolish people, and live without financial worry. Develop faith in yourself now that you will make it. Because you were able to read this book at this distance, I have faith in you that you have won already. I can see you participating in the glory of life. You will make it undeniably. You don't have to do those things you used to do that kept you down or unfocused anymore. You weren't made with poverty, but it was imposed upon you by the devil, which you must remove from your life. Nature will not deny you if you push to succeed. So, you must see poverty as an enemy characteristic and fight it in your life. It wasn't part of the elements that God used to put you together, either. Know who your God is. God was still a decent God, and He is still decent and will forever be decent, blessing mankind. He blessed you long ago, which is why you met the world here. He has already done those things you need to develop for you. Value this about yourself: your human body is made up of the earth, which means you belong to having power on earth as well. No angel was made with the dust of earth except you and me, which means you and I are what earth is supposed to be as good. Step yourself up to reach your level of power now. Thank God for reaching this distance in your reading. I am so happy that, finally, you will make up for your life and make it for your future now!

Angels will not come down to earth to tell you to wake up from where you are until others do what I am doing for you now. Angels will not stand physically or tangibly before you to push you. They are invisible beings who don't belong to earth apart from humans like you, and they should be educated about the power given to you, especially as you are reading this book, which is meant to push you to your level. Angels can only give you a message from God from the spirit realm. Everything on earth is controlled by humans. But physically, making you succeed takes humans like me, which I am doing, meant to push you to your level of greatness. Open your ears and eyes. Open your mind now. There is no time to waste anymore because now is the time to wake up. Now is the time you must try to bring yourself out to the world. Start working skillfully now rather than working hard for nothing.

Remember, the day you realize that you're truly part of those who own earth and should possess and enjoy it by taking your position here, you will have joined the party with successful people whose confidence got them to the point of gaining recognition. I can see that you will make it by taking your place concerning this now. As long as you have been able to read this book, you have penetrated the dark power of poverty and brought about a state of light for yourself. You just need to build a conscience concerning your life in you. Thank you so much for taking the steps you have taken to buy this book to read and come this far. Believe that the distance of success you want to go depends on you. Stop sitting and start meditating on your life by getting out of poverty now.

References

1. The Holy Bible, King James Version. (n.d.). *Galatians 6:7*. New Testament.
2. The Holy Bible, King James Version. (n.d.). *Genesis 1:26*. Old Testament.
3. The Holy Bible, King James Version. (n.d.). *I Thessalonians 5:18*. New Testament.
4. Kiyosaki, R. T. (n.d.). *Rich Dad Poor Dad* [Audiobook].
5. Principle of Personal Economics. (n.d.). Retrieved from
6. http://www.principleofpersonaleconomics.com
7. The Holy Bible, King James Version. (n.d.). *I Corinthians 5:17, II Corinthians 6:16*. New Testament.
8. The Holy Bible, King James Version. (n.d.). *St. John 1:1-4*. New Testament.

9 788119 524112